Following God

Enhancing YOUR MARRIAGE

A WOMEN'S BIBLE STUDY

Enhancing
YOUR
MARRIAGE

A WOMEN'S BIBLE STUDY
BY
Judy Rossi

Advancing the Ministries of the Gospel

AMG Publishers™

God's Word to you is our highest calling.

Following God

ENHANCING YOUR MARRIAGE

© 2004 by Judy Rossi

Published by AMG Publishers. All Rights Reserved.

Third Printing, 2010

ISBN: 0-89957-152-2

Cover design by Daryl Phillips at ImageWright Marketing and Design, Chattanooga, TN
Layout by Rick Steele
Editing by Karen Brunson, Jonathan Wright, and Rick Steele

A free leader's guide for this Bible study is available at:
www.amgpublishers.com
www.eymministries.org

Printed in Canada
15 14 13 –M– 8 7 6 5 4

This book is dedicated to

every woman who desires to
follow God in her marriage.

He won't disappoint you.

Acknowledgments

To the Author of marriage, God the Father, for loving us all so much that He gave us the Bridegroom, Jesus the Christ, and our perfect example in the marriage relationship, and the Holy Spirit, our Counselor, Helper, Teacher, who ensures that we have everything we need for life and godliness.

To the many women who have taken my class, "Enhancing Your Marriage: A Women's Bible Study," and urged me to pursue its publication. My special thanks goes to Beth Carey, the study's strongest advocate (and whose encouragement to publish bordered on nagging!); to Mikell Calkin and Lori Smith who provided passage into the world of publishing; and to Jill Brandt and Mikell who faithfully and prayerfully perused each lesson. Their love, encouragement and constancy throughout the writing process were priceless gifts to me. Thank you.

To those who covered this project in prayer, especially Mikell, Jill, Linda Selden, Gail Nittle, Claudia Duff, and so many others within our Northern Virginia community and worldwide military women's ministry, the Protestant Women of the Chapel (PWOC). Many meals accompanied your prayers. You all have my incalculable gratitude.

To Dr. Jack Elwood, senior pastor of Burke Community Church in Northern Virginia, Randy Newman of Campus Crusade for Christ, and Chaplain (Colonel) Jim May, United States Army, for their valuable input on some very tough topics. Thank you.

To Dan Penwell who saw the study's need, value and potential, and Rick Steele for his patience and kindness as he coached me through the editing process; and for the editing skills of Karen Brunson and Jonathan Wright. I've learned so much.

To my daughters, Dana and Leslie, whose faithful prayers, encouragement, and support were unwavering. They are both a delight to this mom, and will be to the future Mr. Righteous in each of their lives.

And finally, with profound love and gratitude, to John, my bridegroom of thirty years, who deserves a trophy for his marathon patience, encouragement, love, balance, and wise counsel over the last ten months. We've learned a lot together throughout the years. And we know there's more. He is my hero—and I won't stop telling him.

JUDY ROSSI

About the Author

Judy Rossi began teaching marriage-focused Bible studies in 1986. This experience has shown her the tremendous need for women to address their unique roles in their marriages. God's call to speak to that need is presented in her first written work, *Enhancing Your Marriage: A Women's Bible Study.* Judy now speaks regularly on the subject of marriage at women's retreats and conferences across the country.

Judy has a degree in Special Education, dealing with exceptional children, speech pathology, and audiology. She has been married for thirty years and has two grown daughters, Dana and Leslie. Judy and her husband, John, a retired U. S. Army Colonel, live in Fairfax Station, Virginia.

A free leader's guide for this book and more information concerning Judy are available at:

www.eymministries.org

About the Following God Series

Three authors and fellow ministers, Wayne Barber, Eddie Rasnake, and Rick Shepherd, teamed up in 1998 to write a character-based Bible study for AMG Publishers. Their collaboration developed into the title, *Life Principles from the Old Testament*. Since 1998, these same authors and AMG Publishers have produced four more character-based studies—each consisting of twelve lessons geared around a five-day study of a particular Bible personality. More studies of this type are in the works. New authors have recently been acquired, and new types of studies have been published in an ongoing effort to add fresh perspectives as to what it means to follow God. However, the interactive study format that readers have come to love remains constant in all of our newest titles. As new Bible studies are being planned, our focus remains the same: to provide excellent Bible study materials that point people to God's Word in ways that allow them to apply truths to their own lives. More information on this groundbreaking series along with a free leader's guide for this study can be found on the following web page:

www.amgpublishers.com

Preface

Enhancing Your Marriage: A Women's Bible Study was born nineteen years ago while my family and I were stationed in Toronto, Canada. I was asked to assess the needs of a lovely group of women with whom I fellowshipped and teach their Winter/Spring Bible study. As I got to know these women a little better, it was easy to see that most of them yearned for a real relationship with their husbands, longing for more depth in their marriages. As I sought God on how to approach the teaching, He began to unfold a new Bible study, one that was revealing my greater need of Him in my life and in my marriage. Over the ensuing years, God continued to refine my role as John's wife while refining my relationship with His Son. I was learning how intricately interwoven these two relationships were and how important it was to convey this to other wives.

Being in a love-relationship with Jesus Christ can't help but influence our love-relationship with our husbands. Jesus will see to that. He calls us to Himself and gently and lovingly begins to re-tool our souls. And much of this work takes place in the workshop of our marriages.

My prayer is that *Enhancing Your Marriage: A Women's Bible Study* will challenge you to follow God in your marriage, to let Him have full access to your life, to permit Him to re-tool your role as your husband's wife in accordance with His truth, all the while shaping you into the image of His Son. I also pray that you will commit the time, will, and energy God requires of you to complete this study; to view each lesson not only as "home" work, but "heart" work. Your investment will pay huge, lifelong dividends.

Whether you are studying this book on your own or with a group, know that your Teacher is the Holy Spirit. He will not only help you learn and apply the truth, He will help you unlearn and discard the lies. He will teach you to enjoy and maximize the perks of your marriage while building in you a new freedom and confidence to address the problems of your marriage. Your relationship with your husband will become an exciting, purposeful adventure.

Keep in mind that a free leader's guide is available for download at my Web site (www.eymministries.org) and at AMG's site (www.amgpublishers.com).

May God bless the time you spend with Him in this book. Give Him everything you've got, and He'll return it to you *"pressed down, shaken together, running over"* (Luke 6:38).

In His love,

Judy

Table of Contents

1

Knowing God Better: The Key

"*S*ometimes it seems as if my husband and I are complete strangers."

"I just wish I knew what he was thinking."

"I don't think we love each other anymore."

Have you heard these statements before, or have you said them? I don't know a woman who doesn't long for a deeper, more intimate relationship with her husband, one that's rich and rewarding. This Bible study is designed to that end. But before you examine your relationship with your husband, you must first examine your relationship with your God—the way your heart responds to His drawing you to Himself. He longs for you to long for Him, to know Him, to perceive, recognize, and understand His ways—intimately. John 17:3 is the key that will unlock all of God's best for your life. It's the starting point for this study: *"Now this is eternal life: that they may know you, the only true God, and Jesus Christ, whom you have sent (NIV)."*

Knowing God and the One He sent is the sure foundation on which to build healthy lives and marriages. Enhancing your marriage hinges on your personal walk with God through Jesus Christ. To *know* Him is to love Him. The Greek word translated "know" in John 17:3 is *ginōsko,* which means to perceive, recognize, become acquainted with, and understand. The degree to which you know and love God is the degree to which you can know and truly love your husband.

Knowing God and the One He sent is the sure foundation on which to build healthy lives and marriages. . . . The degree to which you know and love God is the degree to which you can know and truly love your husband.

So let's get to know God better; that's the focus of this week's study. Approach each study day with a teachable heart. Answer the questions thoroughly and honestly. Don't skip over any scriptures, no matter how familiar they are to you. Ask God to *"give to you a spirit of wisdom and of revelation in the knowledge of Him . . . that the eyes of your heart may be enlightened"* (Ephesians 1:17–18). He loves to answer that prayer.

Knowing God Better: The Key

DAY ONE

KNOWING GOD AS AUTHOR

The Creator of the universe has a plan, and we, along with our husbands, have been a part of it from the beginning. We're a part of His plan because we are a part of His purpose. At the very least, this should give us hope for our lives and our marriages. Let's examine how God unfolded His plan and what it means for us and for our marriages today.

📖 Read Genesis 1:1–31 as if for the first time. Then in the side margin on the left make a list of what God created each day, noting anything unique about the sequencing of His creation.

The earth is described as formless, an empty waste, and dark. The Holy Spirit was hovering, brooding over the waters, poised to work the will of God. It's no mistake that the very first thing God did was to create light and separate it from the darkness. He continued to use lights in the heavens to separate day from night, as well as for signs and seasons. In later lessons, illuminating the darkness will get very personal.

God created all things according to their own kind, meaning "species" (verses 11, 12, 21, 24, and 25). He was deliberate in His creation, imaginative in His variety, and ingenious in His groupings. He is not about evolution. He is all about originality. Some time ago, a well-known comedian asked a thought-provoking question: "If we evolved from monkeys, why are there still monkeys?"

Throughout the first chapter of Genesis, God saw that what He had made was good. The Hebrew word translated "good" in this chapter can also mean "pleasant, beautiful, excellent, lovely, delightful."[1] Could God have been more pleased? Let's see.

What else did God make, and what distinguished this creation from all else that He formed (verses 26–27)?

_____

_____

_____

What do you think is meant by "Our image" and "Our likeness"? To whom does "Our" refer?

_____

_____

_____

📖 When God is speaking here, He refers to Himself in the plural form, "indicating plenitude of power and majesty and allowing for the [New Testament] revelation of the tri-unity of the Godhead."[2] Think about verse 26. What do the following verses say about who was involved in creation?

Genesis 1:1

_____

_____

Genesis 1:2

_____

_____

Colossians 1:15–17

_____

_____

The entire Godhead—God the Father, God the Son (in the person of Jesus Christ), and God the Holy Spirit—was involved in creation. Humanity was made in Their image, likeness, or resemblance, "not an exact duplicate," but the "shadow of a thing."[3] That human beings were made in the shadow, or likeness, of the triune God should tell us that the Eternal is indelibly engraved on our souls. It is an image that can be filled only with Himself. And no matter what we try to stuff into that God-shaped image, our souls will never be satisfied until He fills them.

Years ago, I had a silhouette of my daughter cut from black construction paper, mounted, and framed. No features were distinguishable, just the contour of her head, nose, chin, neck, and hair. Even so, this "shadow" was recognizable as that of my daughter. And so it is with our being created in the image of God. In His love, wisdom, and power, He placed within the human spirit the capacity to love, respond to, have fellowship with, and reflect Him. Although the nature of that capacity changed when sin entered the world, to this day we still possess the longing to fill this God-shaped void with whatever will satisfy.

In each of the three verses that follow, underline the reason God created humanity.

> _Thou art worthy, O Lord, to receive glory and honour and power: for thou has created all things, and for thy pleasure they are and were created_ (Revelation 4:11, KJV).

We were created for God's pleasure, as a "result of the will . . . as an expression or inclination of pleasure towards that which is liked, that which pleases and creates joy. When it denotes God's will, it signifies His gracious disposition toward something."[4] God deliberately created us to bring Him joy and pleasure.

 Have you ever before considered that you were created for God's pleasure? Think about that. What does that mean to you? How does it affect your concept of God?

_____

_____

_____

God deliberately created us to bring Him joy and pleasure.

Bring My sons from afar, and My daughters from the ends of the earth, every-one who is called by My name, and whom I have created for My glory, whom I have formed, even whom I have made (Isaiah 43:6–7).

Bringing God glory is how His own make Him known to others. If His character is recognizable in a Christian, it reflects who He is, making Him credible and desirable to others. This is what we were created to do.

APPLY How is God made known to others in your life, especially to your husband?

_____

_____

_____

_____

_____

When You said, "Seek My face," my heart said to You, "Your face, O Lord, I shall seek" (Psalm 27:8).

God called David to seek Him, and David responded, "Yes!" Can you imagine it? Have you ever experienced God's wooing you toward Himself, calling you to find some time to sit quietly and seek His face, prompting you to bring to Him who you really are, warts and all (even though He knows you perfectly), so that He can show you who He really is?

APPLY When was the last time you sat with Him, responding to His call? What is your time with God really like? Is it hit-and-miss and distracted, or is it consistent and focused? Describe it.

_____

_____

_____

_____

_____

Can you imagine being created to bring God pleasure, to bring Him glory, and to respond to Him? From the beginning, we were intended to have an eternal, win-win relationship with God. Let's see what else God has in store for us.

📖 What were God's instructions in Genesis 1:28? Why do you think God gave humans authority over all His creation?

_____

_____

_____

_____

_____

Who else could know God's heart but one created in His image? Who else but a human being could be "God's responsible representative and steward on the earth, to work out his Creator's will and fulfill the divine purpose"?[5]

📖 Let's look specifically at the creation of man and woman in Genesis 2:4–23. How did God create Adam (verse 7)?

_____

_____

_____

_____

_____

With all of God's creating, what did He declare was missing for Adam (verse 18–20)?

_____

_____

_____

_____

The scripture refers to Adam's need of a "help meet" (KJV), "helper meet" (AMP), or "helper suitable" (NASB and NIV). Even while surrounded by and naming all of God's birds and beasts, Adam experienced a natural loneliness. Verse 20 indicates that no fitting helper was found. Nothing around him could satisfy this natural need that God had created in him. There was none on earth like him—no companion. Did God make a mistake? Did He forget something? Perhaps He wanted to be sure Adam understood that only He could fill Adam's need His way.

According to verses 21 and 22, what was God's solution to Adam's loneliness?

_____

_____

_____

_____

_____

How did God create woman, and why do you think He created her as He did?

_____

_____

_____

_____

_____

Woman was "made" (NIV, KJV), "built up" (AMP), "fashioned" (NASB) out of the man and for the man, with perfect specifications to complete him—physically, intellectually, emotionally, spiritually. Because she was taken from his side, this is where she was intended to stand, as an equal alongside him. God created someone who would respond perfectly to her male counterpart, completing him by her response to him. In short, woman was created to be the responder.

📖 It's interesting to note that the word "help" in "help meet" is also used in Psalm 46:1 (NIV), which reads, _"God is our refuge and strength, an ever-_

> **"Then the LORD God said, 'It is not good for the man to be alone; I will make a helper suitable for him.'"**
>
> **Genesis 2:18**

> **God created someone who would respond perfectly to her male counterpart, completing him by her response to him. In short, woman was created to be the responder.**

present help in trouble." Consider this awesome parallel. How does it further define a wife's role in her marriage?

_____

_____

_____

_____

_____

What was Adam's reaction to this new creature (verse 23)?

_____

_____

_____

_____

Adam's declaration was a profound and intimate response! He understood and acknowledged without hesitation God's intent for this newly created being who was masterfully fashioned from his own body. Eve was created to be for Adam what God knew he needed. She was essential to her husband and to all he was meant to become. As Christian wives, we're essential to our husbands in the same way.

 Is this a revelation to you? What's your response to the reason Eve was created for Adam? How does this influence your perspective on your own marriage?

_____

_____

_____

_____

📖 Read Genesis 2:24. This is the foundational scripture of God's intent for His holy institution of marriage. What were God's commands to the first couple?

_____

_____

_____

_____

Adam and Eve were commanded by God to leave all others, to cleave to no others, to become one flesh with only the other. God's intent was an exclusive relationship—one woman for one man for all time. Oneness: what a picture! What a plan! And because it was God's perfect plan, it was very good.

 Does the "very good" that God intended exist in your marriage? Where are you in your marriage right now? Check all below that apply:

"For this cause a man shall leave his father and his mother, and shall cleave to his wife; and they shall become one flesh."

Genesis 2:24

- ☐ I'm a newlywed and want a solid foundation for a lifetime.
- ☐ I have a good marriage, and want it to continue to grow.
- ☐ I want to rekindle the love I used to have.
- ☐ I've never loved my husband, but I want to.
- ☐ I don't love my husband anymore.
- ☐ I'm working on our marriage, but my husband is indifferent or unco-operative.
- ☐ My husband is considering divorce.
- ☐ I'm considering divorce.

If you were to ask God to do one thing in your marriage, what would it be?

_____

_____

_____

_____

Ponder God as your Creator and your husband's Creator. Each day of your lives was written in His book before your first breaths were taken (Psalm 139:16), including your wedding day and each day thereafter. His desire is that you remain one. This reality should be an encouragement, in that the God who created you both knows exactly how you should fit together. (If you or your husband have experienced divorce, please see my note on p. 22 above the "Works Cited" section.) Release and entrust your husband to his Creator; then ask Him now to meet you right where you are—in your places of pleasure as well as your places of pain. Trust Him to help you grow from there.

KNOWING GOD AS ABBA

We all have a picture of what an earthly father is and what an earthly father should be. It's indelibly engraved in our minds as a result of our growing-up experiences, good or bad. Consider the ideal earthly father, and write as many characteristics as you can think of that would describe him:

_____

_____

_____

_____

_____

It's more common to view God as a far-off, detached ogre, ever poised to level retribution on wrongdoers. Can you imagine your Heavenly Father as possessing all of the characteristics you wrote above, and more?

In the Old Testament, one of the many descriptions of God's relationship to His chosen nation, Israel, is that of patriarchal father. Although the concept of God as a father is not used much in the Old Testament, when it's used, it usually depicts His relationship to the people of Israel as a whole rather than to individuals. The Israelites' concept of God was also one of authority, such as that which a king exercised over them. The use of the father–child imagery, however, softened the picture, giving it a touch of loving protection and tenderness. Describe the Father on the basis of each of the following scriptures:

Deuteronomy 1:30–31

_____

_____

Deuteronomy 32:8–14

_____

_____

Isaiah 64:8

_____

_____

Yes, we have a heavenly Father who will fight for us and carry us through difficult and dangerous times. He will also mold us—pinching and pressing with the purposeful pressure of the potter (but, oh, the compassion of His fingers!). How He longs for us to desire what He knows is best for us in the midst of our trials, testings, and tragedies, not just in our joys. How He desires us to acknowledge our need of Him, to fear (revere) Him with holy awe!

APPLY Does this sound like the God you grew up with? If not, how do you see Him differently now?

_____

_____

_____

_____

_____

In the New Testament, Jesus—God's Son—introduces us to a personal father. From the following scriptures, what insights can you gather concerning their special and unique relationship?

Matthew 3:16–17

_____

_____

Matthew 11:27

_____

_____

> **Yes, we have a heavenly Father who will fight for us and carry us through difficult and dangerous times. He will also mold us—pinching and pressing with the purposeful pressure of the potter (but, oh, the compassion of His fingers!).**

_____

_____

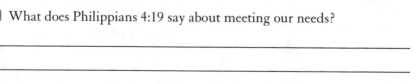 Although we're not children of God by nature, God presents us with the opportunity to be His children. Read John 1:12–13, along with Romans 8:15, 16 and Galatians 4:6. How do we become His children? What rights do we have as His own?

_____

_____

_____

_____

_____

As believers in Jesus Christ, we not only have the right to be called the children of God, but we've also received the privilege of calling God "Abba." The word "Abba" is of Aramaic origin (the language used in Palestine during the time of Christ). It means "father" but conveys more of a warm, intimate sentiment similar to the affection displayed by children when they address their fathers as "Daddy." The Jews did not refer to God in this fashion, but Jesus uses this term when addressing God in prayer, as in Mark 14:36, and teaches His disciples (including us) to regard God as our "Abba."

God is our Abba, to whom we can respond with an attitude of affection, trust, confidence, and openness, just as a small child would respond to his or her loving earthly father. That's relationship, and it's real.

Perhaps you didn't have an earthly father who was a good example of the Father's love, and the past is painful. Maybe it's time for you to recognize that you need your heavenly Father, time to accept Him as your ultimate Parent and not to avoid Him, time to press into His heart, where the healing is. No human heart is beyond His healing balm. Believe that, and ponder it as you participate in this study. He'll meet you right where you are and take you where you need to go.

Accepting God as our Father means that we have security in everyday life. He is much more able to love us and care for us than our earthly fathers are. As our Father, God knows intimately what we, His children, need.

 What does Philippians 4:19 say about meeting our needs?

_____

_____

_____

_____

 Because we're His children, God the Father desires to meet all our needs. Do you believe this—totally trust, depend on, and rely on it? If there are "impossibilities" in your marriage that you haven't yet identified, identify them now, and write them down.

 **Word Study**
BELIEVE

The word "believe" (*pisteuo* in Greek) is used nearly one hundred times in the Gospel of John alone. It means to totally trust, to rely on, to cleave to, to depend on. It goes far beyond mere intellectual agreement, and becomes the heart of our Christian journey, reflecting our total dependence on Who Jesus is and what He has done on our behalf to ensure our right to be called children of God.

_____

_____

_____

_____

_____

_____

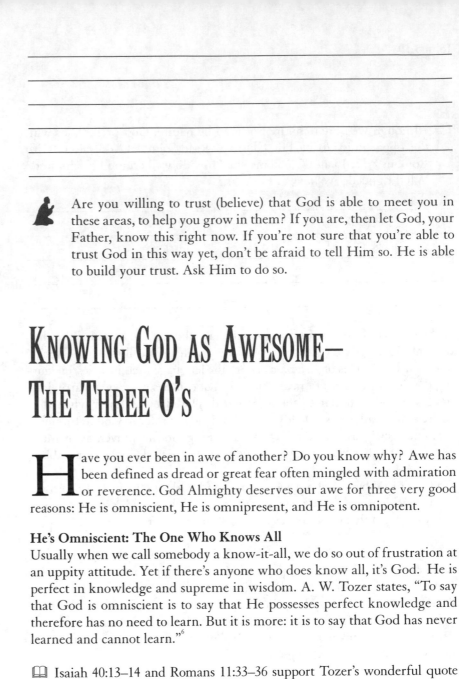

Are you willing to trust (believe) that God is able to meet you in these areas, to help you grow in them? If you are, then let God, your Father, know this right now. If you're not sure that you're able to trust God in this way yet, don't be afraid to tell Him so. He is able to build your trust. Ask Him to do so.

Knowing God Better: The Key

DAY THREE

KNOWING GOD AS AWESOME— THE THREE O'S

Have you ever been in awe of another? Do you know why? Awe has been defined as dread or great fear often mingled with admiration or reverence. God Almighty deserves our awe for three very good reasons: He is omniscient, He is omnipresent, and He is omnipotent.

He's Omniscient: The One Who Knows All

Usually when we call somebody a know-it-all, we do so out of frustration at an uppity attitude. Yet if there's anyone who does know all, it's God. He is perfect in knowledge and supreme in wisdom. A. W. Tozer states, "To say that God is omniscient is to say that He possesses perfect knowledge and therefore has no need to learn. But it is more: it is to say that God has never learned and cannot learn."[6]

📖 Isaiah 40:13–14 and Romans 11:33–36 support Tozer's wonderful quote concerning God's omniscience. How do these scriptures affect your understanding of God?

_____

_____

_____

_____

There's nothing our God doesn't know and understand absolutely. There's no heart, no mind, no spirit, no personality, no relationship, no problem, no joy, no puzzle, no pain, no secret, no desire that escapes His deep knowledge and intimate understanding. And if the knowledge of God is perfect, then the wisdom of God is perfect—His wisdom that addresses the heart, the mind, the spirit, the personality, the relationship, the problem, the joy, the puzzle, the pain, the secret, the desire.

Serving a God who knows and understands all things with all wisdom should be comforting. But it can also be intimidating, especially if we have something to hide. The marriage relationship is fertile ground for hidden thoughts, feelings, motives, and agendas. Until we gain knowledge of and respect for our omniscient God, we will keep hiding—from Him, from our husbands, from our marital difficulties, and from ourselves. "God knows" should be one of the most comforting phrases in our vocabulary.

📖 What does Psalm 139:1–6 reveal about God's knowledge of you?

_____

_____

_____

_____

God searches us with penetrating scrutiny. He knows us down to our depths. He inspects our public day-to-day paths as well as our private, most intimate ones, day and night. And He keeps us under His close watch for our own protection. This can be a comforting reality (or not).

📖 Jesus said in Matthew 10:29–31 (NIV), *"Are not two sparrows sold for a penny? Yet not one of them will fall to the ground apart from the will of your Father. And even the very hairs of your head are all numbered. So don't be afraid; you are worth more than many sparrows."* What do these words mean to you?

_____

_____

_____

_____

It astounds me that the Lord knows even the number of hairs on my head, a number that changes from moment to moment (hairs are either falling out or growing in). Now that's paying attention to the details of my life! Nothing escapes Him.

A dear friend who was fighting cancer with chemotherapy lost all but a few thick strands of her hair. Still determined to cling to the strands that were left, she styled them as best she could. Losing them nonetheless, she finally surrendered to the One who knew her and her plight intimately. Yielding those strands to loss was yielding to her Lord every physical and emotional need during a difficult time—a step in faith toward her omniscient God.

🛑 **APPLY** What parts of your marriage are you unwilling to relinquish to God—areas that you refuse to let Him touch?

_____

_____

_____

> *Until we gain knowledge of and respect for our omniscient God, we will keep hiding—from Him, from our husbands, from our marital difficulties, and from ourselves. "God knows" should be one of the most comforting phrases in our vocabulary.*

What details of your life are buried because you think God is unaware of them or not even interested in them? Be candid and specific.

_____

_____

_____

_____

We know that God is involved in even the smallest details of our lives and marriages. Oswald Chambers in his wonderful devotional *My Utmost for His Highest* writes,

> The great, mysterious work of the Holy Spirit is in the deep recesses of our being which we cannot reach. . . . The psalmist implies—"O Lord, You are the God of the early mornings, the God of the late nights, the God of the mountain peaks, the God of the sea. But, my God, my soul has horizons further away than those of early mornings, deeper darkness than the nights of earth, higher peaks than any mountain peaks, greater depths than any sea in nature. You who are the God of all these, be my God. I cannot reach to the heights or to the depths; there are motives I cannot discover, dreams I cannot realize. My God, search me."[7]

APPLY What a powerful plea! Is it one that you can make? How can awareness of God's omniscience influence your life?

_____

_____

_____

_____

If God knows you this well, would you agree that He also knows your husband as well? How can acknowledging this change the way you relate to your husband?

_____

_____

_____

_____

Are there areas of your life or your marriage that you're not willing to open and expose to God's wisdom, counsel, change, and healing? Know that whatever is hidden in darkness will continue to master you and will remain an obstacle in your faith walk and in your marriage. If you're afraid to address these areas, your Father already knows. Take a step in faith, and yield the hidden parts and details to your all-knowing God.

He's Omnipresent: The Grand Champion of Hide and Seek

📖 Read Psalm 139:7–12. What does this passage reveal about God?

_____

_____

_____

_____

The psalmist asks, "What can I hide?" In His omniscience, God would answer, "Nothing." The psalmist asks, "Where can I hide?" In His omnipresence, God would answer, "Nowhere." We can't go up, down, east, or west without His finding us (verses 8–9). We can run, but we can't hide. And we can't escape the loving supervision that He imposes by His right hand. There is no place where He is not.

APPLY Does this passage comfort you personally? If so, how?

_____

_____

_____

_____

Are there places in your life where you would rather God were not present? What are they?

_____

_____

_____

_____

_____

God's omnipresence applies to our husbands' lives as well as our own, even if he's not a believer. In what specific areas can this truth relieve you of potential worry about your husband?

_____

_____

_____

_____

No one can hide from God—not in body, mind, or spirit. Nor should we want to if we desire His best for ourselves, our husbands, and our marriages. Nothing blindsides Him. And because He's in our every moment—whether good or ugly —He can influence us right there with His truth, His wisdom, His peace, His comfort, and His restraint. Let Him know daily that you welcome His presence and His influence in your life and in your marriage.

He's Omnipotent: God of Power and Might

Read Jeremiah 32:17, 26–27; and Luke 1:26–37. What single, faith-building, hope-reviving truth flows from these scriptures?

_____

_____

_____

_____

There is no other like our God. He said so Himself.

> *The psalmist asks, "What can I hide?" In His omniscience, God would answer, "Nothing." The psalmist asks, "Where can I hide?" In His omnipres-ence, God would answer, "Nowhere."*

> *"I am the LORD, the God of all mankind. Is anything too hard for me?"*
>
> *Jeremiah 32:27 (NIV)*

📖 Read Genesis 17:1. Who does God say that He is? What does this name mean to you?

_____

_____

_____

_____

_____

Only the God of the Bible, the one true God, has all power. His power is incomprehensible—unfathomable and inconceivable to our finite minds. And He reigns! Once we grasp by faith the power of God, His existence takes on new meaning, as do our lives and experiences.

APPLY Do you believe that nothing is too hard, that nothing is impossible for God Almighty, especially if you're in a seemingly impossible marriage? How does your knowledge of God's all-powerful nature compare with the level of your faith in His ability? Consider this carefully, and answer honestly.

_____

_____

_____

_____

_____

How can embracing the all-powerful nature of God change your approach to your marriage?

_____

_____

_____

Do you believe what you've been reading in His Book? If you're struggling, don't despair. Just be willing to let Him work with what you have. Be encouraged—He is able!

Every day acknowledge and anticipate God's omniscience, omnipresence, and omnipotence working in your life. How you choose to respond to His three O's will determine your outlook on your life's circumstances and on your marriage. It can take you from hopeless to hopeful, from empty to empowered. Choose to yield to these divine attributes, and let God be God in your life and your marriage.

Knowing God Better: The Key

DAY FOUR

KNOWING GOD AS OUR ALL

God wants us to recognize Him as our All. He is everything that is good and perfect for us. With regard to what He says, there's no other absolute.

God Is the "I AM"—All We Need

Whenever we want to impart information about ourselves, we use the words "I am." Knowing that this phrase can't stand alone, we finish the description with the rest of the story, such as "I am a redhead" or "I am a systems analyst" or "I am tired." Get the picture? We can speak about ourselves only in finite terms, because there are only so many descriptions that define us. It's not so with God. He calls Himself the "I AM" because He is *everything*. Our finite language can't adequately characterize the God of the universe. He is infinite—in time, in space, in knowledge, in power, in all that He is, in all that He's capable of. This revelation was given to Moses at the burning bush, as recorded in the Book of Exodus. The Israelites deemed this name that God calls Himself so sacred that they wrote it without vowels so that it couldn't be spoken. Their approach to writing the name was just as reverent: scribes bathed before writing it and afterward destroyed the writing implement. There was nothing casual about their concept of the I AM.

God is the timeless foundation of all existence—the One who makes or causes things to happen. Literally, *"YHWH"* or "I Am Who I Am," God is self-existent or eternal, because He had no origin. By His own power, He always was and is and will be. Nothing happens apart from the I AM, period.

Before we join Moses at the burning bush, let's look over some background details. The Hebrews had been enslaved by the Egyptians for four centuries and were treated brutally after the death of Joseph. The great number of Hebrews in Egypt were perceived by Pharaoh to be a threat; he was fearful that they would join his enemies against him. He therefore ordered that all Hebrew boy babies be slaughtered at birth. Moses, protected for his first three months by his mother and then set afloat on the Nile in a basket, was rescued by Pharaoh's daughter and raised as an Egyptian. In his adulthood, Moses killed an Egyptian in defense of a fellow Hebrew, and in so doing he declared his heritage. Pharaoh attempted to kill him, so Moses fled to the country of Midian.

Moses had jumped the gun in his role as Israel's liberator, so he was sidelined until the I AM was ready to use him for that purpose. Forty years later, at age 80, Moses saw the burning bush. It is interesting to note that a burning bush in the desert in that region was not an unusual sight. What was unusual was that this bush was not consumed by the fire.

📖 Read Exodus 3:1–22. Briefly summarize what transpired between God and Moses. Note Moses' response to God's holiness and then his reaction when God explained the mission He had in mind for Moses.

_____

_____

_____

_____

📖 Doubt is a powerful deterrent to carrying out the will of the I AM. List the assurances God gives to Moses in this passage.

_____

_____

_____

_____

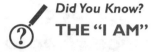

Did You Know?
THE "I AM"

"I AM," translated from the Hebrew *YHWH* or *Yahweh*, is masculine (just in case you wondered), singular, and is used approximately six thousand times in the Old Testament.

"And God said to Moses, 'I AM WHO I AM.'"

Exodus 3:14

📖 Moses should have been willing to carry out the command of the One who makes things happen, right? Briefly summarize Moses' exchange with God in Exodus 4:1–17.

_____

_____

_____

Even after God's assurance that the elders would listen to Moses (Exodus 3:18), Moses couldn't refrain from asking, *What if . . . ?* (Exodus 4:1). What was he thinking? We can almost hear God saying, "Moses, work with Me here!"

When God sets out to accomplish His purpose (which is usually the impossible, by human wisdom), what He intends is what's going to happen, no matter what resistance He meets. But it's most desirable to accomplish the impossible when human resistance isn't part of the equation. Wouldn't you want the One who makes things happen, the I AM, to go before you, accomplishing the impossible?

By the time God's will is made clear to the heart of an obedient child such as Moses, the outcome has already taken place in the heavenly realm. God's timing then unfolds it here on the earth. This is important to understand and remember when we're faced with seemingly impossible circumstances, such as those that Moses was about to experience. To liberate more than two million Israelites, Moses had to persevere through numerous obstacles. These included an unrelenting pharaoh whose heart God hardened, nearly unbearable oppression of the Israelites by the Egyptians, Moses' own anguish and doubt (Exodus 5:22–23), ten plagues (Exodus 7—11), the awesome terror of the first Passover (Exodus 12), and the Egyptians' hot pursuit of the fleeing Israelites.

God accomplished His mission in His way and in His time, not only to answer the cries of His people but also to make Himself known to Jews and Egyptians alike. Because only He is the I AM!

 Let's try some honest reflection: Can you identify with Moses in his doubt? Has the I AM recently required anything of you that you questioned or resisted (and continue to question or resist) because of your doubt in His ability? In what areas of your marriage do you doubt that the I AM could work the impossible?

_____

_____

_____

_____

The I AM is *bigger* than all your circumstances. Remember that you were created to bring Him pleasure, to glorify Him, and to respond to Him. He will do in your life whatever is necessary to accomplish all three purposes if you'll let Him. Will you?

God Is Holiness—All That We Can Become

We just read about Moses' encounter with God. It was no ordinary experience for him. As a matter of fact, God told him how he was to respond to their encounter: *"Do not come near here; remove your sandals from your feet,*

> **By the time God's will is made clear to the heart of an obedient child such as Moses, the outcome has already taken place in the heavenly realm. God's timing then unfolds it here on the earth.**

for the place on which you are standing is holy ground" (Exodus 3:5). And when God revealed Himself to Moses, *"Moses hid his face, for he was afraid to look at God"* (verse 6). Being ushered into the holy presence of the Lord God Almighty is supposed to elicit a holy response.

📖 What do the following scriptures reveal about the holiness of God?

1 Samuel 2:2

_____

_____

Psalm 77:13

_____

_____

Isaiah 5:16

_____

_____

Isaiah 6:1–5

_____

_____

In your own words, describe God's holy nature.

_____

_____

_____

_____

_____

📖 Read 1 Peter 1:13–16. What does God require of us, and why? What do you think this means?

_____

_____

_____

_____

> **"But the LORD of hosts will be exalted in judgment, and the holy God will show Himself holy in righteousness."**
>
> **Isaiah 5:16**

Our response to our holy God should be one that acknowledges His purity, His perfection, His sacred majesty, since there is no equal. And everything associated with God is holy "consecrated, devoted . . . set apart from a common to a sacred use,"[8] to include His men and women. How else will we make Him known?

(APPLY) Think seriously about the holiness of God. What does it mean to you? Does it challenge a casual attitude or convict a prideful heart? Can you identify with Moses as he stood on holy ground, or with Isaiah as he viewed God in His majesty? What *is* your response to God's holiness? What is your response to God's making *you* holy?

_____

_____

_____

_____

How does the concept of holiness apply to your marriage? How does it apply to your growth as a wife?

_____

_____

_____

_____

If the Creator of the institution of marriage is holy, then the institution itself is holy. (Now there's a spiritual perspective worth pondering!) Can you imagine that your marriage is a "consecrated . . . dedicated . . . hallowed [thing]"[9] intended for God's use, even if you didn't know Him at the time you tied the knot? According to Malachi 2:14, the Lord witnesses the covenant between a husband and wife at the time of their marriage. Marriage was a sacred covenant in Old Testament days, and it's a sacred covenant now.

Because marriage is God's holy institution, it's not only a place in which God can use you well, but it's fertile ground for your own growth in holiness. A husband, whether or not he's a believer, should greatly benefit from his wife's growth in the Lord. Has your growing as a woman of God benefited your husband? If so, in what ways?

_____

_____

_____

God Is Truth—All We Need to Know

Christian pollster George Barna found that twenty percent of respondents between twenty-six and forty-four years old believed that there is "no absolute truth, that different people can define truth in different ways and still be correct."[10] Of those who were described as born-again Christians, twenty-seven percent strongly disagreed with the statement, whereas fifty-two percent agreed with it.

📖 What do Numbers 23:19 and Titus 1:1–2 assert about God?

_____

_____

_____

_____

Do you believe what God says in the Bible? Can you trust what He says when everyone else says something different? When we're used to hearing no truth or half-truths from surrounding cultural influences, absolute truth can be daunting and tough to trust. Because God is truth, it's impossible for Him to tolerate anything less.

When we're used to hearing no truth or half-truths from surrounding cultural influences, absolute truth can be daunting and tough to trust. Because God is truth, it's impossible for Him to tolerate anything less.

Have you acknowledged God as the author of truth? Do you believe that His truth is absolute, no matter where we are in human history? If so, will you believe that what He ordained for marriage from the beginning stands today? Does this in any way alter your attitude toward marriage in general? If so, how? Does it alter your attitude toward your own marriage in particular? If so, how?

_____

_____

_____

_____

 Now is a good time to take a few moments to thank God for all He is. Entrust yourself, your husband, and your marriage to Him and to the holy standard of His truth, and watch Him work. Will you do so right now?

KNOWING GOD AS LOVING AUTHORITY

Have you ever felt frightened by the uncertainty of change, or help-less and hopeless when life seemed out of control, or empty when there didn't seem to be a scrap of love left? What do we do in times like these? Where do we go? To whom? Let's examine three more power-ful attributes of God for the answers.

God Is Immutable—The Changeless Master of Change

Change: we fight it, deny it, ignore it, abhor it. It's scary, and it's inevitable. Did you know that we serve a God who can't change? In His perfection, He can't change for the better. In His holiness, He can't change for the worse. He can't change His truth, His agenda, His character, His standard, His purpose, His mind. He'll never become the "I Was." It's impossible for the I AM to become other than who He is.

📖 What do Psalm 102:25–27 and James 1:17 say about our immutable, changeless God?

_____

_____

_____

James 1:17 says there's *no variation* with the Father. Therefore, we can trust that God still means today everything He has said from the beginning.

Although God Himself is changeless, He is always about change: morning/evening, spring/summer/fall/winter, birth/death, unregenerate humanity/new creature. Charles Wesley said, "All things as they change pro-claim the Lord eternally the same."[11] He is the uncreated creating, perfection perfecting, holiness making holy.

 As you continue to know God—to recognize, perceive, and under-stand who He is—can you see how His immutable character tran-

James 1:17 says there's no variation with the Father. Therefore, we can trust that God still means today every-thing He has said from the beginning.

scends time and culture? Can you perceive our changeless God moving in you toward change? In what areas? Identify those here.

_____

_____

_____

Do these areas affect your relationship with your husband? If so, in what way?

_____

_____

_____

God Is Sovereign—The Divine Controller of All Things

It's so easy to say that God is in control when we run out of ways to manage our circumstances, or when we feel helpless and can no longer manipulate the people or events that make our lives a challenge. But do we truly understand the power behind the word "sovereign"?

"Sovereign" has been defined as "supreme in power, possessing supreme dominion or jurisdiction; royal; free of outside influence or control." The infinite attributes of the I AM pronounce Him absolutely free to exercise His will anytime, anywhere, and with anyone. If He were faulty, weak, or constrained in any of His attributes, He could not be in control.

📖 What do the following Scriptures reveal about God's sovereignty?

Job 42:1–2

_____

_____

Psalm 33:10–11

_____

_____

Psalm 103:19

_____

_____

Isaiah 55:8–11

_____

_____

Matthew 10:29

_____

_____

Romans 8:28

_____

_____

The infinite attributes of the I AM pronounce Him absolutely free to exercise His will anytime, anywhere, and with anyone. If He were faulty, weak, or constrained in any of His attributes, He could not be in control.

APPLY What does God's sovereignty mean for you in your life? How can His sovereignty encourage you in your marriage, regardless of its condition?

_____

_____

_____

If we believe that God is the supreme authority over whom no other can have or gain control, then we'll eagerly welcome Him into the midst of our lives and marriages. He personally and deliberately invades our own tiny specks of His universe by engineering whatever circumstances are necessary to draw us, change us, test us, and keep us growing as His own women. And the situation in which that is the most revealing and challenging is marriage; it's where our walk with Him must be the most credible.

APPLY What areas of your life—and perhaps even your husband's life—are you holding onto tightly? Are you controlling, manipulative, refusing to depend on God's sovereign control? Write your assessment here.

_____

_____

_____

God Is Love—Our Foundational Example

Scripture is emphatically clear: God is love. In His love, He seeks only our best, even when that hurts. His love compels Him to commit to us wholeheartedly, to remain faithful to His promises, to never leave us or forsake us, to never fail us.

📖 Read Jeremiah 31:3. According to this passage, what is unique about God's love?

_____

_____

He woos us to Himself, not with contempt or condemnation for our failings but with a loving-kindness that will never end. Could you possibly have been drawn to God in any other way than what's described in Jeremiah?

📖 Read 1 John 4:19–21 with your husband in mind. What effect can God's love for you have on your love for your husband?

_____

_____

APPLY Do you know God's love? Have you experienced it? If so, give an example of how God's love has been manifest in your life. If you don't know this love yet, anticipate it—you'll know it soon. These lessons will demonstrate how the love of God can transform hearts—beginning with your own.

> *"I know that you can do all things; no plan of yours can be thwarted."*
>
> *Job 42:2* (NIV)

_____

_____

_____

 Are your life and your circumstances firmly in your own grip right now? Do you sense that God has some changes in store for you? Consider God's immutable, sovereign, and loving character as He applies His attributes to your life and to your marriage. Don't be afraid of them. This is His love in action. Instead, ask Him to prepare your heart for whatever He knows is best for you. Loosen your grip, and grasp the loving, sovereign hand of our changeless God.

Author's note: A wonderful query came up recently in my classroom. It was "Can God possibly be interested in or even bless our marriage if one or both of us have been divorced? How much of this study can apply to us?" My answers to these questions are: "Absolutely!" and "All of it." Why? Because God knows where we have been and desires to meet us right where we are now. We serve a forgiving, forward-moving God, one who doesn't want us "stuck" in past sins and mistakes (ours or our husbands'), but desires to bless us as we ask His forgiveness and follow Him in our current marriages. So my encouragement to any of you who have been remarried as a result of divorce, or are married to men who have been divorced, is to not permit yourselves to be distracted by that. Keep your eyes fixed on the Author and Finisher of your faith, and let Him move in _this_ marriage. You can glorify Him there—for as long as you and your husband both shall live.

Works Cited

1. Spiros Zodhiates, Warren Baker, eds., _The Complete Word Study Old Testament_ (Chattanooga, TN: AMG Publishers, 1994), #2896, 2320.

2. Charles C. Ryrie, ed., _The Ryrie Study Bible, New American Standard Translation_ (Chicago: Moody Press, 1978), 7.

3. Zodhiates, Baker, eds., _The Complete Word Study Old Testament,_ #6754, 2358.

4. Spiros Zodhiates, Warren Baker, eds., _The Complete Word Study Dictionary New Testament_ (Chattanooga, TN: AMG Publishers, 1992), #2307, 721.

5. Charles F. Pfeiffer and Everett F. Harrison, eds., _The Wycliffe Bible Commentary_ (Chicago: Moody Press, 1962), 4.

6. A. W. Tozer, _The Knowledge of the Holy_ (New York: Harper & Row, 1961), 61.

7. James Reimann, ed., _My Utmost for His Highest: The Golden Book of Oswald Chambers_ (Grand Rapids, MI: Discovery House, 1992), January 9 devotional.

8. Zodhiates, Baker, eds., _The Complete Word Study Dictionary New Testament,_ #40, 70.

9. James Strong, _The Exhaustive Concordance of the Bible_ (McLean, VA: MacDonald Publishing Company, #6944, 102.

10. George Barna, _What America Believes_ (Ventura, Calif.: Regal Books, 1991), 84-85.

11. Quoted in Tozer, _The Knowledge of the Holy,_ 58.

2

The Savior and the Helper

*L*ast week we studied the Father God of all creation, the I AM—the God who on the sixth day of creation saw that all He had made was very good, and then He rested. How satisfied He must have been! He couldn't improve on His perfection. Male and female were the epitome of His creative energy and became His pleasure and glory, His delight. He commanded them to become one flesh. And so they did—inseparably one. How sweet their fellowship in that garden paradise was! But that would soon change.

In these next five days we'll discover the reasons marriage can be so difficult. We'll examine our personal relationship with our heavenly Father through His Son, Jesus Christ, and its impact on our relationship with our husbands. And finally we'll identify the vital role of the Helper-Counselor in our spiritual walk and in our marriages.

I encourage you to give this lesson your utmost energy and attention; it may set the course for the rest of your days.

I encourage you to give this lesson your utmost energy and attention; it may set the course for the rest of your days.

Why is marriage so tough?

THE DOWNFALL

Think about the most beautiful, restful place you've ever been, and multiply that by perfection. Imagine inhabiting that place indefinitely, in perfect peace with the Lover of your soul. That's what God designed for Adam and Eve—an environment of intimate oneness with Him and with each other.

But something was about to go radically wrong. Poised in the garden was Satan, the enemy of our souls. Taking up residence in the body of a serpent, he waited for an opportune time to intercept the man and his helpmeet and to draw them into his bondage of sin. Adam would choose his own will over the will of God; his pursuit of self would destroy God's original intent and tarnish the image of God in which he was created. Sin was to reign on earth, but the war for human souls would rage in heaven.

The question "Why is marriage so tough?" repeatedly plagues those of us who are married. Let's take a look at one of the most critical events in Scripture, the event that set humanity's course against God, destroyed relationships, and turned the paradise He had made into the imperfect world we now know.

📖 Read Genesis 2:8–9. Describe the garden's contents and the people God put in it.

_____

_____

_____

📖 In Genesis 2:15–17 we read that God gave the man his first area of responsibility and the first command. What was Adam's duty in the Garden? What command did God give him? What would happen if he disobeyed?

_____

_____

_____

God put Adam in the middle of the garden and charged him with the responsibility of cultivating it and guarding it, a task that was intended to be pleasurable. God also gave Adam the freedom to eat from any of the trees, with the exception of the tree of the knowledge of good and evil. Should Adam violate this command, a sobering consequence would occur: death.

It's significant that the instructions and command were given to Adam alone. We serve a God of order, and God established Adam's headship by the order of His creation: *"It was Adam who was first created, and then Eve"* (1 Timothy 2:13). From the beginning, Adam was intended to be the accountable and responsible leader, protector, and provider in his environment. To this day, God's intent hasn't changed.

 Consider these previous two sentences. How does this concept affect your view of your husband's role? Is this a tough truth for you or an affirmation of what you already know to be his role? What's your response to it?

_____

_____

_____

Author Nancy Wilson encourages us to "cultivate a high view of our husbands and a high view of their God-given jobs." She states, "You have the privilege of being God's appointed helper for him. Have a high view of this calling and a biblical view of your responsibilities associated with this calling."[1]

📖 Read Genesis 2:18–25 to refresh your memory. Adam had a need that only God could meet. Eve was created, and they became one flesh. Two bodies united, naked and unashamed, two souls flawlessly suited for each other physically, emotionally, intellectually, and spiritually.

Adam and Eve's fellowship with God and with each other was perfect. They knew only peace in a world whose elements were their friends. Their interaction as a couple was complete in every way, loving intimately, totally, freely, as God had intended. There were no judgmental attitudes, no wrongs committed against the other, no guilt, no fear, no jealousy. It's important to examine what changed all of that, because what destroyed their harmonious relationship with God also shattered their relationship.

📖 Read Genesis 3:1–6. In these verses we see Satan using an array of tactics to accomplish his goal: severing oneness between the man and God, then between the man and his wife. I call these tactics the five Ds: distraction, doubt, debate, deception, and desire, which lead to the ultimate D—downfall. Let's take a look at the Enemy's strategy. In the first part of verse 1, what distraction got Eve's attention?

_____

_____

Because we can assume that the only conversations taking place up to this point were between Adam and Eve and their Creator, a speaking serpent had to be distracting. Satan's agenda has always been separation. Distraction remains his first tool in the trek toward sin, because it diverts our focus from the One who can keep us from sinning.

 Consider the things that distract you from staying on God's path, tempting you toward sin. What are they, and how are they used to distract you?

_____

_____

_____

Once the Enemy had Eve's attention, he was able to reel her in with the second D. According to verse 1, how did the serpent plant doubt in Eve's mind?

_____

_____

According to rabbinic legend, the serpent was a stunning, two-legged animal. When Satan entered this creature, it was given the ability to speak. Genesis 3:1 describes the serpent as subtle and crafty. The Hebrew word translated "subtle" alludes to extraordinary shrewdness. Our enemy, Satan, is no different today. He convincingly speaks deception into the minds of his victims, those easily deceived by his lies, with exceptional cunning.

The words Satan used with Eve are just as effective today in creating doubt in our own hearts about the truth of God. Satan's question, *"Did God really say, 'You must not eat from any tree in the garden'?"* (Genesis 3:1, NIV) introduced suspicion about God and His motives, plus inaccuracy about what God had actually said. Satan planted suspicion in Eve's innocent mind to erode her trust in the One who loved her most.

APPLY Satan's tactics haven't changed. Doubt is still the precursor to unbelief. Do you believe that God desires to work in your life and your marriage? If not, identify your doubts: *Did God really say. . . .*

_____

_____

_____

Reread verses 1–5, and explain how Satan's next tactic, *debate,* unfolded.

_____

_____

_____

> ## "He said to the woman, 'Did God really say...?'"
> ## Genesis 3:1 (NIV)

Eve valiantly attempted to defend God's command and correct Satan's misrepresentation. However, she did so by exaggerating God's truth. No match for the serpent's shrewdness, Eve was easily goaded into debate, which caused confusion and more doubt, laying the groundwork for deception.

It is during debate that either the truth or the lie is taking shape. The painful truth is this: when we exaggerate a truth to defend our stand, we don't believe what we think we believe. Exaggeration should alert our minds that deception is taking shape! How does Proverbs 10:19 back up this point?

_____

_____

_____

> ## The painful truth is this: when we exaggerate a truth to defend our stand, we don't believe what we think we believe.

In his craftiness, Satan distracted Eve, caused her to doubt God, and goaded her into debate. She was now ripe for the next *D.*

Carefully look at verses 4–5. What is the lie? Can you discern the deception?

_____

_____

_____

The serpent's blatant lie, *"You will not surely die"* (Genesis 3:4, NIV) was coupled with the truth that when they ate the fruit God had forbidden, they would become like Him, knowing good and evil (verse 22). That was the deception—just enough truth to make the lie believable. Satan also distorted God's motive, deliberately inferring that God was selfishly withholding the desirable. And Eve believed him—no more debate.

If we don't know or are not convinced of the character and truths of God, we'll be susceptible to the same confusion and doubt when His Word is challenged. Our daily fork in the road is to choose whom we'll believe: God or Satan.

During painful seasons in marriage, Satan wants us to pursue a way out, not the way through. His persistent goal is to sever oneness, to drive a couple apart and destroy the family. He'll try to imbed such thoughts as *Why would God want me to stay in an unhappy marriage? . . . Surely there's someone better for me. . . . Why would God want me to love (forgive, respect) someone who doesn't deserve it? . . . We've never been right for each other. . . . We don't have anything in common. . . . We don't love each other anymore. . . . This is too hard.*

Satan will attempt to distort God's Word, His standard, and His intent. He wants us to question God's motives for permitting trials in our lives and marriages. If that doesn't work, he'll try to convince us that God is not so easily offended—that we can go against His Word if our happiness is at stake. But God *is* offended when His Truth is compromised. He won't alter His standard just because His answers to our questions are difficult to accept.

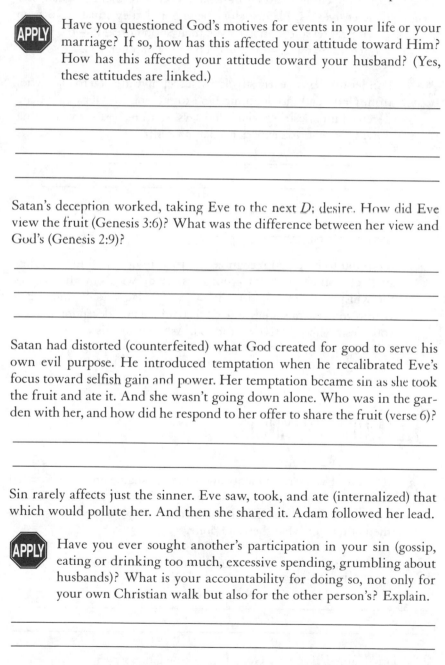

APPLY Have you questioned God's motives for events in your life or your marriage? If so, how has this affected your attitude toward Him? How has this affected your attitude toward your husband? (Yes, these attitudes are linked.)

_____

_____

_____

_____

Satan's deception worked, taking Eve to the next *D*; desire. How did Eve view the fruit (Genesis 3:6)? What was the difference between her view and God's (Genesis 2:9)?

_____

_____

_____

Satan had distorted (counterfeited) what God created for good to serve his own evil purpose. He introduced temptation when he recalibrated Eve's focus toward selfish gain and power. Her temptation became sin as she took the fruit and ate it. And she wasn't going down alone. Who was in the garden with her, and how did he respond to her offer to share the fruit (verse 6)?

_____

_____

Sin rarely affects just the sinner. Eve saw, took, and ate (internalized) that which would pollute her. And then she shared it. Adam followed her lead.

APPLY Have you ever sought another's participation in your sin (gossip, eating or drinking too much, excessive spending, grumbling about husbands)? What is your accountability for doing so, not only for your own Christian walk but also for the other person's? Explain.

_____

_____

_____

_____

Extra Mile
MANKIND'S FALL

Read 1 John 2:15–17. What is the parallel between the things of the world, as described in this passage, and the events that led to the Fall?

When Adam and Eve ate the fruit, their eyes *"were opened"* (Genesis 3:7, NIV) to a sudden miracle, but it was not a good one. They were suddenly fully aware of the magnitude of their choice, and they experienced a rude awakening of their sense of right and wrong. Having been exposed to nothing but God's good, they now realized that evil would constantly compete for their life choices.

In Genesis 3:7–13 the moment of truth—God's truth—kicked in. When Adam and Eve ate the fruit, their eyes *"were opened"* (Genesis 3:7, NIV) immediately, and they miraculously possessed the knowledge they desired, but it was not what they had expected. List all the ways in which this sudden miracle affected them.

_____

_____

_____

What a devastating experience for Adam and Eve! The joy and comfort, the goodness and blessing they had with God and with each other were gone forever. Into their place flooded the powerful, frightening emotions of shame and fear, opening the door to behaviors new to them—denial, self-deception, defensiveness, blame. How bewildered they must have been, how filled with regret and remorse over their sudden reality—the separation of the once inseparable—and the deep agony of loneliness.

APPLY Ponder this lesson earnestly. How susceptible are you to distraction from God's path, to doubting God to the point of debate, to being deceived into desiring what God says isn't His best for you? What downfalls have you experienced as a result?

_____

_____

_____

_____

 Ask God to help you recognize the road to downfall in its earliest stage of distraction, before your eyes are drawn from Him, before the whisper of "Did God really say. . . ?" places doubt and debate within you and raises lies above His truth, before deception elevates your desires above His own for you. Ask to hear His voice that says, *"This is the way, walk in it"* (Isaiah 30:21).

The Savior and the Helper

DAY TWO

THE CONSEQUENCES

A dam and Eve were suddenly awakened to shame and its associated inhibitions. Each hid from the other and from God because of their nakedness. They were totally vulnerable—exposed and afraid. And they blamed others for what they had done.

In Genesis 3:12, whom did Adam blame? (Look closely.) In verse 13, whom did Eve blame?

_____

_____

Adam blamed Eve and God. Eve blamed the serpent. Who *was* to blame? In Genesis 3:14–19, God made that clear as He leveled curses and judgments on the serpent, the woman, the ground, and the man.

What was God's curse on the serpent, as noted in verse 14? Why did God curse it?

_____

_____

What were God's judgments against Eve (verse 16)?

_____

_____

What was God's curse on the ground? Why did He curse it (verses 17–18)?

_____

_____

In verses 17–19, what was God's judgment against Adam, and why?

_____

_____

_____

APPLY How do you think your marriage is affected by God's judgments against Adam and Eve?

_____

_____

_____

_____

God's curses and judgments affect us all. Because of Satan's deception, God subjected all of creation to death and decay (Romans 8:20–21), and the serpent became a humiliated yet feared belly-crawler, eating from the dust of the ground.

God held Eve accountable for being so easily deceived instead of standing firmly on what she knew to be true. As a result, physical and emotional suffering would be associated with all aspects of childbearing and childbirth, including painful menstrual cycles, infertility, miscarriages, difficult pregnancies, stillbirths, excruciating pain in childbirth, and the problems associated with menopause.

The Fall had also changed the character of Adam and Eve's physical and emotional relationship. Prior to their sin, they *were both naked, and they felt no shame* (Genesis 2:25, NIV). But afterward, areas of their deepest intimacy were shaken. Their oneness became separateness. And Eve was now to be subject to her husband's leadership (Genesis 3:16), an edict that predicted the relationship's potential for contention. This reality hit home for me. I realized how resistant I had been to my husband John's headship in our home. I did vie for control in our marriage, even in minor areas, challenging him sometimes without words, but with a look or with my body language. There was also an everpresent tension in our sexual relationship. And emotionally, we were often like strangers. The truth was biting. Instead of being my husband's completer, I was his "competer." I knew God had some work to do in my heart.

Instead of being my husband's completer, I was his competer.

APPLY Is your husband's God-ordained authority in the home an issue for you? Do you vie for control? In what areas? Finances? Parenting? Career? Color-coordinating his clothes? What does competition in your home look like? How is it impacting your relationship? Prayerfully consider this before the Lord, and write your insights here.

_____

_____

_____

Is sexual intimacy an issue in your marriage? It may not even be an openly contended issue. Your distress (and his) may be lurking beneath the surface, unspoken, hidden. Be willing to admit it to the Lord. How is it affecting your marriage?

_____

_____

_____

God's judgment against Adam was for more than his eating the forbidden fruit. What was the first part of God's rebuke, according to verse 17?

_____

_____

God first rebuked Adam for succumbing to Eve's persuasive tactics, and then for not obeying His command. Satan had not deceived Adam—Adam had chosen to ignore God's face-to-face command not to eat of the tree of the knowledge of good and evil. Instead, he chose to listen to his wife. This act of rebellion bought him a lifetime of exhaustive work in order to provide for his family. The ground that had yielded effortlessly and bountifully would now require strenuous human effort to produce food. Today a husband's career and time spent on the job are often causes of contention in the home, but they may not be the only reasons for job-centered strife in a marriage. Many wives have entered the workforce either by necessity or by choice. However, the luxury or need of dual incomes doesn't always translate into shared responsibilities between a husband and wife, especially in the areas of housekeeping and parenting, which create more relational stress.

APPLY Are your husband's job and the hours he puts into it an area of contention in your home? If so, how is this contention displayed in your relationship?

_____

_____

_____

If you're a dual–income family, are there added tensions? If so, what are they? How have they been affecting your relationship?

_____

_____

_____

Whether or not we're in a dual-income marriage, it's necessary to drive home a very important point here: the frightening reality is that God will hold every husband accountable for his God-ordained role in the home as leader, provider, and protector, even if he's not a believer. That role was established in his soul from the beginning. A wife's competition for her husband's role as head of the family will yield one of two reactions from him: either he'll withdraw and let her take over, or he'll fight back. If she deliberately and willfully cajoles, manipulates, and nags in order to impose her will in an area of her husband's responsibility (which is not the same as offering wise counsel), she is in sin. If he allows her to take over his role, he is in sin.

 Is your husband fighting to establish his God-given place in your home? If so, how can you tell? Has he withdrawn from taking the lead in the family? If so, why do you think he's done so? Do you long for him to lead but believe that your way is better? Honestly assess your husband's role as head of your home, as well as your part in support of it. Write your assessment here:

_____

_____

_____

_____

God created the helpmeet to be a strong, positive influence on her man. She was the "one who could share man's responsibilities, respond to his nature with understanding and love, and wholeheartedly co-operate with him in working out the plan of God."[2] What God ordained from the beginning is still possible today, even if our husbands are unbelievers or slow-growing believers. Applying God's biblical principles—His truth—to our role of godly wives will enhance our marriages. And unless our husbands' hearts are like stones (which only God can determine), they'll respond.

📖 There was one final consequence of Adam and Eve's first sin. Read Genesis 2:9 again, and note that only the fruit of the tree of knowledge of good and evil was forbidden. Now read Genesis 3:22–24. From what tree were Adam and Eve no longer permitted to eat? Why? How do you think this affected their relationship with God?

_____

_____

_____

Barring Adam and Eve from the tree of life because they had eaten the fruit of the tree of knowledge guaranteed physical death for humanity, as God had warned in Genesis 2:17. Death is a consequence not of God's wrath and retribution but of His justice and mercy. Immortality in a sin-filled world would be a living hell for us. Life is tough enough with our days numbered.

📖 But there was another death that took place that day—the death of a relationship. Adam and Eve were now spiritually dead in their sin, alienated from their Creator. Read Romans 5:12 followed by 3:23. What impact did Adam's disobedience have on all who came after him?

_____

_____

_____

> **A wife's competition for her husband's role as head of the family will yield one of two reactions from him: either he'll withdraw and let her take over, or he'll fight back.**

The inheritance of sin—what a legacy! Adam fell short of the glory of God, for which he was created, and charted the course of sin and death for every one of us.

📖 Read Romans 1:18–32 with a sober heart. Describe what the sinful nature born in every human being is like.

_____

_____

_____

Pay particular attention to verses 21–25. What is the indictment here against humanity? What was darkened (verse 21)?

_____

_____

_____

Exchanging the truth of God for a lie, habitually practicing every ungodly behavior, and applauding others who do the same is rebellion against God—willful disobedience. The human heart that was created to respond to the Creator was now darkened—hardened to the things of God—and would fuel the sinful nature. And the resulting behavior would not only grieve God but also invite His wrath.

"Death" is a terrible word, but it's the destiny of all (Romans 6:23). In faithfulness to His holy character, God could not permit sin to go unpunished. His punishment was not only the death of the physical body (*"When you eat of it you will surely die,"* [Genesis 2:17, NIV]), but also death to spiritual oneness with Him (*"After He drove the man out, he placed on the east side of the Garden of Eden cherubim and a flaming sword flashing back and forth to guard the way to the tree of life"* [Genesis 3:24, NIV]). Formerly God's pride and joy, humanity was now a doomed creation.

📖 But in His goodness, loving-kindness, and mercy, God tended to this first couple. What did He do for Adam and Eve, according to Genesis 3:21?

_____

_____

God could have annihilated His first couple on the spot. But in a prophetic display of love, He shed the blood of animals not only to cover the nakedness of the two who had just rejected Him, but also to foretell the substitutionary payment that would take place in the fullness of time.

📖 God knew that neither fig leaves nor any other human endeavor would be enough to pay the price that Adam inflicted on all those who would follow him. So, according to Genesis 3:15, God declared war! The serpent (Satan) would have a formidable foe. Who do you think He is?

_____

_____

_____

"They exchanged the truth of God for a lie. . . ."

Romans 1:25 (NIV)

Doctrine
SUBSTITUTION

Since the fall of Adam and Eve, the holiness of God established that human beings, as the wrongdoers (sinners), could not make restitution for their wrongdoing (sin). Only holiness could accomplish the restoration to holiness, and human holiness was destroyed in the garden of Eden. Only One was qualified to substitute Himself for us, to take our place. So Holiness took on unholiness; the sinless One, Jesus Christ, took on our sin. *"He made Him Who knew no sin to be sin on our behalf, that we might become the righteousness of God in Him"* (2 Corinthians 5:21).

The Genesis 3:15 passage is called

the *protevangelium*, or the 'first gospel,' the announcement of a prolonged struggle, perpetual antagonism, wounds on both sides, and eventual victory for the seed of woman. God's promise that the head of the serpent was to be crushed pointed forward to the coming of Messiah and guaranteed victory. This assurance fell upon the ears of God's earliest creatures as a blessed hope of redemption.[3]

Isn't it good of God to prophesy His plan to restore the relationship that was destroyed in the Garden of Eden? What a promise!

 God's plan unfolds throughout the Old Testament records of Abraham, of Moses and the Israelites, of the Law and the Prophets—God was preparing, warning, revealing. A wonderful foretaste of what was to come is given in Ezekiel 36:25–28. What is the promise given there?

_____

_____

_____

APPLY Consider what you've learned today. What do you think of our God, who desires redemption and reconciliation rather than retribution for his wayward creation? What does this reveal about His character? How does this revelation apply to your own life? To your marriage?

_____

_____

_____

 Thank God for His mercies and for His commitment to His creation. May He show you your part in His plan and in your marriage—day by day.

THE REDEMPTION

The Savior and the Helper
DAY THREE

In our spendthrift society, we can get caught up in the buy-now-pay-later mentality. Much like the proverbial frog in the pot, before we're even aware that the heat is increasing, we can become laden with debt that takes months, perhaps years, to repay. That debt becomes our bondage.

In similar fashion, sin creates the spiritual debt we owe God as fallen creatures. And no matter how hard we work, no matter how great our works, we can't satisfy this debt. It, too, is bondage. We can't redeem ourselves from what we owe God. He won't (*can't*) forgive our debt based on what we do. The harsh reality is that we owe a price we can't pay, and God requires payment for our debt.

So He paid the price for us Himself. *"The Son of God appeared for this purpose, that He might destroy the works of the devil"* (1 John 3:8)—works that

"The Son of God appeared for this purpose, that He might destroy the works of the devil."

I John 3:8b

had left humanity hollow and hopeless, pursuing whatever would fill the void within.

📖 Isaiah prophesied the Savior's mission, as told in Isaiah 61:1–3. Jesus confirmed it in Luke 4:14–19. What did the Messiah come to do, as described in these passages?

_____

_____

📖 Read Luke 4:20–21. As the crowd waited expectantly (knowing there was more), what proclamation did Jesus make?

_____

_____

The devastating effect of humanity's sinfulness was bondage to Satan, manifesting itself in many forms. But prophecy was fulfilled as Jesus Christ set out to destroy the works of the Enemy. He went forth with the good news, filling the empty cups of the spiritually impoverished. (Is your cup empty?) He healed the brokenhearted. (Is your heart breaking?) He set free those held captive by the Enemy. (Are you in bondage to Satan's bidding?) He restored sight to the blind. (Are you unable to see Jesus and His truth clearly?) And He delivered those who were oppressed. (Are you downtrodden, bruised, crushed, and broken by circumstances?) Jesus' mission is to restore to life that which is dead so that we *"will be called oaks of righteousness, The planting of the LORD, that He may be glorified"* (Isaiah 61:3).

 Do you know this Jesus? Even if you've been a believer for years, are you more intimately acquainted with Him this year than last? Is your understanding of His ways becoming progressively clearer, especially as you let Him walk you through your tough spots His way? Is your prayer time growing deeper and richer? Knowing Him like this should be our continual, habitual practice (John 17:3), so that we become oaks of righteousness, established by Him and in Him. This is how we glorify Him. Let's discover Jesus afresh.

📖 What do the following scriptures reveal about Jesus Christ?

John 1:1–2, 14

_____

_____

Colossians 1:15

_____

_____

Hebrews 1:3

_____

_____

In your own words, who is Jesus?

_____

📖 Very plainly, Jesus Christ is God revealed. How did Jesus convey this in John 10:30; 14:8–11?

_____

_____

Jesus said that if we've seen Him, we've seen the Father (John 14:9). Who Christ is, God is. A youth pastor used to tell my daughters that Jesus is "God with skin on." Every attribute of Jesus communicates God the Father to us.

📖 What powerful declaration did Jesus make in John 8:58?

_____

_____

📖 In declaring Himself the I AM, Jesus equated Himself with Jehovah, the *I AM WHO I AM* of Exodus 3:14. Below are seven verses that contain "I AM" statements made by Jesus. Review the following scriptures, and fill in the blanks.

John 6:35, 41, 48: I am the _____

John 8:12: I am the _____

John 10:7, 9: I am the _____

John 10:11, 14: I am the_____

John 11:25: I am the _____

John 14:6: I am the _____

John 15:1, 5: I am the _____

JESUS IS . . .

◆ The Bread of life—the sustainer of our souls;

◆ The Light of the world—the only One who can separate us from Satan's darkness;

◆ The Door for the sheep—the One through whom our salvation is sure;

◆ The Good Shepherd—the One who gathers us in His arms and carries us close to His heart;

◆ The Resurrection and the Life—the ultimate and only victor over death and its sting, raising us to life abundant;

◆ The Way, the Truth, and the Life—the only way to the Father; the only truth from the Father; the only life in the Father;

◆ The True Vine—the only real and genuine source of growth and blessing.

📖 Jesus Christ is also the supreme authority over all. Read Colossians 1:15–20, and list all that indicates His supremacy.

_____

_____

_____

🛑 **APPLY** I'm struck by the phrase noting that in Him *all things hold together* (Colossians 1:17). What a revealing and relieving hope! By His authority the universe and everything in it hold together. And I'll

> "Jesus said to them, 'Most assuredly, I say to you, before Abraham was, I AM.'"
>
> John 8:58 (NKJV)

take this a step further: because my life is in Him, He holds it together, no matter what (poor health, challenging marriage, wayward children). Because I have accepted Him as the supreme and final authority, I can trust Him as my life's "glue." What can this mean for your life? How can this truth affect your marriage, even if your husband is not a believer?

_____

_____

_____

_____

📖 Read Philippians 2:6–11. Write in your own words what transpired between Jesus and His Father as described in this passage.

_____

_____

_____

> **By the compelling authority of His name, all people will acknowledge His supremacy, whether they want to or not. What an awesome event to consider!**

By the compelling authority of His name, all people will acknowledge His supremacy, whether they want to or not. What an awesome event to consider!

📖 Read John 10:14–18. What was Jesus willing to do for us? How would He do it, and by whose authority?

_____

_____

_____

According to Romans 5:18–19 and 1 Corinthians 15:21–22, why was it necessary for Jesus to die for us?

_____

_____

_____

📖 Read John 3:16 and Romans 5:8. Why did God sacrifice His Son for us?

_____

_____

> **"But God demonstrates His own love toward us, in that while we were yet sinners, Christ died for us."**
>
> **Romans 5:8**

God's love compelled Him to sacrifice the only sinless One who could reconcile the whole human race to Himself, reestablishing relationship as it was in the beginning. No one else would qualify, *"for there is no other name under heaven . . . by which we must be saved"* (Acts 4:12, NIV). That's why there's nothing to be done but to receive the gift that God offers us through Jesus Christ.

"God so loved the world . . ." (John 3:16, NIV). Can you sense the intensity of His love? Did He love us so much that He simply forgave our sins? No. He gave His only Son to *pay* for our sins.

📖 Let's explore what this gift cost the Giver. Read Mark 14:32–36. What transpired between God the Father and God the Son in the Garden of

Gethsemane? What was Jesus' response to what He knew the Father was requiring of Him?

_____

_____

_____

_____

What disobedience to the will of God had destroyed in the Garden of Eden, obedience to the will of God restored in the garden where Jesus now prayed, *"Yet not My will, but Yours be done"* (Luke 22:42). Jesus knew what awaited Him—the betrayal, the abandonment, the flogging, the pummeling, and most painful of all, the cross.

📖 Read the accounts of the crucifixion in Matthew 27:32–51 and John 19:30. Briefly recount what took place. (Note what happened to the curtain or veil in the Temple, according to Matthew.)

_____

_____

_____

The cross was the place where divine fury was unleashed against the Enemy's works of sin and death. It was the place of the Son's *separation* from the Father as Jesus bore every sin known to humanity. How painful that must have been for the both of Them. And yet Jesus bore our sin willingly in submission to the Father. It was finished.

📖 Now read Hebrews 6:19–20 and 4:14–16 in that order. What insight do these passages give you into the symbolism of the torn veil or curtain?

_____

_____

_____

The veil, or curtain, separating humanity from the dwelling place of God was torn in half from top to bottom, giving all who would call on the name of Jesus access to the Father forever. What a Savior!

📖 The story didn't end with Jesus' death on the cross—there's more. Read Matthew 28:1–10. What happened after Jesus died?

_____

_____

_____

Jesus lives, resurrected from the dead by the power of the Holy Spirit and raised in victory over sin and death. And because He lives, we, too, can have eternal life!

📖 How do we acquire new life in Christ? Jesus speaks about this in John 3:3–8. What truth is Jesus imparting in this passage, and what do you think it means?

_____

_____

> **The Cross was the place where divine fury was unleashed against the Enemy's works of sin and death.**

Jesus' declaration, *"I tell you the truth, no one can see the kingdom of God unless he is born again"* (John 3:3, NIV) has troubled and even offended millions for two thousand years. But if Jesus said it, then it's so. New birth means new life born of water (cleansed) and of the Spirit (regenerated and transformed by the Holy Spirit). Remember Ezekiel 36:25–28? When we're born anew, we're reconciled to and are now in relationship with our Father, as Adam and Eve were in the beginning.

It has been over two decades since I was wooed by God to confront my empty heart. Mine is not a unique story. I had a wonderful husband, two precious daughters, a warm roof over my head, friends, activities, possessions, and so on. But I was empty. My soul was yearning for something that the things of the world could not provide. A song that was popular at the time typified my life. It is Peggy Lee's "Is That All There Is?" The title said it all.

I knew there was more. I discovered that *"if you confess with your mouth Jesus as Lord, and believe in your heart that God raised Him from the dead, you shall be saved; for with the heart man believes, resulting in righteousness, and with the mouth he confesses, resulting in salvation"* (Romans 10:9–10). In 1982, at the age of 34, I gave my life to Christ, and He gave me His.

 Consider Christ. What is your response to the sacrifice He made for you? Who is He in your life? Are you truly grateful to Him as Savior and committed to Him as Lord? Is there anything you must do to put Christ back on the throne of your daily life? What might be squeezing Him out of His rightful place in your heart? Ask Him to show you any such persons, things, or issues. Write them here.

_____

_____

_____

_____

_____

 Take a moment with Him now, and recommit your life to Him. Return to Him all that you are, all that you do, and all that you have—your husband, your marriage, your children, your job, your very life—entrust them all to His care and to His will.

 If you don't know Christ as Savior and Lord, do you sense that something is missing from your life, that there is a God-shaped hole in your soul that yearns to be filled? Remember that you were created for this relationship. A wonderful journey through the rest of your life can begin with Him now. He is real, and He desires to make Himself known to you. Come and yield to the only true God and to Jesus Christ, His Son. Below is a special prayer for you.

 In a quiet place before Him and in your own words, **acknowledge** that you have sinned and that you desire to please Him and glorify Him with your life (Romans 3:23; 6:23.) **Turn** from (repent of) your old life and embrace Him, trusting in your heart that His death on the cross was enough to pay your sin debt. Then **receive** His forgiveness. To do so is called faith (Hebrews 7:25, 27.) **Confess** that He is Lord. **Give** Him permission to permeate your life with His own, to dwell in you by His Holy Spirit, to begin transforming you into

My soul was yearning for something that the things of the world could not provide. A song that was popular at the time typified my life: Peggy Lee's "Is That All There Is?" The title said it all.

the person He has always intended for you to become. Then **thank** Him for His love and for His sacrifice on your behalf. That's it. Jesus Christ is now your Savior and Lord, and you are His *forever*.

Whether you have recommitted your life to Christ today, or received Him as your Savior and Lord, you have a future ahead of you that promises everything that Christ desires for you. It will be sweet and tender and at other times tough, but always fulfilling.

THE ASSURANCE

Charles Stanley says it well: "God loved. God gave. We believe. We have. Period."[4] That's called grace, God's undeserved favor, mercy, and blessing. Therefore, it's not what *we do* (our works), it's what *Jesus did* that acquits us, declares us righteous, gives us right standing with God.

📖 What insight does Ephesians 2:1–10 provide regarding grace versus works?

_____

_____

_____

We're not saved *by our* works—we're saved *for His* works—by grace through faith. Salvation is a free gift. If we could earn our own salvation by what we do, we would brag about it, measure our works against those of others, and declare ourselves righteous. And God won't have any part of that. Only He is qualified to declare us righteous.

📖 How do the following verses assure us that we are His forever, that our salvation is secure?

Romans 8:1–2; Colossians 1:21–22 _____

_____

Romans 8:38–39 _____

_____

2 Corinthians 5:17 _____

_____

2 Corinthians 5:21 _____

_____

Hebrews 7:25 _____

_____

God didn't just cover our sins—He removed them. Jesus' victory over Satan, sin, and death is our victory. Satan is now powerless to enslave a believer to a lifetime of accusation and habitual sin. Jesus took on our sin; we took on His righteousness. God now sees us through the blood of His Son—

The Savior and the Helper
DAY FOUR

"For by grace you have been saved through faith; and that not of yourselves, it is the gift of God; not as a result of works, that no one should boast."

Ephesians 2:8-9

God didn't just cover our sins—He removed them.

pure, holy, and free from accusation—acceptable in His sight forever. Oswald Chambers states, "We are acceptable to God not because we have obeyed, nor because we have promised to give up things, but because of the death of Christ, and for no other reason."[5]

It is our challenge as Christians to believe these truths of assurance. Our mistakes, weaknesses, and repeated human failings may cause us to doubt that God still loves us or that our salvation is secure. Sometimes we may even doubt that we're saved. The Enemy whispers, *"Did God really say . . .?"* (Genesis 3:1, NIV). But God thunders, *"I will never desert you, nor will I ever forsake you"* (Hebrews 13:5) and *"You are not your own; you were bought at a price"* (1 Corinthians 6:19, NIV). In other words, He's saying, "You're Mine!"

Our old nature is dead to sin, finished, over. Our eternal life has begun; we now have a new nature that is *"alive to God in Christ Jesus"* (Romans 6:11, NIV). He is not refurbishing our old selves—He's creating each of us as new creatures. A life in Christ is a life that's changing.

 Do you believe that you're accepted and declared righteous by God? What does it mean to you to be put into right standing with Him because of what Christ did for you?

_____

_____

_____

_____

How can knowing that God loves and accepts you help you in your marriage, starting right now?

_____

_____

_____

📖 One of the most encouraging scriptures that speaks to this truth of new life is Isaiah 43:18–19. Read this passage, and record your response to it. What hope does this passage give you with regard to your marriage?

_____

_____

_____

Our level of faith is determined by what we're willing to believe. And the by-product of believing God's Messenger, Jesus Christ (John 6:29), is hope—hope for our futures, hope for our marriages. *"Now may the God of hope fill you with all joy and peace in believing, so that you will abound in hope by the power of the Holy Spirit"* (Romans 15:13).

📖 There's one last profound scripture to look at. Read Revelation 22:13–14. What did Jesus restore for those of us who call Him Savior and Lord? Do you have any insights into this revelation?

_____

_____

_____

> **"I am the Alpha and the Omega, the First and the Last, the Beginning and the End. Blessed are those who wash their robes, that they may have the right to the tree of life and may go through the gates into the city."**
>
> **Revelation 22:13–14 (NIV)**

Humanity has been brought full circle from what happened in the Garden of Eden. What a generous, loving God, that we should be given the right to the tree of life! Jesus *is* the Beginning and the End!

 Take time now to thank God for loving you lavishly, for calling you to Himself and investing in you by pouring out His grace and mercy on your life. It's His life in you now. And He's doing a *"new thing . . . do you not perceive it?"* (Isaiah 43:19, NIV). Let Him know that you willingly believe in Him and in the One He sent. If there are areas where your belief is weak, or even areas where you fail to believe entirely, ask Him to make His truth real to you and to strengthen you in His truth.

THE PROVISION

The Savior and the Helper
DAY FIVE

When you read about the Holy Spirit in your Bible or hear of Him in a sermon, what vision does He create in your mind? Who is He to you? What role does He play in your life and marriage? How vital is He to your Christian walk? Today's lesson will clarify or remind us of who He is and how crucial He is to our growth in Christ.

Pause and think about the Holy Spirit for a few minutes, and then answer these questions:

Are you aware of the Holy Spirit's presence in you? _____

Do you daily acknowledge His presence in your life? _____

Do you daily anticipate His working in your life? _____

Do you sense promptings and nudgings but don't know whether or not they're from the Holy Spirit within you? Explain.

_____
_____

Who do you think the Holy Spirit is? How relevant do you think He is to your walk of faith? Explain.

_____
_____
_____
_____

Forgetting, misunderstanding, or ignoring the Holy Spirit in our lives is like having all the conveniences in our homes—heat, telephone, water, electricity—and not using them, then wondering why we're cold, lonely, thirsty, dirty, and sitting in the dark.

📖 According to Galatians 4:6, how does the Holy Spirit come to inhabit a person?

_____
_____
_____

"Because you are sons, God sent the Spirit of his Son into our hearts, the Spirit who calls out, 'Abba, Father.'"

Galatians 4:6 NIV

Jesus provides the means by which His Spirit dwells in our hearts. Every child of God, everyone who has received and believed Jesus Christ as Savior and Lord, has been given the Holy Spirit. God is now our Father, our Abba, and He is able to get very personal with each of us through the indwelling of His Holy Spirit.

📖 Read Psalm 139:7–13, Luke 1:35, and 1 Corinthians 2:9–11. From these scriptures you can deduce certain major attributes of the One who takes up residence in our hearts. What do you discover?

_____

_____

_____

Could you discern the omniscience of the Holy Spirit in 1 Corinthians? His omnipotence in Luke? His omnipresence in the psalm? 2 Corinthians 3:17 says, *"Now the Lord is the Spirit."* The Holy Spirit shares all the attributes of God and Jesus Christ.

 Can you use help in your spiritual growth, guidance in becoming the wife God has called you to be, comfort in a time of trial and need, counsel in decision-making? Carefully read the scriptures listed in the chart below. Prayerfully consider each purpose of the Holy Spirit so that you'll know and understand who is available to you and how He can influence your life and your marriage.

Scripture	Purpose of the Holy Spirit	Effect on Your Life	Effect on Your Marriage
John 14:16–17			
John 14:26			
John 15:26–27			
John 16:8–11			
John 16:13			
John 16:14			
Acts 1:8			
Romans 5:3–5			
Romans 8:26–27			
1 Corinthians 2:6–14			
1 Corinthians 6:11			
Ephesians 1:13–14			
Ephesians 3:20–21			
Titus 3:3–7			
2 Peter 1:3			

Now who do you think the Holy Spirit is to you *personally*? (Really consider this question as it relates to your growth as a godly wife.)

_____

_____

_____

_____

📖 In John 6:63 (NIV), Jesus said, *"The Spirit gives life; the flesh counts for nothing. The words I have spoken to you are spirit and they are life."* Based on this truth, what can you expect to happen in your life as a Christian?

_____

_____

_____

📖 Read John 15:1–5. What's the indicator in our own lives that the Holy Spirit is in fact living within us?

_____

_____

_____

📖 Read Galatians 5:22–25. Just what is this fruit that Christians possess?

_____

_____

_____

Let's look at the fruit of the Spirit (the word "fruit" being singular in this case) as analogous to an orange. An orange has many components: the peel, membrane, pulp, seeds, juice, fragrance, flavor, and so on. All these parts make up the full character of the orange. So it is with the Holy Spirit. The components of His fruit are love, joy, peace, patience, kindness, goodness, faithfulness, gentleness, and self-control. If He's in us, His fruit is in us—that is, we contain all the components of who He is.

No branch eats its own fruit, but instead, it bears fruit for *others* to consume. In the same way, the Holy Spirit cultivates the fruit in us to nourish others. The more fruit we give away (use, put into practice, or exercise), the more we produce. In so doing, our need for love, joy, peace, patience, and so on will be met. What a great spiritual dynamic!

📖 Read 2 Corinthians 3:17–18 and record what's taking place in this passage. How does this apply to each of us?

_____

_____

_____

_____

As followers of Christ, we find that the Holy Spirit is working a process of change in us, a process that's guaranteed to bear His fruit. This process lasts

"The Spirit gives life...."

John 6:63 (NIV)

a lifetime. It touches and deals with every facet of our lives every day. The Bible calls this process of change sanctification, being molded into the image of Christ by His Holy Spirit. As we remain teachable, not only our lives but also our marriages will reap rich rewards.

📖 What is Paul's admonition in Ephesians 5:18?

_____

_____

_____

"...be filled with the Spirit."

Ephesians 5:18 (NIV)

The Holy Spirit is the power of God in us—the same power that raised Jesus Christ from the dead. Many of us fail to acknowledge this in our own lives, and we therefore fail to use it. Yet in Ephesians we're commanded to be filled with His Holy Spirit, the result of which is our continuous walking in, being led by, and drawing from the Source that's within us. And it's *our* responsibility to ask the Holy Spirit to regularly fill us with Himself in response to God's command. This keeps us aware that it is He who supplies the daily power to face the stuff of life.

 You can get into the habit of acknowledging the Holy Spirit in your life by asking God to fill you with His Spirit each day. Anticipate His working in you toward change. It's the Holy Spirit who makes your life what Jesus wants it to be, and it's a walk you can enjoy.

Works Cited

1. Nancy Wilson, *The Fruit of Her Hands* (Moscow, Idaho: Canon Press, 1997), 18.

2. Charles F. Pfeiffer and Everett F. Harrison, eds., *The Wycliffe Bible Commentary* (Chicago: Moody Press, 1962), 5.

3. Ibid., 8.

4. Charles Stanley, *The Glorious Journey* (Nashville: Thomas Nelson Publishers, 1996), 139.

5. James Reimann, ed., *My Utmost for His Highest: The Golden Book of Oswald Chambers* (Grand Rapids: Discovery House, 1992), October 29 devotional.

3

Pleasing God: A Study on Obedience

You're probably wondering why this third lesson doesn't deal specifically with marriage. It's because I know that my relationship with my husband is indelibly linked to my relationship with Jesus. If my relationship with Jesus is broken or impeded, my relationship with my husband will likely suffer as well. Conversely, if all is flowing well between my Lord and me, the "right stuff" will also flow toward my husband. How I respond to my Lord is how I likely will respond to my husband. And unless I daily surrender that part of me that gets in the way of God's conforming me into the image of His Son, the two primary relationships in my life—the one with my Lord and the one with my husband—will suffer.

For me to see improvement in my own marriage, it was crucial for God to bring me through the teaching that I'll be sharing with you in the third and fourth lessons—a tough teaching but a necessary one. So present a teachable heart to God, and ask Him to help you learn the truths contained in these lessons. I believe that by doing so your marriage will be exceedingly blessed.

Unless I daily surrender that part of me that gets in the way of God's conforming me into the image of His Son, the two primary relationships in my life—the one with my Lord and the one with my husband—will suffer.

DEFINING THE PROBLEM

Whether you're a brand-new creation in Christ Jesus or have been His for years, a tension exists in the human heart as God works His character into it "little by little." Daily we're challenged to respond to all that's happening around us with the Presence that's within us. Our response should not be about following rules and regulations but about pleasing God. The Holy Spirit will contend daily with our selfish tendencies that are prone to sinfulness. These behaviors are still independent of God, because we refuse to bring them under the authority of Christ and the power and leading of His Holy Spirit in us. This selfish or worldly bent is characterized by thinking, "Life is about me. I want what I want when I want it." In Scripture, our selfish tendencies are called "the flesh" (see Matthew 26:41).

The apostle Paul wrote a letter to the believers in the church of Corinth who were struggling with their fleshly, or worldly, nature. Here's a little background. The city of Corinth, located between the Adriatic and Aegean seas, was a bustling, wealthy seaport. Its population was multinational (Greek, Roman, and Asian). Athletic competitions entertained the people in an outdoor theater that seated twenty thousand. Taverns abounded, and the city teemed with sexual immorality and pagan practices. Its temple of Aphrodite alone had a thousand prostitutes. The Corinthian culture was so decadent that "the Greek term *Korinthiazomai* (literally, 'to act the Corinthian') came to mean 'to practice fornication.'"[1] With the immorality surrounding these Christians as the norm, is it any wonder that they were having problems with their own behavior and attitudes?

What parallels do you see between the Corinthian culture and our present culture?

_____

_____

_____

_____

📖 What difficulties did the church have, according to the following scriptures?

1 Corinthians 1:10_____

_____

1 Corinthians 3:3_____

_____

1 Corinthians 5:1–2_____

_____

1 Corinthians 6:1–8_____

_____

> Daily we're challenged to respond to all that's happening around us with the Presence that's within us. Our response should not be about following rules and regulations but about pleasing God.

1 Corinthians 6:18–20 _____

_____

_____

_____

What are the similarities between the Corinthian church and the Church today? (The word "Church" with a capital "C" refers to all believers.)

_____

_____

_____

📖 Read 1 Corinthians 3:1–3. How does Paul characterize these Christians? Why?

_____

_____

_____

> **"I gave you milk, not solid food, for you were not yet ready for it. Indeed, you are still not ready. You are still worldly."**
>
> **1 Corinthians 3:2–3 (NIV)**

In these verses Paul distinguishes between two kinds of Christian lifestyles: **carnal** (meaning fleshly or worldly) and **spiritual.** The carnal believer is one who's converted to Jesus Christ but who, like an infant, is still following the inborn human nature, with its emphasis on pleasing the self. He or she is not walking in full fellowship with Jesus Christ and has not fully surrendered to the Spirit of God. The spiritual believer, on the other hand, has a more mature relationship with the Lord, being led by the Holy Spirit and drawing from His attributes (or fruit) within.

📖 According to Galatians 5:19–21, what are the practices of the carnal nature?

_____

_____

📖 Take a moment and reacquaint yourself with Galatians 5:22–23. What is the fruit of the Spirit?

_____

_____

_____

> **"But the fruit of the Spirit is love, joy, peace, patience, kindness, goodness, faithfulness, gentleness and self-control."**
>
> **Galatians 5:22–23, (NIV)**

Unlike carnal believers, spiritual believers have yielded their lives to God, desiring to do His will. Their lives are evidence that they're controlled, or led, by the Spirit, because the fruit of the Spirit is being produced. The fruit grows naturally in believers' lives as they respond to the Holy Spirit's leading.

🛑 **APPLY** As Christians, we must honestly ask ourselves how we're living our lives. How would you characterize your life at present? Are you being ruled more by your personal passions, desires, and self-centered reactions (focusing on you) than by the Holy Spirit (focusing on God)? Write your honest assessment here:

_____

_____

_____

> *"And He died for all, that they who live should no longer live for themselves, but for Him who died and rose again on their behalf."*
>
> *2 Corinthians 5:15*

📖 Read 2 Corinthians 5:15. How does this verse confront a believer's self-centered attitude?

_____

_____

_____

📖 In 1 Corinthians 3:2, what does Paul mean by saying that he had to give the church members milk instead of solid food?

_____

_____

_____

📖 In Hebrews 5:11–14 the writer also addresses a group of Christians who apparently were not progressing as they should in their Christian lifestyle or "walk." Summarize what the author has to say about their level of spiritual development.

_____

_____

_____

How does the training take place, and for what purpose (verse 14)?

_____

_____

_____

Paul challenged the Corinthians by writing, *"You are still worldly. . . . Are you not acting like mere men?"* (1 Corinthians 3:3, NIV). Paul boldly admonishes them for behavior that is identical to those who are unsaved. Think about this: Paul first preached the gospel to the Corinthians in A.D. 50. He wrote the letter that we know as 1 Corinthians six years later. What exactly is the point he's driving home here?

_____

_____

_____

Paul was looking for evidence of growth after six years in the faith. The by-product of applying God's truth to daily circumstances is *maturity*. His comparing the Corinthians to infants is forthright and lovingly confrontational. Consider what you would feel if your own child, after six years of "new life," still wanted only milk, refusing solid food—showing no signs or evidence of appreciable growth. Frustrating? Absolutely.

Spiritual growth is a choice, and constant use (practice) of what has been learned is the best training method. Yet there are believers who go from sermon to sermon, Bible study to Bible study, mentor to mentor, always learning but not putting into practice what they know. Such a choice is lazy and dangerous.

 Let's personalize this. How long have you been a Christian? Unless you're a fairly new Christian, would you say that you've graduated from milk to solid food? Can you look back and see where you were when you accepted Christ, and then compare that with where you are now? Is there a difference? Are you growing and maturing? Are you *changing*? If your answer is yes, how do you know that you've grown, matured, changed? If your answer is no, list some evidences that prove you haven't changed?

_____

_____

_____

_____

What impact has your growth, or lack of growth, had on your response to daily and long-term challenges, stresses, and frustrations? (Carefully think about this question before candidly answering.)

_____

_____

_____

_____

What impact has your growth, or lack of growth, had on your marriage thus far?

_____

_____

_____

_____

 Prayerfully assess your maturity in the Lord. Are you daily becoming more of an image-bearer, reflecting the image of the One who has claimed you as His own? If you are a new Christian, your spiritual growth process is just beginning. Look forward to it. If you have been a Christian for a while and confess to having little maturity, that can change instantly. Ask God to open your heart to His goal for your life, and then be willing to follow His leading. You won't be disappointed.

THE DISOBEDIENCE OF UNBELIEF

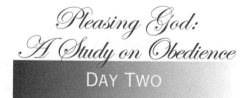

In 1 Corinthians 10, Paul uses the Old Testament example of Moses and the Israelites to emphasize God's displeasure with those who lived as self-pleasing and self-reliant "people of God." Before we go into this New Testament teaching, we need a little historical background.

God was about to rescue the Israelites, His chosen people, from four hundred years of Egyptian oppression. In Lesson 1, Day Four, we read the exchange between Moses and God in Exodus, chapters 3 and 4. The I AM called Moses to lead His people out of captivity.

📖 God led Moses and the Israelites on a long journey to the Promised Land. At every step along this journey, God provided for His chosen

Extra Mile

LIBERATION

Carefully read Exodus 5 through 14. Note the following: (1) what God's people went through to gain their freedom, (2) what God did to make Himself known to both the Egyptians and the Israelites, (3) what was required of the Israelite leaders (Moses and Aaron), and (4) the events that finally led to the Israelites' freedom.

people. However, the Israelites were an obstinate bunch. They constantly murmured and disrespected Moses as God's appointed leader. A description of their seemingly endless sin cycle is told in Psalm 78:12–54. After reading this passage, answer the following questions.

If you were an Israelite who had experienced God in spectacular ways, what would you conclude about Him? What would your level of loyalty to God be?

_____

_____

_____

_____

APPLY Has there been a time when God's work in your life was evident, when He went before you and either removed obstacles or helped you overcome them one by one, until deliverance was sure? Explain.

_____

_____

_____

_____

How did this experience shape your walk with Him then? How does it influence your walk with Him now?

_____

_____

_____

_____

The Psalms passage we just read shows us how easy it is to forget the power and goodness of God, in spite of all He does for us. The passage suggests that there were countless incidents when Israel tested the patience of Almighty God. We'll now look at one of those incidents recorded in the Book of Numbers. The Israelites, now freed from Egypt, were on their way to the land God had promised Abraham generations before. Canaan, the land of milk and honey, was just a few short miles away. God commanded Moses to send twelve spies—one leader from each of the tribes of Israel—to check out the land and its inhabitants.

📖 Read Numbers 13:1–33. What were Moses' instructions to these tribal leaders (verses 17–20)?

_____

_____

_____

After an initial glowing report and evidence of the abundance of the land (verses 23–27), another report began to emerge from ten of the twelve explorers. What was it (verses 28–33)?

_____

_____

📖 Now read Numbers 14:1–38. How did the Israelites react to the two reports (verses 1–4)? Note that each of these four verses reveals a different behavior. Identify each behavior.

_____

_____

_____

_____

The bad report that the ten leaders spread so plagued the Israelites with fear and doubt that they wailed and wept (verse 1); they grumbled against God's chosen authorities (verse 2); they accused God Himself of leading them to their death, leaving their children as prey (verse 3); and they threatened to replace Moses and head back to Egypt, where they had been oppressed and miserable (verse 4). How quickly they had forgotten their faithful God—in just one short year!

APPLY Are the Israelites' reactions familiar to you? Have you ever been tempted to go back to a bad situation because its familiarity and perhaps even its oppression were more palatable than what God was requiring of you now? Do you wish you were somewhere else or with someone else rather than face "giants" with the Lord and move forward in Him? Do you ever think that perhaps being a Christian is too hard and that life was easier the way it used to be for you? In what areas of your life might you be wishing that you could "go back to Egypt?" Explain your answers to these questions.

_____

_____

_____

_____

The Israelites refused to apply what they had learned of their mighty and faithful God. And Joshua and Caleb's distress was evident in the tearing of their robes. What truth and admonition did Joshua and Caleb give the Israelites (verses 6–10), and what was the Israelites' response (verse 10)?

_____

_____

_____

APPLY Joshua and Caleb gave the Israelites wise counsel based on God's truth. Yet the people rejected it. Can you imagine yourself responding in the same way, especially in a situation in which you're consumed with fear? How do you respond to your challenging circumstances? What do you say to wise counsel when you're frightened, grieved, or grumbling, especially if the counsel comes from an authority figure God has placed in your life, perhaps your husband? How have you responded?

_____

_____

_____

What do you say to wise counsel when you're frightened, grieved, or grumbling, especially if the counsel comes from an authority figure God has placed in your life, perhaps your husband?

Circumstances can't destroy us; only our responses to them can.

Take a good look at verse 10. How is God's appearance described? Why do you think God appeared at this time?

_____

_____

_____

_____

On the basis of what you read in verses 11–12, what was God's response to the Israelites? How would you characterize His frame of mind?

_____

_____

_____

_____

God said to Moses, *"How long will these people treat me with contempt? How long will they refuse to believe in me, in spite of all the miraculous signs I have performed among them?"* (Numbers 14:11, NIV). If you've read Exodus 7—14, you should get a better understanding of this profound statement. Signs, miracles, protection, liberation . . . God wasn't exasperated—He was angry. At that moment His majesty as well as His wrath were displayed in His glory. What a combination! Focus on the phrase *"refuse to believe."* Doesn't that imply an act of will? The Israelites chose unbelief—a very poor choice.

APPLY The facts of our personal circumstances are the facts. Yes, there are giants in the land, perhaps lots of them. Yet circumstances can't destroy us; only our responses to them can. Our responses will always expose our belief systems. Is your response "Did God really say. . . ?" or "Thus says the Lord. . . ."? What insight do you have into how you respond to tough circumstances?

_____

_____

_____

_____

What was Moses' appeal to God, and how did God respond to it (verses 13–20)?

_____

_____

_____

_____

Although God forgave the Israelites as Moses asked, He did impose judgments for their actions. What were they in verses 21–23, 26–30, 32, and 34–35?

_____

_____

_____

_____

How were the Israelite children affected by their parents' bad behavior (verses 31–33)?

_____

_____

_____

_____

Caleb and Joshua were allowed to enter Canaan because they were whole-hearted in their loyalty and unwavering in their belief that God was bigger than the giants of the land. The younger generation, too, was allowed to enter the Promised Land. But the sad reality is that those who eventually inherited it were first subjected to forty years of desert suffering and hardships. This generation, along with Joshua and Caleb, entered the land God gave them, but not before they endured consequences of their parents' unfaithfulness. What insight does this give us into the impact of our own sin on others, or the consequences of another's sin on us?

_____

_____

_____

_____

APPLY If we think that our children are unaffected by our choices, we're sadly mistaken. The consequences of poor behavior are far-reaching. They affect not simply the one choosing disobedience. Consider your role as a Christian wife. Do your children hear you grumbling against your husband? Do they read disrespect on your face? Do they witness it in your body language? What statement are you making to your children about your relationship with their father? Honestly examine yourself. Are you a good example of a godly wife for your children so that your daughter can be one and your son can choose one?

_____

_____

_____

_____

What was the fate of the ten explorers other than Caleb and Joshua (verses 36–38)?

_____

_____

The other ten explorers, like Caleb and Joshua, were leaders in their respective tribes. The bad report that they spread eroded the people's faith, causing them to grumble against God, Moses and Aaron. The explorers were given a powerful responsibility, because their faith influenced that of countless others. Whether we realize it or not, as women of God, we're all in a place of influence—in our marriages, homes, workplaces, neighborhoods, communities, and churches. In the midst of challenging circumstances, we're responsible for standing firm in the faith, trusting God rather than believing and spreading a bad report that potentially weakens others.

> *Are you a good example of a godly wife for your children so that your daughter can be one and your son can choose one?*

God forgave, but His consequences were firm. And it all began with the Israelites' response to a tough situation. Grieving their circumstances led to grumbling. Their grumbling led to accusing God. Their accusing God led to rejection of sound leadership. Their rejection of sound leadership led to the threat of murder. This blatant rebellion invited God's judgment.

 The Israelites' grumbling (murmuring) was key to their demise, because it led to progressively worse behavioral choices. Before now, have you ever considered grumbling a sin? Do you grumble against any of God's appointed leaders in your life—your boss, your pastor or church leader, your husband? Where has your grumbling led in the past? How do you think God responds to your grumbling?

_____

_____

_____

_____

📖 Now read Hebrews 3:7–19. The author of Hebrews speaks to believers about the Israelites' willful unbelief, which landed them in the desert for forty years. According to verse 19, what caused God's anger?

_____

_____

The Greek word for "unbelief" in this passage, *apeitheia,* means "disobedient . . . unwillingness to be persuaded, willful unbelief, obstinacy . . . opposing the gracious word and purpose of God."[2] The Israelites' unbelief was a choice that led to their refusal to obey God by trusting Him and the leaders He had appointed. The by-product of unbelief is rebellion, whether in the form of fearful, passive resistance to the will of God or through blatant defiance of His will. According to verses 12–15, what can we do to avoid the sin of unbelief?

_____

_____

APPLY Is your heart hardened because you don't believe God is trustworthy in your challenging circumstances? Do you see a problem in your own walk with disobedience (willful unbelief)? Has it led or is it leading to rebellion against God or any of His appointed authorities in your life? Explain.

_____

_____

_____

What are some areas of unbelief in your life right now, areas that you don't believe God can or will affect?

_____

_____

_____

_____

If unbelief is willful, then so is belief. We choose one or the other.

📖 Back to the Corinthians: in 1 Corinthians 10:1–12, Paul referenced the wrongs committed by the same crew of Israelites after God relegated them to the desert for forty years. Read this passage and answer the following questions.

Why is Paul telling the Corinthian church this story (verses 6, 11)?

_____

_____

_____

In verse 12, what sober warning does Paul give, and how do you think it applies to the believer's life?

_____

_____

_____

📖 Paul follows his warning with a powerful promise. Carefully read the passage that follows, underlining its points of hope-filled encouragement: *"No temptation has overtaken you but such as is common to man; and God is faithful, who will not allow you to be tempted beyond what you are able, but with the temptation will provide the way of escape also, that you may be able to endure it"* (1 Corinthians 10:13).

Unless it's acted upon, temptation itself is not sin. It's actually necessary to our Christian growth. Temptation requires and tests our patience, which builds and strengthens our endurance. We learn to trust in and depend on God to get us through periods of weakness (Hebrews 4:15–16) that prepare us for the more difficult periods to come. God's deliverance from a temptation can come in numerous forms and scenarios, but the last few words of 1 Corinthians 10:13 suggest that there will likely be exertion on our part. This can be an excellent exercise when we allow God to use it to build our spiritual muscle.

APPLY Has the Holy Spirit been nudging you, warning you about temptations that you consistently act on that result in sinful behaviors? Is there a trial in your life that's enticing you to sin in your thought life, speech, or behavior? If so, in what ways are you being tempted? How do Paul's encouraging words in 1 Corinthians 10:13 apply to your temptations? Be open and honest with yourself as you write your answers.

_____

_____

_____

How can the encouragements in 1 Corinthians 10:13 apply specifically to your marriage?

_____

_____

_____

If unbelief is willful, then so is belief. We choose one or the other.

"No temptation has seized you except what is common to man. And God is faithful; he will not let you be tempted beyond what you can bear. But when you are tempted, he will also provide a way out so that you can stand up under it."

1 Corinthians 10:13 (NIV)

Is believing God difficult for you? Do you believe that your temptations to sin are greater than His Spirit in you? Are your hope, confidence, and expectancy in the Lord alone, or are they in another? Yourself, perhaps? Take a few moments now and answer these questions before the Lord. And where your belief is weak, ask God to make your belief stronger (Mark 9:14–24).

LOVE THE LORD YOUR GOD

"Love the Lord your God with all your heart and with all your soul and with all your strength."

Deuteronomy 6:5 (NIV)

The Old Testament is not merely a history of the struggling Israelites. It's a fascinating love story about God's relationship with the nation Israel and Israel's prophetic role in the advent of the Messiah.

The Old Testament reveals powerful instruction in what God expected from those He called His own and from those who acknowledged Him as their God. It also clearly defines the consequences for those who did not. Before his death (close to the end of the forty-year desert experience), Moses gathered the Israelites to give them God's instructions on how they were to enter the Promised Land under Joshua's leadership. The land was inhabited by hideously wicked nations that followed evil religions. The natives were a corrupt and brutal people whose customs included prostitution of both sexes, infant sacrifice, and every act of evil and worldly behavior imaginable. Moses prefaced the instructions with a reminder of whom the Israelites were to serve and obey.

📖 Read Deuteronomy 6:1–25. Record the commands and instructions that God expected the Israelites to obey as found in the verses shown. Also record the reasons He gives for requiring their obedience. Be as thorough as you can.

Deuteronomy 6:1–25

Commands and Instructions	Reasons for the Commands
Verses 1–9	Verses 2–3
Verse 12	Verses 10–11
Verses 13–14	Verse 15
Verses 16–18	Verses 18–19
Verses 20–25	Verses 24–25

In verses 1–9, 20–24, God is seen establishing himself in the hearts of His people as their one and only God. And He wanted them to do the same in the hearts of their own children. Why do you think this was necessary? (Consider the mission on which they were about to embark.)

_____

_____

APPLY Have your children asked about God's activity in your life? Do they understand what it means to love Him with all their heart, soul, and strength? How do you convey your love of God to them? Give an example. Why is it important to honestly share with your children your walk with Christ?

_____

_____

_____

What point does God make in verses 10–12? Why is it important for us to attribute all we have to God's generosity?

_____

_____

_____

If we forget to acknowledge with gratitude everything that God gives us— our lives, salvation, husbands, marriages, children, friends, homes, material possessions, and successes—we become complacent, careless, or even reckless with His gifts. And when we forget to be grateful for His many blessings, we're vulnerable to the other gods that beckon us to follow them.

📖 We rarely think of jealousy as a positive trait. But Deuteronomy 6:13–15 states that God is a jealous God. Read Exodus 20:1–6 and Isaiah 42:8. What do you think it means that God is a jealous God?

_____

_____

According to John MacArthur, "God is zealous to protect what belongs to Him. He will not allow another to have the honor that is due to Him alone."[3] God's love requires that we respond to Him with total allegiance and faithfulness and that we teach our children to do the same. Our love for Him should motivate us to obey His commandments, and only such obedience can ensure our well-being and righteousness. Is it any wonder that God calls us to love Him with all of our heart, soul, and strength?

APPLY Although we've just walked through an Old Testament instruction, God's jealousy for those of us who belong to Him remains the same today. It will not change. Is He competing for your allegiance? Are you giving "other gods" honor that's due Him alone? Who or what might these other gods be? What does or doesn't motivate you to obey His commands? Give your candid answer to these questions.

_____

_____

_____

_____

📖 In Deuteronomy 6:16, the Israelites were commanded not to test the Lord as they did at Massah. Read about what happened at Massah in Exodus 17:1–7. Based on this account, what do you think it means to test God? Why is testing God a sin?

> "Be careful that you do not forget the Lord, who brought you out of Egypt, out of the land of slavery."
>
> Deuteronomy 6:12 (NIV)

_____

_____

The people, still led by God after their exodus from Egypt (Exodus 13:21–22), were traveling toward the Promised Land. Despite God's miraculous signs and liberation, they contended with Moses for water, failing to acknowledge that the God who freed them was still with them. Instead of following Moses' lead and turning to God in their need, the Israelites complained against Moses. How frustrating it must have been for God to have His faithfulness challenged!

 Have you ever questioned or challenged the faithfulness and goodness of God? If yes, what was your circumstance? How did it affect your attitude toward Him? What was the outcome? What affect did the outcome have on your attitude? If you're currently questioning God's faithfulness, how is it affecting you and your relationship with Him?

_____

_____

_____

According to Deuteronomy 6:25, what was the people's reward for obeying God?

_____

_____

📖 Read Mark 12:28–30. What does Jesus validate? Read John 14:21. How does Jesus define love for Him?

_____

_____

Our love for God compels us to obey His commands, to do His will. This is what pleases Him. Our obedience is evidence of our love for Him. And God is faithful—He will reveal Himself to us as we obey. Would this not compel us to obey Him all the more?

 Do you understand what it means to love God with your whole heart, soul, mind, and strength? Is there competition for His place in your life or in your marriage, especially if either is or has been challenging? Is it easier to consider what God hasn't done for you than what He has? Think about your love for God, and ask Him to increase your desire to please Him. Take time now to remember where you've been and where He's brought you. Just as important, anticipate where He's taking you. And thank Him.

THE DISOBEDIENCE OF COMPROMISE

When we were very young, we began to receive instructions from our parents designed to promote our best interests. The first were simple, one- or two-word commands such as "No!" and

> "I am the Lord, that is My name; I will not give My glory to another, nor My praise to graven images."
>
> Isaiah 42:8

"Hot!" and "Don't touch!" Though we didn't realize it at the time, in their profound love, our parents were protecting us from danger. We come to a full understanding of our parents' intent for our good, and the import of our obedience to their requirements, when we have children of our own.

The Israelites were *"the children of the LORD"* (Deuteronomy 14:1, NIV). And no one but the Father knew what was best for them. What could be better than the land He promised them, with splendid cities others had already built, houses already full of good things, hewn cisterns already dug, vineyards and olive orchards already planted? Even the Canaanites, who presently occupied the land, weren't going to get in the way of what God ordained. As the Israelites stood poised to enter, God gave His people final instructions that would ensure long, prosperous, and secure lives for them. Let's take a look at His directives.

📖 Read Deuteronomy 7:1–26. Note the commands and instructions that God gave Moses to pass along to the Israelites and the reasons they needed to fully obey. Then answer the questions that follow.

According to verses 4, 6, 16, and 25–26, why did God want the Canaanites and everything consecrated to their gods destroyed? (For now, we'll use the word "Canaanite" to represent the inhabitants of the seven enemy nations that were already in the Promised Land when the Israelites arrived.)

_____

_____

_____

What were the consequences if the Israelites didn't carry out these instructions completely and without compromise (verses 4, 10)?

_____

_____

Again, we see that God will reward those who are obedient to Him. What does He promise His people (verses 9, 12–15)?

_____

_____

The Israelites were afraid of the Canaanites. Why (verses 1, 17)?

_____

_____

What was God's command with regard to their fear (verse 18)? How will God deal with the Israelites' enemies (verse 19)?

_____

_____

God reminded His people of where they had been and where they were going, what He had done for them in the past, and what He had promised for their future. Therefore, the "in-between" was securely in His hands as well. So He encouraged them with *"Do not be afraid . . . remember well . . . You saw with your own eyes"* (Deuteronomy 7:18–19, NIV). In other

> *"Whoever has my commands and obeys them, he is the one who loves me. He who loves me will be loved by my Father, and I too will love him and show myself to him."*
>
> **John 14:21 (NIV)**

words, He was saying, "Trust Me. If I brought you into this, I'm going to bring you through it. Just do as I command, and watch Me reveal Myself."

📖 Revisit Deuteronomy 7:20–21, and read Exodus 23:27–28. What about those enemies that were hiding? How would the Israelites conquer them?

_____

_____

_____

_____

The hornet seems to be used here in a figurative sense, to represent the awesome terror of God, which would produce panic and chaos when He unleashed His power on Israel's adversaries. The *Wycliffe Bible Commentary* states, "The fact that certain species of hornets in Palestine build nests underground and in rock crevices suggests the appropriateness of the figure to the destruction of Canaanites in hiding."

📖 Read Deuteronomy 7:22–24 and Exodus 23:29–30. Here God promises to drive out the sinful nations "little by little." Why? How will God ensure Israel's success against the Canaanites? Why doesn't He want them to eliminate the Canaanites all at once?

_____

_____

_____

_____

> *"Little by little I will drive them out before you, until you have increased enough to take possession of the land."*
>
> **Exodus 23:30 (NIV)**

"Little by little"—what an encouraging phrase! The Israelites would *gradually* gain control of the land that was inhabited by their foes. If they destroyed the Canaanites too quickly, the effects of warfare would decimate the land that sustained the wild animals, potentially putting the Israelites at risk. Their great and awesome God would be with them (verse 21), and little by little they would increase in strength until their enemies were defeated.

📖 Read Psalm 81:13–16. Record what God promised to do with the enemies in the land and the conditions under which He was eager to do so.

_____

_____

In studying Deuteronomy 6—7, we find that the Israelites' total victory over the Canaanites was dependent on what?

_____

_____

God was establishing a maintenance agreement—"Listen to Me! Follow My ways! Don't compromise!" Obedience was crucial to Israel's relationship with Him. And it's crucial for believers today.

 Obedience is a troubling word. We may not like the sound of it or even what it means, and yet God says we can't live for Him without it. As you process today's lesson, consider what your obedience means to God. What does your obedience mean to *you*? Can you admit compromise in your walk that you need to bring to wholehearted obedience? If so, would you confess it to Him now? Will you ask Him to help you obey Him with your whole heart, soul, mind, and strength?

EMBRACING THE SOLUTION

During today's study, be mindful of how God's instructions to the Israelites also apply to you in your own land. This "land" is your heart—your center of thought, emotion, and will—the engine behind your every action. Proverbs 4:23 (NIV) describes the heart as *"the wellspring of life,"* which is to be guarded above all else. Sins and human weaknesses can still have a hold on each of us, inhabiting our hearts and impeding life's flow. Let's consider them our personal Canaanites. It's time to confront them.

The Israelites faced formidable foes in those who occupied the land that God gave them. Without absolute obedience to God's commands, they were powerless and would be defeated. Although His instructions sometimes seemed harsh, they resulted from His plan for His chosen and reflected His merciful benevolence toward them. Israel's total dependence on Him would be their strength. If they compromised with their enemies, there would be no victory. As they were commanded to destroy their adversaries, *"Make no treaty with them, and show them no mercy"* (Deuteronomy 7:2–3, NIV)—so we are commanded to disavow whatever would tempt us away from God and cause us to sin. Therefore, God requires our unwavering obedience in order to deal effectively with the Canaanites in our personal spheres.

Just what tempts us away from God and causes us to sin? Satan's goal from the beginning was to get us to focus on self. Anything that has us focused inward distracts us from focusing upward—our sin, weaknesses, bad habits, conditioned responses, negative attitudes and behaviors. For example, one's feeling of inferiority ("I'm not smart [pretty, skillful] enough") is just as self-focused as one's feeling of superiority ("I'm the best!"). Hurtful anger is quite self centered ("I don't need to control myself"). And so is guilt ("I'm not good enough to be forgiven") and unforgiveness ("I've been wounded, and I have the right not to forgive"). Self-centeredness is the epitome of carnal living.

📖 Read Galatians 5:16. How can we be victors over our inner enemies? As new creations in Christ, we have a choice to make. What is it?

_____

_____

_____

📖 Ponder Galatians 5:17. What's the nature of the relationship between the flesh (our human nature independent of God) and the Spirit?

_____

_____

_____

If we walk in or live by the Spirit, He helps us apply the truths of Scripture to our daily lives. It's an ongoing activity, the result of which is progress in

> **Satan's goal from the beginning was to get us to focus on self. Anything that has us focused inward distracts us from focusing upward—our sin, weaknesses, bad habits, conditioned responses, negative attitudes and behaviors.**

> ## "But I say, walk by the Spirit, and you will not carry out the desire of the flesh."
>
> ### Galatians 5:16

our growth toward Christlikeness. When we willingly submit to the Holy Spirit's control, we'll live to please God. Therefore, His Spirit is able to put to flight any sin that persists in our hearts—little by little.

 The following are some "Canaanites," or inner enemies, that plague us even as Christians. Don't panic if you're currently dealing with a number of them. I circled quite a few early in my Christian walk. How comforting it is to look at them now and to know that, with the help of the Holy Spirit, I've made steady progress over the years. What a faithful God we serve—abounding in love and merciful in His training methods! We would be well served to remember His admonition to the Israelites in Deuteronomy 7:18: *"You shall not be afraid of them* [the Canaanites]; *you shall well remember what the LORD your God did"* and what He'll continue to do for His own. Carefully look over the following list, and circle the "Canaanites" with which you struggle.

Canaanites in Our Land

anger	guilt	selfishness	bitterness
doubt	ill temper	obscenity	deceit
worry	inferiority	envy	laziness
gossip	fear and anxiety	unforgiveness	disrespect
pride	lack of discipline	superiority	idolatry
jealousy	self-pity	grumbling	disobedience
self-reliance	approval-seeking	covetousness	self-hate
insecurity	discouragement	arrogance	overindulgence
shame	sexual sin	adultery	depression
resentment	hopelessness	impulsiveness	conceit
dishonesty	impatience	self-centeredness	procrastination
apathy	lovelessness	judgmental nature	foolish talk
alcoholism	coarse joking	complacency	hate
rebellion	materialism	quarrelsome nature	unbelief
self-deception	gluttony	lying	controlling nature
discontent	love of money	greed	critical nature
manipulation	blame	negativity	self-justification

Are any enemies in your land not on the list? Write them here:

_____

_____

Sometimes the antagonists in our "land" bully us from the dark crevices of our souls. We let them hide in the darkness, not realizing that their hiddenness is their power over us. Frances Frangipane said, "The areas we hide in darkness are the very areas of our future defeat."[5] But much like the hornet of the Israelites' time, the Holy Spirit is prepared to expose the enemies in our territory so that we can destroy them entirely. As the Israelites were to gradually take possession of the land God gave them, so we are to claim every inch of our hearts for God. And we're not to fear the process. God knew the Israelite's limitations, and He knows ours.

How are the inner enemies you circled impeding your Christian walk? How are they affecting your marriage? How are they affecting other relationships?

_____

_____

What will you do with those that are determined to survive in your land, hiding like cowards but surfacing long enough to wreak havoc? What do you *want* to do with them? Based on how the Israelites were to deal with their Canaanites (Deuteronomy 7:2), how are we *supposed* to deal with ours?

_____

_____

_____

Here's a powerful thought to consider: You can't rid yourself of an enemy you're willing to tolerate.

I thought of many reasons my Canaanites should no longer inhabit my heart: they made me look bad and feel bad (which is self-centered). They also hurt others. But the most important reason, one that I had to get used to, was that *they offended God.*

📖 Read Ephesians 4:30. What do you think this means?

_____

_____

_____

It's the Holy Spirit's job to convict us of sin. God is grieved when we refuse to exchange our old ways for His righteous ways. However, just as God promised the Israelites, He assures us that our land will not become desolate—He will not permit us to be so busy with our enemies that we would ignore cultivating our hearts for Him. Just the magnitude of so many Canaanites to slay in short order would overwhelm us with more: *untamable* stress, guilt, worry, helplessness, and eventual hopelessness—the "wild beasts!" He'll put before each one of us those sins, bad habits, conditioned responses, negative thoughts and attitudes, and consuming negative emotions that we need to confront, one at a time. And we'll soon discover that as we obediently deal with each of them in turn, a train of others will latch on and be driven out as well.

📖 Given all that you've learned thus far, what assurance do you receive from 2 Corinthians 3:17–18?

_____

_____

APPLY Your inner enemies have been around for a long time. If you choose to yield your life to God—all that you are, all that you have, and all that you do—and allow yourself to walk in His precious Spirit, the fact that you've had these behaviors for a long time will no longer be an excuse for hanging on to them, nor will the manner in which you acquired them be an excuse: *I guess I'm like my mother. . . . If my father hadn't been so* (fill in the blank), *then I wouldn't be this way. . . . If only my husband were* (fill in the blank), *then I* (fill in the blank). As you yield to God's will, He'll weaken your inner enemies little by little, all the while strengthening you for their destruction. His

You can't rid your-self of an enemy you're willing to tolerate.

"And do not grieve the Holy Spirit of God, by whom you were sealed for the day of redemption."

Ephesians 4:30

glorious fruit will become more evident in your life each day as your Canaanites become less so.

As a believer, you're accountable to your Lord, learning through obedience that you can be honest with yourself and with God about your enemies within. Prayerfully ask yourself what God has revealed as the number-one "Canaanite" in your life, and write it here:

_____

_____

_____

_____

This week pay attention to the excuses, rationalizations, and denials you use to justify certain behaviors and attitudes. Consider how they affect your relationship with God and your husband. This is an exercise in honesty. Reflect on what you've just studied. Ask God to begin work on the area you just identified as needing change most. How would you like this area to change? Yield to the nudgings of His Spirit, and follow His lead. Take a moment to express your desire for change, in the form of a prayer to the only One who can make it happen.

_____

_____

_____

_____

Works Cited

1. Charles C. Ryrie, ed., *The Ryrie Study Bible, New American Standard Translation* (Chicago: Moody Press, 1978), 1726.

2. Spiros Zodhiates, Warren Baker, eds., *The Complete Word Study Dictionary: New Testament* (Chattanooga, TN: AMG Publishers, 1992), #543, 208.

3. John MacArthur, *The MacArthur Study Bible* (Nashville: Word Publishing, 1997), 256.

4. Charles F. Pfeiffer and Everett F. Harrison, eds., *The Wycliffe Bible Commentary* (Chicago: Moody Press, 1962), 165.

5. Francis Frangipane, *The Three Battlegrounds* (Cedar Rapids, IA: Arrow Publications, 1989), 14.

4

Obedience in Action: The Process of Change

N_o one is able to escape the negative influences that swirl around us. They compete for our thoughts and attitudes so that our behavior will reflect the world and not the One who resides within us. This week's lesson will help you overcome the Canaanites you identified in Lesson 3, those weaknesses, bad habits, conditioned responses, negative attitudes and behaviors—sins—that lurk in your life and threaten your marriage. Perhaps you're hampered by a critical nature (disrespect). Or maybe the sin that besets you is your tendency to emasculate your husband? Or is it fear? Does your "Canaanite" cause you to cling to your husband unhealthily, or perhaps keep you from confronting any potentially destructive behaviors your husband might have? Or is it depression? Is there something you're running from? Anger perhaps? Or self-hate? Is it causing you to withdraw from your husband emotionally and sexually? Let the Holy Spirit boldly address your inner enemies and begin the process of working them out of your life with the assurance that *"He who began a good work in you will perfect it"* (Philippians 1:6).

But before doing so, we must consider two things: the condition of our hearts, and our personal history. Only then can we address the sins that want to rule us and create a chasm between our Lord and us, and between our husbands and us. We'll learn how we can draw the Lord into our responses to life's challenges. His Holy Spirit is eager to lead us through

This lesson will help you overcome the Canaanites you identified in Lesson 3. . . .

every temptation, trial, stress, and frustration in ways that will help us mature, enhance our marriages, and glorify God. He won't waste one opportunity, nor should we.

Do you ever consider that who you are affects who others are or who they'll become?

A MATTER OF THE HEART

Do you ever consider that who you are affects who others are or who they'll become—your husband, your children, your coworkers, even those whom you briefly encounter? To be honest with you, I didn't give it much thought until God challenged me with the reality that who I am matters, because the person I am is supposed to convey whom I belong to. And sometimes my personality doesn't convey that I belong to God. I'm given a profound awareness of when I choose to act independent of God or choose to be controlled by and responsive to His Holy Spirit. Whichever I choose at any given time reveals my heart. Sometimes it isn't pretty, and God lets me know when it's time for a "change of heart," a repetitive occurrence in every maturing believer's life.

📖 Let's examine the heart by looking at the behavior of Adam and Eve's first son, Cain. Read Genesis 4:1–16, and list all the personality traits that you see in Cain, both stated and implied.

_____

_____

_____

_____

What deeds resulted from his sin-filled heart (verse 8)?

_____

_____

How could this happen? How could Cain kill his own brother and then lie to God Almighty? Both Cain, a farmer, and Abel, a shepherd, had honorable vocations. And although Scripture is not definitive, the passage implies that each had an understanding about offering the fruits of their labor to God as gifts of worship. What offering did each bring to the Lord? Why was God pleased with Abel's offering and not with Cain's?

_____

_____

_____

By bringing the fat portions from the firstborn of his flock—the best of the best—Abel understood his God and responded in righteousness. Cain brought an offering of the fruits of the soil (not the *first* fruits) to the Lord. He understood what God required, but he chose to respond inappropriately. His attitude toward God is further revealed in verse 5. What was Cain's reaction to God's disfavor?

_____

_____

_____

Cain's attitude was made obvious by his response to God's displeasure over his offering. His was an unrepentant heart, but he knew his brother's was righteous. Instead of desiring a change of heart, Cain reacted in anger, indignation, dejection, jealousy, and bitterness. God could see everything that made up Cain's thought life and caused his behavior; He knew Cain's heart. What guidance and warning did He give Cain with regard to his ways (Genesis 4:6–7)? What do you think this means?

_____

_____

_____

> *"If you do well, will not your countenance be lifted up? And if you do not do well, sin is crouching at the door; and its desire is for you, but you must master it."*
>
> **Genesis 4:7**

God plainly told Cain that he had a choice to make. Don't we all? Daily we get to choose what's right and stay in God's favor (the Holy Spirit prompts us toward this choice), or what's wrong if we yield to the lurking sin that desires to master us. (The Enemy tempts us toward this one.) Daily we choose to be mastered, either by the Spirit, or by sin.

According to verses 8–9, how did Cain respond to God's warning?

_____

_____

_____

Cain deliberately planned Abel's murder. Evil thoughts and attitudes were so rooted in Cain's heart that he was indifferent to God's counsel.

📖 Proverbs 23:7 (KJV) says, *"As* [a man] *thinketh in his heart, so is he."* How does this verse explain all human behavior?

_____

_____

_____

> *"As [a man] thinketh in his heart, so is he."*
>
> **Proverbs 23:7 (KJV)**

Just what is the heart? It's the very core of our lives, the center of our "desires, feelings, affections, passions, impulses.[1]" It includes our mind, which is the seat of intellect and understanding. And last, the heart "represents especially the sphere of God's influence in the human life . . . soul, the very center."[2] It's where either faith or unbelief takes root. In short, the heart is the pool from which every thought and emotion, every attitude and action flow. And it's only the heart that can be right before God (Acts 8:21). The term "heart," as defined here, is used nearly one hundred times in the New Testament alone.

 Proverbs 23:7 explains why we relate to our husbands in the ways that we do—the attitudes that we cultivate produce the words we use and the ways in which we use them, as well as the things we do or don't do for our husbands. Apply this verse to your attitude toward your husband and your marriage. What does it reveal?

_____

_____

_____

_____

_____

The Enemy wants to dupe us into thinking that we aren't responsible for certain attitudes or actions—that those are usually or always someone else's fault. This is especially true if we're living with difficult spouses. But if our attitudes, words, and behaviors are by-products of what's going on in our hearts, then we need to understand the truth about this center of our very being.

📖 How do the following scriptures describe the heart?

Jeremiah 17:9

_____

_____

_____

Mark 7:20–23

_____

_____

_____

Luke 6:43–45

_____

_____

_____

Yes, the human heart is characterized as evil—thinking evil things, building evil attitudes, and encouraging evil deeds. It is sin-filled. Our "Canaanites" may be running rampant and without restraint. Does this scenario sound hopeless? It is for those without Jesus Christ.

📖 Recall from Ezekiel 36:25–28, which we studied in Lesson 2, that each believer has been given a *new heart*, one that has been cleansed and is now softened toward the things of God. Each has also been given a new spirit—the Holy Spirit—who enables us to be responsive to God and gives us a desire to be obedient to God's truth. Read Hebrews 4:12–13. What's the purpose of God's Word in a believer's life? What astonishing assertion does verse 13 make, and what does this mean for the believer? How can this truth influence us in our marriages?

_____

_____

_____

_____

> **Sin no longer needs to lay claim to a believer's territory demanding to be master. We have a Master; He's the one to whom we must give an account of our lives, and He's now in command.**

Sin no longer needs to lay claim to a believer's territory demanding to be master. We have a Master; He's the one to whom we must give an account of our lives, and He's now in command.

📖 Read 1 John 3:9. What encouraging truth do we receive from this verse about sin in our lives?

_____

_____

_____

Christian minister and teacher Oswald Chambers writes, "To be born of God means that I have His supernatural power to stop sinning. . . . 1 John 3:9 does not mean that we *cannot* sin—it simply means that if we will obey the life of God in us, that we *do not have to sin*."[3] Now that's an empowering statement!

📖 Paul addresses the powerful potential for change in our hearts (guaranteed!) in Colossians 2:6–7, 13–14; 3:1–17. Carefully read through these passages, making a list of what God did and what we're able (and required) to do.

What God Did   **What We're Able and Required to Do**

_____

_____

_____

_____

_____

Christian author Miles Stanford wrote, "Once we see that our death to sin is in the past tense, completed, we are free to count ourselves *alive* to God in Christ Jesus, and to *live*—in the present tense!"[4]

APPLY Will you agree that you have died to sin and are now alive with Christ? If so, what does this mean for the sin that is still entrenched in your heart?

_____

_____

_____

God wouldn't call you to confront a sin only to let it destroy you. There isn't a sin in your life that can't be overcome by the power of God at work in you now. Ask Him to help you set your heart on things above. Then trust Him with the life He saved.

EVERYONE HAS A HISTORY

It's true: we each have a history, a past that shaped and molded us into who we are, one that many of us embrace whenever we need to justify our actions ("I'm this way because…"). Our histories are composed of choices that we made and choices that others made for us, good or bad. The effect that these choices have had on shaping our inner selves can range

> **"For you have died and your life is hidden with Christ in God."**
>
> **Colossians 3:3**

Obedience in Action: The Process of Change
DAY TWO

from wonderfully beneficial to powerfully destructive. In today's lesson, I want to address those who still cling to a painful history.

Although we can't change a painful past, it doesn't have to ruin or run our lives. Wrongs that we committed or that were committed against us were done in the presence of Almighty God. In His divine sovereignty, He knew that we would face these painful experiences. He did not abandon us there; He was with us. And He grieves with us, just as He did over Cain, just as He did over Abel. Satan would have us believe that our past defines our present and shapes our future. In Jesus, however, it does neither. With the indwelling of His Spirit, everything we are and everything *we can become* is now found in Christ alone, regardless of our history.

Jesus Christ not only frees us from the guilt of our own sins, but He can also free us from the anger, guilt, and shame associated with sins committed against us. Because He is the God of justice, He is the only One entitled to repay another for these wrongs. Our responsibility as children of the King is to let Him repay for injustices as He wills. If we choose to cling to our past, we'll remain victimized by it and allow ourselves to victimize others and ourselves because of it, and we'll continue to impede God's process of change in our life. Because of His great love for us, He won't permit us to use our past to justify how we treat ourselves or another.

📖 Read Zephaniah 3:14–20, paying particular attention to verse 17. God is restoring His beloved. How does He do this? How can these words comfort a Christian who needs restoration?

_____

_____

_____

_____

📖 In Jeremiah 29:11–13 God gives powerful promises to the Israelites, who were soon to be released from Babylonian captivity. What are they? What was the Israelites' role in His promise? What application does this passage have in a believer's life today?

_____

_____

_____

_____

📖 Read Colossians 1:21–22, and then explain the effect of our relationship with Jesus on our past experiences. How does God view us now?

_____

_____

_____

We should remember this truth: Because of God's gift of salvation through Jesus Christ, we no longer have a past to condemn us; nor do we have one to use as an excuse. We're to struggle neither with the past nor with the future. Our moment-by-moment journey with the Lord is struggle enough. It's also where our victory lies.

> "The Lord your God is with you, he is mighty to save. He will take great delight in you, he will quiet you with his love, he will rejoice over you with singing."
>
> Zephaniah 3:17 (NIV)

> Because of God's gift of salvation through Jesus Christ, we no longer have a past to condemn us; nor do we have one to use as an excuse.

📖 Read John 8:31–32. Who was Jesus addressing in verse 31? What condition did He set before they could realize the promises He gave them next?

_____

_____

_____

The two promises Jesus gave in verse 32 are (1) *"You will know the truth"* and (2) *"The truth will set you free"* (NIV). What do you think this means for those who believe?

_____

_____

_____

This is one of the most encouraging and liberating scriptures in the Bible. We *who believe Jesus* are called to abide in and obey His truth. As the Holy Spirit progressively imparts biblical truth to us, the action is completed; the Spirit is then able to set us free from whatever holds us hostage!

APPLY Do you have a "history," an area in your life that needs restoration, one that has kept you "stuck," that repeatedly challenges you and your relationship with God? If so, write a brief sketch of your history here. How is it affecting your relationship with God?

_____

_____

_____

_____

Has this area also affected your relationship with your husband? If so, in what ways? Is he helping you overcome your history? If so, how? Is he judging you for it? If so, what kind of behavior does he display? Is he a target of it? If so, how does it take aim? Is he aware of it? If not, why? If it's hidden from him, does this really mean it's not affecting him? Take time to think these questions through, and answer them candidly.

_____

_____

_____

Is the number-one Canaanite you identified in Lesson 3 linked in any way to the area you described above in your "history" that needs restoration? If so, in what way?

_____

_____

_____

_____

> ## As the Holy Spirit progressively imparts biblical truth to us, the action is completed—it is able to set us free from whatever holds us hostage!

> ## "To the Jews who had believed in him, Jesus said, 'If you hold to my teaching, you are really my disciples. Then you will know the truth, and the truth will set you free.'"
>
> ## John 8:31–32 (NIV)

Where have you gone before to gain freedom from this area that consumes or masters you? What were the results?

_____

_____

_____

_____

Jesus said that His Word frees us. Do you *believe* this? Do you trust Him to strengthen you? Do you depend upon Him to restore you? Write down any reservations you might have. Acknowledging them is important to the process.

_____

_____

_____

_____

_____

It's time to permit the truth of God to seep into your soul and confront anything that stunts your growth in Him, chokes His joy in you, or reduces your effectiveness in reflecting His life in you, especially toward the person with whom you are one—your husband.

Do you trust God with your history? Do you believe that He knows exactly what to do with it? Are you willing to release it all into His hands? Are you willing (even if you don't feel ready) to move into your future with Him, no longer pursuing the questions of your past? If so, tell Him in a written prayer here. Thank Him and praise Him for what He's doing and for what He's going to do. Anticipate freedom in the One who has covered your past with His cleansing blood and holds your future in the palm of His hand. Return to this prayer when you need to be reminded that God is faithful to His promises. He will complete in you what He has begun (Philippians 1:6).

_____

_____

_____

_____

Obedience in Action:
The Process of Change

GETTING ON TRACK

Over the next two days you'll become aware of the steps the Lord took me through to confront my Canaanites (my "self"). He and I repeat the process whenever He brings an unwanted characteristic to my attention, or when He needs me to apply a little maintenance to ones I've already overcome (which is necessary to guard against complacency). When these steps are applied consistently, the time from recognizing a sin to its being overcome gets shorter and shorter. You can unlearn negative emotions, attitudes, and behaviors and learn to replace them with the ones God desires for you.

From the list in Lesson 3, what did God reveal as your number-one inner enemy (or Canaanite)? Write it here and then begin to apply the steps that follow. God will do the rest in his perfect timing.

_____

_____

STEP 1: RECOGNIZE YOUR INNER ENEMIES AS SIN

When we recognize an area of sin in our lives, we can hang on to it with excuses such as "That's how I was brought up," "That's just the way I am," or "It's not as bad as what my husband does!" What are some of the things you've said to justify sinful behavior?

_____

_____

_____

📖 What does 1 John 1:5–8 and 10 say about the sins we ignore, excuse, or defend?

_____

_____

_____

Recall that God's very first act during creation was to separate the light from the darkness. It's the first thing He does with a new believer as well (Colossians 1:13–14). Therefore, He'll hold us accountable if we claim to be His yet continue to (habitually) dabble in the darkness.

📖 Paul understood the believer's struggle. Although we have been freed from our sin nature and given a new nature, sinful thoughts and attitudes, habits, and conditioned responses still contend with the Spirit in us. Read Romans 7:14–25. Describe our struggle. What is our hope (verse 25)?

_____

_____

_____

APPLY Can you identify with Paul's description of the believer's struggle? If so, how is it similar to your own?

_____

_____

_____

_____

> "If we say that we have fellowship with Him and yet walk in darkness, we lie and do not practice the truth."
>
> I John 1:6

Be encouraged; recognizing an area of sin is the first step toward eliminating it from your life.

What thoughts, attitudes or behaviors do you struggle with in your marriage that seem difficult to change?

_____

_____

_____

_____

Be encouraged; recognizing an area of sin is the first step toward eliminating it from your life.

STEP 2: DENY YOURSELF

Generally, we don't want to deny ourselves of what we want: thoughts we *really* want to think, attitudes we *really* want to convey, words we *really* want to speak, and conduct we *really* want to display. To do so would be to ignore our own interests. This is particularly true in the marriage relationship, where "self" is front and center. If this is the case for any of us, it's beneficial to see if there's a similar response in our relationship with God.

📖 Read Mark 8:27–38. Note the exchange between Jesus and Peter. What does Peter profess in verse 29? In verse 32, what is Peter's response to a hard truth that Jesus conveyed? What is Christ's rebuke to Peter in verse 33?

_____

_____

_____

_____

In verse 34, Jesus requires three things from His disciples. What are they, and what do you think they mean?

_____

_____

_____

_____

> **"Then he called the crowd to him along with his disciples and said: 'If anyone would come after me, he must deny himself and take up his cross and follow me.'"**
>
> **Mark 8:34 (NIV)**

To deny or refuse ourselves means that we choose to "disown and renounce self and to subjugate all works, interests and enjoyments"[5] to Jesus Christ and His perfect best for us. Then we take up our daily hardships, marital or otherwise, in devoted life-or-death commitment to Him and follow Him habitually, perseveringly, through these hardships no matter what. It's our deepest place of humility and the cost of pursuing Him (Philippians 2:3–11). Is it a price we're willing to pay? Will we ignore our own interests for the sake of Christ's for us? Will we run whatever race He's put before us—with dedication and purpose (a marriage marathon, perhaps)? Will we follow His lead moment by moment?

 Do you profess Jesus as the Christ and then reject tough truths because they don't serve your interests? Perhaps the truths are too hard to accept because of what they would require of you (cost you) as His child or as a wife. How would denying yourself, taking up your cross, and following Jesus change how you're living for Him in general? How would denying yourself, taking up your cross, and following Jesus change how you're living for Him in your marriage?

_____

_____

_____

_____

STEP 3: CONFESS, REPENT, AND RECEIVE GOD'S FORGIVENESS

The three components of Step 3 are inseparable if we want to successfully deal with our sin. What motivates us to confess? What can thwart our getting to the point of confession? What's the condition of our hearts? How does God desire that we respond to those sinful habits, character flaws, and conditioned responses that offend Him and hurt others? What does it take to turn us away from sinful behavior and toward God? God's heart breaks over our sin. Does ours?

Confession isn't what we do just to get something off our chest—to relieve us of the burden of guilt so that we'll feel better. To confess literally means "the same to speak." In confession, we're saying the same thing back to God that He has spoken to us by His Spirit. Therefore, it's not for God's sake that we confess but for our own. In our agreement, we admit that something within us must change.

📖 There's a difference between genuine confession and lip service. Paul talks about two kinds of sorrow in 2 Corinthians 7:9–10. What are they, and where does each lead?

_____

_____

_____

_____

📖 When the Holy Spirit produces constructive guilt (conviction) in our hearts, the by-product is godly sorrow, which leads to repentance. A powerful example is found in Psalm 51. Let's look at David as he dealt with his sin with Bathsheba. Read this psalm. In David's prayer of confession, what was he asking from the Lord?

_____

_____

_____

Even though David's sin was against Bathsheba and her husband, Uriah, what did he acknowledge about his sin (verse 4)? Why was this an important admission?

_____

_____

_____

_____

Extra Mile
DAVID'S SIN

David was considered a man after God's own heart (Acts 13:22). To understand the magnitude of David's sin against God, read 2 Samuel 11. You will understand more fully David's penitent heart.

What did David know about God, especially in light of verses 7, 10, 12, and 14?

_____

_____

_____

📖 According to Psalm 32:3–4, what happens when we don't confess our sins?

_____

_____

What are some personal things that can stand in the way of confessing our sins to God?

_____

_____

_____

_____

📖 One of our biggest barriers to confession is pride. Read James 4:1–10. James is addressing serious sins that only the grace of God could penetrate (verses 1–5). What do verses 6–10 say about pride and its remedy? What results when we apply the remedy (verse 10)?

_____

_____

_____

" 'God opposes the proud but gives grace to the humble.' "

I Peter 5:5 (NIV)

If we choose not to humble ourselves, God will do it for us.

Everything right and righteous springs from humility. And note that it's our choice—*"Humble yourselves"* (James 4:10, NIV). If we choose not to humble ourselves, God will do it for us.

Let's look again at Psalm 51. According to verses 16–17, what does God desire from us more than all we can sacrifice for Him or offer Him? Why is that important to Him?

_____

_____

_____

David was a man after God's own heart, who had done all of His will (Acts 13:22). He understood the magnitude of his sin against God. The reality of his offense brought him to godly sorrow and a desire for a pure heart (Psalm 51:10). Such a transformation is what we call repentance, which means "to change the mind, relent . . . [involving] regret or sorrow, accompanied by a true change of heart toward God."[6] The Holy Spirit produces constructive guilt in believers to motivate change. Such guilt follows the profound realization of having offended God. Because this sorrow leads to repentance, there's nothing left to regret. The slate is clean, and the person is free. When we experience genuine sorrow, God is working. We can rejoice, because this sorrow is achieving the purpose of God in our lives.

Had David approached God with worldly sorrow, he would have merely felt sad about getting caught in his sin. Nothing would have changed, and he would have continued in his downward spiral. Pastor-teacher John MacArthur qualifies worldly sorrow as

> nothing more than the wounded pride of getting caught in a sin and having one's lusts go unfulfilled. That kind of sorrow leads only to [destructive] guilt, shame, despair, depression, self-pity, and hopelessness. People can die from such sorrow.[7]

📖 Read Psalm 32:1–2, 5; 103:12; and 1 John 1:9. What is God's response to heartfelt confession?

_____

_____

_____

📖 Read Psalm 19:12–13; 26:2; 139:23–24. What is the psalmist asking God to do in these verses?

_____

_____

_____

 How do you approach God when you know you have a sinful behavior to confess? What motivates you to confess it to Him? Do you confess because you got caught? Do you confess so that you'll feel better? Or do you confess because you know that you offended Him? Have you ever truly grieved or wailed over something you've said or done? Why? What does humbling yourself in the presence of the Lord mean to you? Ponder all these questions, and give honest insights into how you acknowledge your sin to God.

_____

_____

_____

_____

Not only is confessed sin forgiven, but you're cleansed from the sin and freed from the guilt. And God will never use a confessed sin against you. Do you freely receive His forgiveness when you seek it? And what does receiving His forgiveness mean with regard to your forgiving yourself?

_____

_____

_____

If we know that God has forgiven an offense and yet we won't forgive ourselves, then we're saying that what our Savior did on the cross was not payment enough for what we've confessed. Receiving God's forgiveness is saying, "I agree that I'm forgiven." Jesus said on the cross, "It is finished." When we fully believe this, we can move forward with Him in freedom from our sin.

In Their Shoes
UNCONFESSED SIN

What impact does unconfessed sin have on our lives? According to David's account in Psalm 38:1–11, we can suffer physically, emotionally, psychologically, and spiritually. But our sin also has social ramifications with those closest to us (verse 11). Read this poignant passage of intense sorrow. In what ways can you identify with David's lament?

If we know that God has forgiven an offense and yet we won't forgive ourselves, then we're saying that what our Savior did on the Cross was not payment enough for what we've confessed. Receiving God's forgiveness is saying, "I agree that I'm forgiven."

Have you ever asked the Lord to examine you, test you, and look for anything in you that might be offensive to Him? If so, what prompted you to do so? If not, what has kept you from doing so? What would His examination reveal about you in general? What would His examination reveal about you in your role as a wife?

_____

_____

_____

_____

God's searching and testing is a merciful undertaking, one that all Christians should welcome. So be encouraged. He'll test you and try you until your sins are driven out (little by little) and replaced with Himself.

 If it's not godly sorrow that motivates your confession, ask God to give you a broken and contrite spirit over your sin so that you can truly understand what David prayed: *"Against you, you only, have I sinned and done what is evil in your sight, so that you are proved right when you speak and justified when you judge"* (Psalm 51:4, NIV). Pray Psalm 139:23–24 for yourself regularly. It's a wonderful prayer, though not to be prayed lightly. Praying it will help you to stay on the path God has chosen for you. Tell God that you invite and welcome His change in your life. Pray this with expectancy, believing that He'll respond.

Obedience in Action: The Process of Change

DAY FOUR

FULL STEAM AHEAD

In Day Three we went through the first three steps toward conquering areas of sin: (1) recognizing each area of sin, (2) denying yourself, and (3) confessing that sin to the Lord, receiving His forgiveness, and repenting of it. Today we'll go through the final four steps.

STEP 4: TRUST GOD

After recognizing and confessing sin, we must then trust the Lord to rid us of it in His way, being careful not to approach this step as a matter of *trying* rather than trusting. By relying on our own efforts (even though our desire is to please God by attempting to rid ourselves of sin), we'll set ourselves up for failure.

Remember the struggle Paul talked about in Romans 7? Whenever he wanted to do good, evil was right there with him. He knew that there was only One who could rescue him from his misery (Romans 7:24–25). We're powerless to create lasting change in our own lives. Only God, through His Holy Spirit, can bring about lasting changes (sanctification) in us. We have a cooperative role to play that involves choice. The most active part of defeating sin is to *want* to defeat it. God is looking for a willing spirit. And because He knows our hearts, His Spirit will take over when we choose to entrust our sin to Him.

We're powerless to create lasting change in our own lives.

God commands us to trust Him. According to each of the following scriptures, in what ways are we to trust God? What will be our reward?

Proverbs 3:5–6

_____

_____

Isaiah 26:3

_____

_____

Jeremiah 17:5–8

_____

_____

APPLY Think about the promises in these passages as we choose to trust Him with all our heart, mind, and energy—*He* will keep our paths straight (Proverbs 3:6), *He* will keep us in perfect peace (Isaiah 26:3), and *He* will take us from striving (Jeremiah 17:5,6) to *thriving* (Jeremiah 17:7,8). The more we look outside the Source for answers to our sin problem, the more prolonged our search will be for the solution.

📖 Read Psalm 46:10. How can we apply this verse to our plight against sin?

_____

_____

_____

> *The more we look outside the Source for answers, the more prolonged our search will be for the solution.*

Trusting God means surrendering our sin to *Him* for purging. Only He can create circumstances perfectly tailored to our personalities that will allow us to work offensive behaviors out of our lives. Trusting God to weaken the enemies within and to strengthen us frees us to respond to His leading.

STEP 5: WAIT FOR GOD.

When you willingly and prayerfully trust God with the sins in your life, you're to wait for Him. That's certainly not what we're used to doing. As a matter of fact, waiting for God to move is pretty stressful for most Christians. We want results, and we want them now! Our attitude often can be summed up with the motto, "So what are we waiting for?" Psalm 37:5 says, *"Commit your way to the LORD; trust in him, and he will act"* (RSV), or *"Commit your way to the LORD, Trust also in Him, and He shall bring it to pass"* (NKJV), or *"Commit your way to the LORD, Trust also in Him, and He will do it"* (NASB).

📖 Read each of the following scriptures. What will your waiting yield?

Psalm 37:34

_____

_____

Isaiah 40:28–31 (What a promise!)

_____

_____

> *"Commit your way to the Lord; trust in Him, and He will act."*
>
> *Psalm 37:5 (RSV)*

Isaiah 64:4 (Get ready!)

_____

_____

📖 According to Psalm 40:1–3, how are we supposed to wait, and how will our waiting be rewarded?

_____

_____

_____

When waiting for the Lord, we're not just hanging out until something happens. There's a confidence, an expectancy, and a hope associated with the waiting; it's proactive. We anticipate God's involvement.

Oswald Chambers puts waiting into perspective:

" 'Wait on the Lord' and He will work (Psalm 37:34). But don't wait sulking spiritually and feeling sorry for yourself, just because you can't see one inch in front of you! Are we detached enough from our own spiritual fits of emotion to 'wait patiently for Him'? (37:7) Waiting is not sitting with folded hands doing nothing, but it is learning to do what we are told."[8]

APPLY Have you been waiting for God to remove a frustrating, unwanted character flaw from your heart? How have you waited? Impatiently? With "folded hands"? With expectancy that God will do it? In what ways will you need to change how you wait?

_____

_____

_____

_____

While you're waiting, take the next step in the process.

STEP 6: REJOICE AND PRAY WITH THANKSGIVING

Even though we're tested and stretched, perhaps painfully, during the first five steps of the process, while we're waiting for God, we should begin to rejoice and praise Him.

📖 What do Philippians 4:4–7 and 1 Thessalonians 5:16–18 say about rejoicing and praying with thanksgiving?

_____

_____

_____

Why are rejoicing and praying with thanksgiving necessary in the process of overcoming our inner antagonists, especially when they want to rear up in tough circumstances? (What's the opposite of rejoicing? If you need some help with this, go back to Numbers 14:11, 26–27.)

_____

_____

_____

> **When waiting for the Lord, we're not just hanging out until something happens.**

> **"Rejoice always; pray without ceasing; in everything give thanks; for this is God's will for you in Christ Jesus."**
>
> **I Thessalonians 5:16**

What's the opposite of thanksgiving? How would that attitude affect our response to difficult circumstances?

_____

_____

_____

_____

We praise God and give thanks in difficult circumstances because He's in them, and His purposes will unfold. He is our hope.

STEP 7: OBEY

📖 In the Gospel of John, Christ talks about obedience as the measure of our love for Him. In the chart below there are several verses of Scripture listed. Read each passage and then jot down the blessing promised as a reward for obedience in the space provided next to each passage. Then jot down the effect of obedience on our relationship with Christ based on what you read.

Verse	Blessing	Effect on Relationship with Christ
John 14:21		
John 14:23		
John 15:9–11		

🛑 APPLY Consider the areas of your marriage in which you (not your husband) need to improve (for example: communication, expressions of kindness and respect, sexual responsiveness, submission to your husband's leadership in the home). What are they? How will your obedience to God affect these problem areas of your marriage?

_____

_____

_____

_____

What effect will your obedience to God have on your relationship with your husband?

_____

_____

> _"If you obey my commands, you will remain in my love, just as I have obeyed my Father's commands and remain in his love. I have told you this so that my joy may be in you and that your joy may be complete."_
>
> **John 15:10–11 (NIV)**

Over time you'll be prompted by the gentle voice of the Holy Spirit to address the areas in your marriage that need attention. At first you may resist these promptings, focusing on ways that your husband could improve and praying for the Spirit to speak to him instead. Ask God to help you be quick to put down your self-interests. Speak back to Him the need for change. Trust Him to work in you on these areas. Wait for Him with joy and thanksgiving while He prepares and presents many opportunities to practice obedience.

Obedience in Action: The Process of Change
DAY FIVE

Every willful display of self-centered behavior encourages the slow erosion of the relationship.

STAYING ON TRACK

Marriage provides so many opportunities to practice godliness. I say that with a little snicker, because we all know that it's much easier to practice nastiness! There's a sense of security in marriage that can make both spouses feel safe enough to act out their ugly tendencies. It's false security. Every willful display of self-centered behavior encourages the slow erosion of the relationship. The damage may be imperceptible until that final storm causes a complete breakdown and collapse. Each spouse will want to look to the other for culpability. But God will hold each accountable for his or her own role, as husband or wife.

God holds me accountable every day for how I live my role as John Rossi's wife. That's what I'm responsible for—my life, not my husband's (which is why this is a Bible study for wives). My goal is to honor God in the race that He has marked out before me. And I'm not to regard His instruction and discipline lightly; nor should you.

Let's take a look at how God applies His loving discipline to our lives and for what purpose. Read Hebrews 12:1–13 very carefully. According to verse 1, what is our responsibility? And what has God already done to help us? (Look carefully at the beginning and end of this verse for the answer).

_____

_____

_____

_____

God provided wonderful witnesses who persevered in life by faith (Hebrews 11). We can be motivated to do the same by their example of persistent and patient endurance. The important reality is that God has marked out our race for us. Therefore, we move boldly into whatever He'll use to make us holy witnesses for the encouragement of others.

According to verses 2–3, on whom are we to focus, and why?

_____

_____

_____

In verse 5, we see that the Father's desire is to encourage us and reason with us, not condemn us. How does this approach prepare us for the truth we're about to hear on the subject of God's discipline?

_____

_____

How are we to respond to His discipline (verse 5 and 9)?

_____

_____

_____

Why does the Lord discipline us (verses 6–11)?

_____

_____

_____

In verses 10–11, what are the ultimate goals of God's loving discipline?

_____

_____

_____

What does verse 11 imply is our part in producing the harvest?

_____

_____

_____

God can discipline us all day long, but if we refuse to be trained by it, we can't expect our hearts *or* our circumstances to change for the better. The condition of our hearts and the state of our affairs often go hand in hand. If peace eludes us in our hearts or in our homes, it's fair to ask ourselves if we're making light of the Lord's discipline (verse 5).

What admonition is given in Hebrews 12:12–13? What does this mean?

_____

_____

_____

I love these last two verses. I hear, "Buck up! Let the race that God has marked out for you strengthen you. Keep your paths straight, and remove everything that you could trip over. And keep going in the right direction, so that the parts of you that are still weak will be strengthened and healed. Persevere."

APPLY Have you experienced the Lord's discipline in your life? How did you respond to it then? How would you respond to such correction now?

_____

_____

_____

In Their Shoes

THE HALL OF FAITH

Read Hebrews 11 and note all of the Old Testament saints who encourage believers today by their lives of faith.

"No discipline seems pleasant at the time, but painful. Later on, however, it produces a harvest of righteousness and peace for those who have been trained by it."

Hebrews 12:11 (NIV)

Have you experienced the Lord's conviction and discipline in any area specific to your marriage? If so, what was it? How have you been trained by it (verse 11)? How did it affect your relationship with your husband?

_____

_____

_____

_____

Now that this lesson is completed, how will you respond to God's call to obedience? What have you heard from the Lord about obedience as it applies to your own spiritual journey? to your marriage?

_____

_____

_____

Obedience is a small investment that pays huge dividends.

Obedience is a small investment that pays huge dividends. A popular speaker once said that when we obey God, we get more than we ask for, more than we expect, and more than we deserve. Being under God's authority is our only place of peace, even if our husbands and marriages are challenging. It's also our only source of righteousness, yielding a child of God growing in holiness. Watch and see how faithful your Father is as you're faithful in your obedience.

 Perhaps watching our children's response to our discipline provides a glimpse of our response to our Father's discipline. How do you respond to His loving admonitions, rebukes, or even "spiritual spankings"? Can you see the intensity of His love behind His discipline? Will you thank Him for loving you that much?

Works Cited

1. Spiros Zodhiates, Warren Baker, eds., *The Complete Word Study Dictionary New Testament* (Chattanooga, TN: AMG Publishers, 1992), #2588, 819.

2. Ibid., #2588, 820.

3. James Reimann, ed., *My Utmost for His Highest: The Golden Book of Oswald Chambers* (Grand Rapids: Discovery House, 1992), August 15 devotional.

4. Miles J. Stanford, *The Complete Green Letters* (Grand Rapids: Zondervan Publishing House, 1983), 205.

5. Zodhiates, Baker, eds., *The Complete Word Study Dictionary: New Testament,* #533, 204.

6. Ibid., #3340, 969.

7. John MacArthur, *The MacArthur Study Bible* (Nashville: Word Publishing, 1997), 1775.

8. Reimann, ed., *My Utmost for His Highest: The Golden Book of Oswald Chambers,* August 1 devotional.

5

Marriage: God's Will and God's Way

*S*ome of us may not think our marriages were made in heaven, but I believe God would disagree. He was in on it when we tied the knot, and He's in on it now. God will use whatever condition our marriages are in to make us holy, which is His goal in every believer's life. He can also create, enrich, recreate, revive, or restore love in the best or worst of marriages, even if it seems as if we're working on it alone right now.

As we ask God to breathe new life into our marriages, He wants us to participate. First, we entrust our men to Him—all they are and all they can become. Then we give God ample room to work, recognizing that it's His Holy Spirit's job to change hearts. And He begins with our own.

This week we'll study the different ways God established the permanence of marriage, which is to be as vital and unshakable a bond as His is with us. And He sealed it with a love that only He could design, a love patterned after His own, a love of eternal, binding commitment—covenant love.

> **God will use whatever condition our marriages are in to make us holy, which is His goal in every believer's life.**

BONE OF MY BONES

When we married, we probably didn't really consider what our vows meant, especially from God's perspective. We knew we would be sharing the same dreams, living space, food, money, toothpaste, and so on; we also knew our marriages were supposed to last a long time. But did we realize that we actually became a *part* of each other, that an exchange was made when vows were exchanged, that two souls were melded into one when the marriage was consummated? God purposefully established the holy institution of matrimony. He designed the marital relationship to mean something profoundly spiritual and to represent the relationship with the One who ordained it.

📖 Let's take a look at God's purposeful order in creating a man and a woman. Please reread Genesis 2:7, 18–20. God created enough to keep Adam busy, but a suitable helpmeet was still missing. Why do you think God said a man's being alone was not good?

_____

_____

The Hebrew word translated "alone" in Genesis 2:18 is from the root word *bad* (isn't that intriguing?), meaning "apart from" and can refer to "a part or parts of something such as an amount of an ingredient used to make incense or anointing oil."[1] In the beginning, every other living creature was partnered with a companion of like kind, and yet there was no one else on earth like Adam. Adam needed another part, a companion if you will, to complete him.

📖 Read Genesis 2:21–22. Recount how God resolved Adam's aloneness.

_____

_____

📖 Now read Genesis 2:23. What's the significance of Adam's declaration in this verse?

_____

_____

_____

That God created Adam first and Eve second was no slight to her womanhood. She was created *for* Adam, to respond to him physically, emotionally, intellectually, and spiritually. He was not complete in any of these areas without her responding nature. Adam's declaration in verse 23 acknowledged that Eve was a part *of* him and no longer apart *from* him. God's purposeful plan for them then is still His plan for us today.

Despite today's morally "free" society, many men move through life alone without a committed, monogamous relationship, without a help-meet. God's perfectly designed marriage covenant was stamped on a man and a woman's souls "in the beginning" and has not changed with the times. God's answer to aloneness was not to be found in a series of one-night stands, in out-of-wedlock cohabitation, or in the arms of someone else's husband or wife. It was to be found in a committed marriage relationship.

> **"And the man said, 'This is now bone of my bones, and flesh of my flesh; She shall be called Woman, Because she was taken out of Man.'"**
>
> **Genesis 2:23**

APPLY Have you ever felt alone, especially in your marriage? If yes, to what do you attribute your aloneness.

_____

_____

_____

Would you be happy as a woman alone, without anybody, not just without your husband? Explain why or why not.

_____

_____

_____

Throughout their years together, husbands and wives should be growing toward each other, more attuned, accepting and responsive to each other's natures. As God is maturing and completing us as individuals, we respond to each other in ways that are maturing and completing our marriage relationship. This is the process of growing in oneness—first with the Lord and then with each other. Even if a husband is not Christian, he can still be influenced by God's working in and through his wife (1 Corinthians 7:14). Describe your growth as a couple over the years.

_____

_____

_____

_____

A wife was designed by God to complete her husband by her response to him physically, emotionally, intellectually, and spiritually. How would you assess your response to your husband physically? Has non-sexual, physical affection as well as sexual expression grown over the years, or has it diminished? Explain your answer.

_____

_____

_____

How do you respond to your husband's emotional makeup as it relates to his maleness? How does it differ from your own? Do you think your differences are "normal"? How do you respond to these differences?

_____

_____

_____

How do you respond to your husband's intellect (his ability to understand, reason, and deduce) as you discuss issues and come to conclusions, or tackle problems and arrive at solutions?

_____

_____

> *God's answer to aloneness was not to be found in a series of one-night stands, in out-of-wedlock co-habitation, or in the arms of someone else's husband or wife. It was to be found in a committed marriage relationship.*

How do you respond to your husband spiritually? In other words, how do you relate to him on a spiritual level, whether he's an unbeliever or perhaps a believer who may not be where you are spiritually?

_____

_____

_____

_____

How do you think your husband would assess your oneness physically, emotionally, intellectually, and spiritually? (You might consider asking him, although this may be a difficult question with which to begin a dialog.)

_____

_____

_____

_____

The fact is, the more intimately we relate to the Lord, the more attuned we'll be to intimately relate to our husbands. Conversely, the more detached we are from Him, the more detached we're likely to be from our husbands. It's a spiritual dynamic.

Marriage is about companionship, fellowship, intimacy—in other words, _relationship!_ Adam and Eve's relationship with each other was designed to reflect their relationship with God. And so is ours. The fact is, the more intimately we relate to the Lord, the more attuned we'll be to intimately relate to our husbands. Conversely, the more detached we are from Him, the more detached we're likely to be from our husbands. It's a spiritual dynamic. Once I understood this, my entire perspective on marriage—_my_ marriage—changed.

APPLY In what ways is your relationship with Jesus Christ reflected in your marriage? Can you discern ways in which it's _not_ reflected in your marriage? If so, please explain.

_____

_____

_____

If God had fashioned you from your husband's rib, how might that influence your attitude toward your husband? (Think carefully on this one before writing your answer.)

_____

_____

_____

Ask God to show you your husband through His eyes...

 If you feel alone in your marriage, take time daily to thank God for your husband, even if you may not feel thankful right now. Ask God to help you understand what it means to respond to your husband. Then be willing to follow His leading. Ask God to show you your husband through His eyes in each area of your marriage so that you'll know how to apply His teaching. As you continue growing more deeply in the Lord, may what you receive from Him flow toward your husband as blessing.

AND THE TWO SHALL BECOME ONE

Every marriage has problems. Some are niggling annoyances. Some are agonizing wounds. But all, whether great or small, are traceable back to the violation of the one command that keeps a marriage in the center of God's will. Let's take a look at it.

In God's plan to optimize the joy, companionship, and mutual blessing of this amazing relationship he ordained between a man and a woman, He gave them three commands. Read Genesis 2:24. What are they?

_____

_____

When a man is called to "leave" his father and mother, he is "to loosen, relinquish, release to permit; to set free; to leave, forsake, abandon, leave behind."[2] Carefully consider this entire definition. What message is God sending to the man with this verse?

_____

_____

God directs a man not only to leave his father and mother but to "cleave" to his wife. In the Hebrew, this means he is "to catch by pursuit: abide fast, cleave (fast together), follow close (hard after), be joined (together), keep (fast), overtake, pursue hard, stick, take."[3] The Greek equivalent means "to cement together—to stick like glue—or to be welded together so that the two cannot be separated without damage to both."[4] This is a very active verb! And this definition indicates that the action is ongoing, never-ending. Why do you think God commands the man to cleave?

_____

_____

_____

Why do you think the first two commands are directed to the man and not also to the woman? (Consider your answer in light of their God-ordained roles.)

_____

_____

_____

How do you think God intends a wife to respond to her husband's "leaving" other relationships and "cleaving" to her?

_____

_____

_____

By divine design, God created the man first, assigned him responsibility for the Garden's care, and made him accountable for carrying out His commands, thereby establishing his leadership role in his environment. God also charged him to take the lead in the marriage relationship. That Adam and

> "For this cause a man shall leave his father and his mother, and shall cleave to his wife; and they shall become one flesh."
>
> **Genesis 2:24**

A husband is to leave behind all other relationships of his youth and create a new relationship with his bride, who is to respond in kind.

Eve had no human mother and father to leave is profound. Their primary relationship was to be with God first, who commanded them to make each other their primary earthly relationship. It's no different today. A husband is to leave behind all other relationships of his youth and create a new relationship with his bride, who is to respond in kind.

As we stated earlier, the man is commanded to cleave to his wife, to be inseparably and actively joined to her by his strength, which holds her to him. Her husband is her umbrella of protection, provision, and leadership, and God will hold him accountable for how he lives out his role. God will also hold a wife accountable for how she responds to his role. This is an awesome consideration for today. Accountability in the eyes of God doesn't change just because the cultural mores have.

📖 We can apply this same dynamic of leaving and cleaving to our heavenly Bridegroom, Jesus Christ. How do the following verses convey this?

Matthew 28:20

_____

_____

John 1:1–2, 14

_____

_____

John 10:27–30

_____

_____

Romans 8:35–39

_____

_____

Jesus cleaves to us with such strength, assurance, and care that we desire to cleave to Him in response. He is our spiritual place of protection, provision, and leadership.

Jesus, the Bridegroom, left the establishment of His heavenly realm to come to earth and establish a relationship with us, His Bride. He cleaves to us with such strength, assurance, and care that we desire to cleave to Him in response. He is our spiritual place of protection, provision, and leadership. Nothing and no one can separate us from His love. Nor should we want them to!

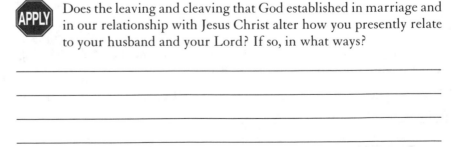 Does the leaving and cleaving that God established in marriage and in our relationship with Jesus Christ alter how you presently relate to your husband and your Lord? If so, in what ways?

_____

_____

_____

_____

With regard to your "leaving," have you really left Mom and Dad? Have you left their leadership, their protection, and their provision in exchange for your husband's? Honestly assess this question, and answer how you *know for certain* that you have or have not.

_____

_____

_____

With regard to your "cleaving," is there anyone or anything taking up space *between* you and your husband that only he should occupy? In other words, is anyone or anything causing you to neglect your husband? If so, what or who is it (children, friends, job, ministry, television, or so on), and how is it affecting your relationship with him? If not, what is the evidence that you and your husband are welded together?

_____

_____

_____

_____

How would you assess your husband's leaving past relationships and cleaving to you?

_____

_____

_____

If our husbands don't leave and cleave in a way that reflects God's command, we should be careful that we don't do the same. When we carry out God's command for us—to leave and cleave to our husbands—He will honor our obedience.

The final command in Genesis 2:24 is that the two will become one flesh. What do you think this means?

_____

_____

_____

The exchanging and binding of two souls into one makes the marriage a new entity, and God accomplishes this through the profound intimacy of sexual intercourse. In the beginning, when God created one male *only* and one female *only* and called the two *alone* to oneness, He established two eternal laws: (1) marriage is a *heterosexual* union, and (2) marriage is a *monogamous* union.

Sexual intercourse is God's ultimate wedding gift! God designed this beautiful act in marriage to result in yet another creation . . . or two, or three, or more. Our children are a natural product of God's natural order—a reward from God, to be used for His purpose.

📖 Just as leaving and cleaving in marriage have a spiritual application, becoming one flesh also has a spiritual application. What do you discover in the following verses?

1 Corinthians 6:17

_____

_____

"But he who unites himself with the Lord is one with him in spirit."

1 Corinthians 6:17
(NIV)

_____

_____

When we entered into our relationship with Jesus Christ, it was by the power of His Holy Spirit that we became one with Him. We are that "new creation," to be used for the purposes of God. What a remarkable God we serve!

APPLY   In what ways is your oneness with Jesus Christ reflected in your life?

_____

_____

_____

_____

If oneness is what God intended for marriage , what does it look like in your marriage? Are you two "one" both physically and in spirit, or are you more like "married singles"? Explain.

_____

_____

_____

_____

Does your sexual relationship with your husband reflect your oneness, bringing you closer together? If so, in what ways? If not, what stumbling blocks are hindering your oneness in this area?

_____

_____

_____

_____

Leaving, cleaving, and becoming one are the foundational building blocks of every marriage relationship, no matter how new or "seasoned" it is. All other relationships are to take a back seat. Nothing is to distract us from our leaving or break the bond of our cleaving. Nor is anyone or anything to divide our oneness—not parents, not children, not friends, not outside intruders, not activities, not even self. And we build this same inseparable bond with Jesus Christ.

Every trace of marital discord can be found in the violation of one or more of the three commands in Genesis 2:24. If the Holy Spirit is prompting you to acknowledge difficulty in leaving, cleaving, or becoming one, bring it to the Lord without delay. If your husband is falling short in any one of these three areas, pray for his eyes to be opened to God's truth while anticipating that God will do what's necessary to align you with His will for your marriage. Be encouraged that He's doing a work—first in you, then in your marriage.

The Covenant Love of God

What do you think of when you hear the word "covenant"? There are many synonyms that help define it, such as "pledge," "vow," "commitment," "contract," "agreement," "oath," "promise," and so on. With any one of these words, we usually think in terms of permanence. But we've all experienced, either first-hand or through others, pledges forsaken, vows ignored, commitments abandoned, contracts cancelled, agreements violated, oaths dishonored, and promises broken. I believe our conventional understanding of covenant today is that of a mere agreement. We often think that any time the terms of the agreement are no longer to our satisfaction, then we're free and justified to walk away.

But what is covenant to God? It's the very essence of who He is, and the covenant theme fills the pages of the Bible from cover to cover. God covenanting with human beings is His solemn, sacred, eternally binding pledge of commitment to His creation. Fred Lowery writes,

> Covenant was in the heart of God from the day he created mankind. It's a term that describes God's unique relationship with his people and carries with it the guarantee of all the benefits and blessings of that relationship. Covenant is how he chose from the beginning of time to demonstrate his love and his desire to fellowship with his creation. The truth is, our God is a covenant God, the Bible is a covenant book, and we are a covenant people.[5]

We've already seen a glimpse of God's covenant heart with His creation, described in Genesis 1. It was evident in His commitment to life on earth and its care through the rule and dominion of human beings, who were to reflect their Creator's glory and love.

Then we see His covenant love toward Adam and Eve as He clothed them in skins to cover their nakedness and sin, grieving over their choice of allegiance and yet promising the Deliverer from Eve's "seed" or descendents (Genesis 3:15). He was determined to win humanity back to Himself.

📖 We track the "Seed" (capitalized for a very important reason) through Noah's family. Even in God's judgment of humanity's inhumanity, He remained faithful to His covenant. Read Genesis 9:8–17. What does this passage reveal about God's commitment to His creation?

_____

_____

_____

God's covenant with Noah was never to destroy His creation by flood again, and He sealed this promise with His rainbow. However, knowing that the unbridled, rebellious, continually evil human heart would prevail, He would "do what a flood of judgment [could not] do; He would change the heart of man."[6]

📖 God affirmed His covenant of the promised Deliverer as He passed the "Seed" from Noah's son Shem to Abraham. The "Seed" that was to

> **What is covenant to God? It's the very essence of who He is and fills the pages of the Bible from cover to cover. It's His solemn, sacred, eternally binding pledge of commitment to His creation.**

come from Abraham would bless every nation on earth as it passed through Abraham to his son Isaac, through Isaac to his son Jacob, through Jacob to his son Judah, and through the tribe of Judah into the lineage of David. Generations later, the fulfillment of God's covenant would be realized. Read Galatians 3:16. Who is the "Seed"?

_____

Through many centuries from Adam to Noah, all the way to Mary the mother of Jesus, God chose certain human beings to continue the messianic bloodline. Throughout the Bible, the word "seed" is often used to describe someone's offspring or descendents. In many cases, it refers to the messianic line beginning with Adam that extends through many generations—all the way to the promised Messiah, the "enmity" alluded to in Genesis 3:15 that would come between humanity and Satan. Jesus Christ is this promised Messiah, the fulfillment of the covenant love of God. He is the one who will bruise Satan's head, ultimately defeating the devil and the forces of evil forever. Through Christ, God is winning humanity back to Himself, one heart at a time. And if we're Christ's, we, too, are Abraham's seed and heirs according to the promise (Galatians 3:29).

📖 In the following verses, what do we learn about our covenant-making God?

Genesis 17:7

_____

_____

Deuteronomy 7:7–9

_____

_____

Psalm 89:19–37

_____

_____

Psalm 105:8

_____

_____

Ezekiel 36:26–28

_____

_____

Hebrews 6:13–19

_____

_____

God's covenant love promises that

- His covenants are everlasting
- His constancy holds even when ours falls short; His faithfulness will never fail
- He'll never go back on the promises He makes; they stand forever
- His covenants are confirmed by His binding oath, and there is no one holier or greater by whom He can swear

Extra Mile
COVENANT

To round out your appreciation for God's covenant promises through the "Seed," Jesus Christ, you can read about the Abrahamic Covenant in Genesis 12, 15, and 17; the Mosaic Covenant in Exodus 19—24 and Deuteronomy; the Davidic Covenant in 2 Samuel 7 and 1 Chronicles 17; and the New Covenant in Jeremiah 31—33 and Hebrews 8—10. God is faithful from cover to cover.

"I will establish my covenant as an everlasting covenant between me and you and your descendants after you for the generations to come, to be your God and the God of your descendants after you."

Genesis 17:7 (NIV)

- He'll never forget the promises He makes
- His is an everlasting covenant of peace, because He'll establish Himself among us forever
- He'll never change His mind, because He can't lie; He'll do what He said He's going to do
- We can anchor ourselves surely and securely to His promises, no matter how storm-tossed our circumstances

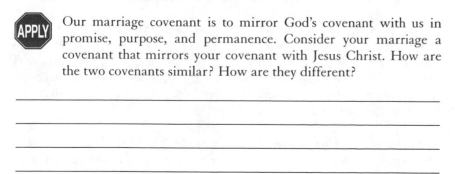 **APPLY** Have you ever felt that God failed you, that He didn't keep a promise? What was the circumstance? What happened? How did you resolve the issue with God?

_____

_____

_____

_____

When you consider God's covenant-keeping character, how could you re-evaluate the notion that He let you down?

_____

_____

_____

Marriage is a covenant relationship that God puts on the same plane as His covenant relationship with you and me. Even if we've never considered our marriages from the context of covenant, God does. And nothing is to break a covenant that's sacred in God's eyes—not disappointment, not circumstances, not boredom, not a changing of the mind, not loss of love, not adultery—nothing but death, because in God's view, the consequences are eternal. That was the binding commitment God intended for marriage from the beginning, and neither time nor cultural inclination can change His changeless mind. As Kay Arthur pointedly declares, "No matter what it costs, a covenant is a covenant is a covenant."[7]

God obviously has high standards for marriage. Our frail personalities often do not live up to these standards, however, and it is likely that some of you reading this study will feel like you have already blown it. Perhaps you are divorced and remarried by now. Maybe the divorce was not your choice. Though your first marriage may not have met God's expectations, always know that you are serving a forgiving God. You can be restored and vow to turn your current marriage over to a loving, compassionate God. He can make our crooked paths straight (see Proverbs 3:6).

APPLY Our marriage covenant is to mirror God's covenant with us in promise, purpose, and permanence. Consider your marriage a covenant that mirrors your covenant with Jesus Christ. How are the two covenants similar? How are they different?

_____

_____

_____

_____

_____

You're in a covenant relationship with our Lord Jesus Christ. You're also in a covenant relationship with your husband. As you ponder the significance of what this means in each relationship, especially when storms arise, pray for the willingness and the perseverance to hold firm to the Anchor that will hold you to your two covenants. May God give you a new determination to reflect His covenant in promise, in purpose, and in permanence.

Marriage: God's Will and God's Way

DAY FOUR

Our marriage covenant is to mirror God's covenant with us in promise, purpose, and permanence.

THE MARRIAGE COVENANT— A BIBLICAL PERSPECTIVE

Our nation's divorce rate has skyrocketed, with one out of every two marriages dissolving. This should be a sobering statistic for us all and an alarming one for the Christian community, since the percentage of divorced, "born again" Christian adults is in a statistical dead heat with the national divorce rate.[8]

Divorce used to be for many the last resort. For too many today, it seems to be the only resort. Although most couples still make the traditional vow, "as long as we both shall live," what many of them seem to mean is "as long as we both shall *love.*" Sacred vows are broken, and God grieves. Christian marriages are being ensnared by cultural compromise and devoured by "no fault" divorce. Couples are under the erroneous assumption that divorce will solve all their problems, oblivious to the greater troubles that it often creates.

God's covenant love is the foundation of our relationship with Him, and it's to be the foundation of our relationship with our spouses. Since He created the institution of marriage and set the ground rules, the most crucial test of covenant love in our marriages must be "Do I please God in my marriage?" not "Do I please my husband?" or "Am *I* pleased?" And we are able to please God in our marriages as we rely on His Holy Spirit for truth, guidance, and counsel. *He* will enable us to meet God's standards.

📖 Let's look at the seriousness with which God views covenant, first with Himself and then within marriage. Read Malachi 2:1–16. What's God's complaint against Israel's spiritual leaders (verses 1–9)?

_____

_____

The prophet Malachi delivered a stern rebuke to Israel's priests. Their hard-hearted disregard for God's love and His laws had caused the people to stumble. The Jews had broken faith with God, and their unfaithfulness spread to their marriages as they divorced their Jewish wives and turned to foreign wives with foreign gods. God would deal justly with each one who had done this (verse 12).

Malachi describes God as a "witness" in verse 14. The Hebrew word translated "witness" in this verse means "to protest or testify." A literal translation of this verse reads, "And ye have said, 'Wherefore?' Because Jehovah hath testified between thee and the wife of thy youth, that thou has dealt treacherously against her, and she thy companion, and thy covenant-wife."[9] What part did God play in the marriages of these men and their Israelite wives? What insight does that give us into the part God plays today in our marriage vows?

_____

_____

Malachi's description of their wives reminds the Israelite men that monogamy was God's plan for His people. List three ways the wife is defined in verse 14?

_____

_____

_____

How does monogamy help children to become "godly offspring" (verse 15)? What implication does this have for children of Christian parents in today's divorce-saturated culture? Seriously consider this question before answering.

_____

_____

What sobering declaration does God make in verse 16? Why do you think He feels this way? (Ponder verses 14–15 for your answer.) What warning does He repeat from verse 15?

_____

_____

_____

" 'I hate divorce,' says the Lord God of Israel…"

Malachi 2:16 (NIV)

Our Lord used strong language when He said He hates divorce. God knows the destruction divorce leaves in its wake. Therefore, He warns in the strongest terms against that which would destroy the one-flesh relationship that He made and witnessed between a husband and the wife of his youth—his companion, his wife by covenant.

You may ask, "If God hates divorce, why did He permit it?" Divorce is a byproduct of fallen, hardened humanity. That God permits it doesn't mean He condones it. The law that God delivered to Moses permitted husbands (only) to divorce their wives for infidelity, an offense worthy of death (see Leviticus 20:10; John 8:3–5). However, men divorced their wives for any and every reason, which God abhorred. God sought through Moses to protect the innocent wife from being stoned or socially ostracized, by commanding a certificate of divorce from the husband who sent his wife away (divorced her) for any reason other than marital infidelity (Deuteronomy 24:1–4). The certificate also permitted the innocent wife to remarry without the stigma of being labeled "adulteress."[10]

📖 Through Malachi, God forcefully asserted to his people the necessity to stick to His command in Genesis 2:24. Read Matthew 5:31–32; 19:1–9; Mark 10:2–9. In what ways did Jesus affirm God's command?

_____

_____

_____

> **The most crucial test of covenant love in our marriages must be "Do I please God in my marriage?" not "Do I please my husband?" or "Am I pleased?"**

Although Jesus explained that Moses permitted divorce because men's hearts were hard, He asserted that divorce was never part of God's plan from the beginning (Matthew 19:4, 8; Mark 10:6). In the Matthew and Mark passages, Jesus was reigning in those who were "putting away" their spouses for reasons other than unrepentant, persistent marital unfaithfulness. His validation of the marriage union as a binding, life-long covenant was significant to the culture then, and it is just as significant to ours today. God has not and will not change His mind about the permanence of marriage.

Ed Wheat laments the devastation that results from ignoring God's standard for marriage: "The leaving, cleaving, and knowing each other results in a new identity in which two individuals merge into one—one in mind, heart, body and spirit. This is why divorce has such a devastating effect. Not two people are left, but two fractions of one."[11] *God* made them one. Divorce destroys that oneness. Is there any question why God hates divorce?

The damage of divorce goes beyond the one-flesh couple. It's also a violation of a commitment to children, the ones who would be the continuation of God's covenant people. Divorce destroys God's plan for the family, leaving the children torn between two loyalties and disillusioned by parents who were intended to credibly model responsible adulthood. These children are often shaken in their faith and in their security as they struggle secretly with self-blame, guilt, and "if onlys." God grieves—not only for them but also for the glory that could have been His had His couple (even if only one is Christian) persevered, prayed through their problems, sought biblical counsel, and determined to remain steadfast to the covenant He had witnessed.

> **"So they are no longer two, but one. Therefore what God has joined together, let man not separate."**
>
> **Matthew 19:6 (NIV)**

Couples should not even utter the word "divorce" in their marriages, since it plants a seed that Satan longs to cultivate. His goal is to destroy what God has joined together. But our goal should be to uphold our marriage covenant and to help others uphold theirs, to persevere through the rocky times and not pull out. As Christian marrieds, we have a high calling—forgive, reconcile, restore—the very message of the cross.

That same spirit of forgiveness and reconciliation should also be extended to those who are divorced. Those who are divorced should be told that God can bring healing and restoration to their lives, though He may not choose to restore former marriages. God's covenant love can never be dissolved, even if a marriage already has been.

There are well-respected, biblically grounded theologians who agree that Jesus permits divorce and remarriage only in the case of hard-hearted, unrepentant marital infidelity (Matthew 5:31–32; 19:7–8). Some believe that Paul by implication permits divorce and remarriage in the case of an unbeliever abandoning his or her believer spouse (1 Corinthians 7:15). Although divorce may be allowable in these two cases, we must consider that neither is a mandate. This is evident in the story of Hosea and Gomer (Hosea 1—3:5). Hosea's love and loyalty toward his faithless wife, Gomer, were relentless. Although she abandoned him to pursue her lovers, and their marriage ties were severed, Hosea did not abandon her. He waited. One day he saw her worn, naked body on the slave block in the market square, and he bought her back (redeemed her). Over time, he restored her. Does this sound familiar? It's the beautiful plan of God's covenant love and relationship with Israel. It's the message of the cross once again.

That Scripture may offer two grounds for legitimate divorce (unrepentant marital unfaithfulness, and abandonment by an unbelieving spouse) doesn't mean that divorce is always God's solution in these circumstances. A marriage that is in one (or both) of these painful places is its own unique story. Therefore, no two marriages can be treated alike. Each has two different people with two different hearts producing different dynamics within their marriage. Only God knows how working in one heart can potentially reach the other, which is why clinging to the Word of God, receiving solid biblical counsel, and following the Holy Spirit's leading are so critical. God's desire is always repentance and forgiveness, reconciliation and restoration, commitment, unity, and love. If this is our hope, then we're to give Him everything we have toward saving our marriages. Cling to Spirit-driven hope, and watch for God's many victories still in the making; choose to trust Him, and relentlessly persevere (James 1:2–4). Marriages in the worst places have known the greatest victories when a believing spouse has yielded to God's grip on her life and not given up. And God is glorified.

 At this point you may be asking, "But what if . . . ?" Let's examine a few of the more common questions:

But what if . . . ? What if your husband has had an affair? What if *you* have had an affair? Again, you must remember the message of the cross—forgiveness, reconciliation, and restoration. Have you and your husband taken these steps? How have you proceeded, and what's been the outcome? Is your relationship maturing since the affair? If so, in what ways? Or did you "pick up where you left off" prior to the affair, leaving buried and unspoken what must yet be healed? If so, please consider seeking the biblical counsel necessary to effectively rebuild what only God can restore, even if you have to do so alone. Assess your relationship here.

_____

_____

_____

_____

_____

But what if . . . ? What if you're currently dealing with an unrepentant, adulterous husband? The Lord is able to lead you step by step in your response to him. You may hear from those who hurt with you that divorce is always justified in this situation and that he deserves whatever he gets. Measure what you hear from others by the yardstick of God's Word. Seek biblical counsel as quickly as possible, especially if you're confused and unsure about who or what to believe. Remember that confusion is a tool that Satan uses to cause us to doubt God and reject His plan for us. Meditate on what God says in the Bible about the solemnity of your marriage covenant. Stay in His Word *daily*. Wait patiently for God to dispel your confusion. Trust Him. Be willing to wait for Him to act and to lead you. Seek God's peace about not rushing toward a decision, and give your emotions a rest. God will make "the next thing" clear to you—one step at a time. Above all, battle for your husband on your knees, praying diligently for God to rescue him from the clutches of the Enemy, to soften his heart, to draw him to Himself and then back to you and your family. Persevere in this, the most difficult of all marital scenarios. It's one with which God is intimately acquainted. What insights is God giving you right now into your circumstances?

In Their Shoes
HOSEA 1—3:5

The book of Hosea is about God's covenant love for an idolatrous people. It is about their sin, God's judgment, and His faithful commitment to them, as told metaphorically through the marriage of the prophet Hosea to his adulterous wife, Gomer. Since creation God has dealt with the unfaithfulness of His people, but His love and His commitment to His covenant are relentless. Understanding His love will help us stand firm in our two most important covenants: that with our Lord, and that with our spouse. (Author Francine Rivers also wrote an excellent novel based on the book of Hosea entitled, *Redeeming Love*. It is a poignant depiction of covenant love.)

You may hear from those who hurt with you that divorce is justified and that he deserves whatever he gets. Measure what you hear from others by the yardstick of God's Word.

_____

_____

_____

_____

But what if . . . ? What if you're in an abusive marriage? Consider a few tough questions: Are you in physical danger? Are your children in physical danger? How have you responded to the abuse? Why do you allow your husband to abuse you or your children? Do you think you deserve it or they deserve it? Are you afraid to seek help? Why? Do you think confronting the problem by seeking help is being disloyal or unsubmissive to your husband?

Here's a tough truth: If you *don't* seek help, nothing will ever change. Faithful, biblical love is not about empowering sinful, abusive behavior (physical *or* mental). It says instead, *Don't run away* from the problem. *Run toward* the solution, not only for your sake, but also for your husband's and your children's sakes. Learn what's available to you. Pursue biblical counsel so that both you and your husband can benefit, even if he refuses to participate. Seek shelter from physical harm until he gets the help he needs. Don't rule out skilled intervention. Abusive behavior is *not* OK with God! Let His truth strengthen you with the courage, resolve, and perseverance you need to bring this darkness to light. Then allow the Holy Spirit and experienced biblical counselors to show you the path that leads to healing and restoration in your lives and in your marriage.

But what if . . . ? What if you've been divorced, and not by reason of infidelity or the abandonment of an unbelieving spouse? What do you do about that? For those of us who have been divorced and are remarried, Dr. Wheat offers this wise and encouraging advice:

> Whatever your past mistakes in the area of marriage and divorce, ask God's forgiveness and accept it, knowing that you have been set free from guilt. He always deals with us in the now, and you have every opportunity to go forward in a new way, "forgetting what lies behind and reaching forward to what lies ahead" (Philippians 3:13). With your eyes on Jesus and your mind shaped by the Word, you can make a new life for yourself and your partner from this moment forth.[12]

Will you make the commitment to do so right now?

Christian author Gary Thomas pointedly states,

> One of the reasons I am determined to keep my marriage together is not because doing so will make me happier (although I believe it will); not because I want my kids to have a secure home (although I do desire that); not because it would tear me up to see my wife have to "start over" (although it would). The first reason I keep my marriage together is because it is my Christian duty. If my life is based on proclaiming God's message to the world, I don't want to do anything that would challenge that message. And how can I proclaim reconciliation when I seek dissolution?[13]

Scripture is a love story about a stiff-necked, adulterous people being bought back by their loving Husband. Because of His covenant love, we were

Extra Mile

MARRIAGE VOWS

In 1 Corinthians 7, Paul gave key instructions specific to marriage vows. Read verses 10–16 and 39. Identify the instructions and record what you learn.

redeemed, having experienced His forgiveness, reconciliation, and restoration. As Christians, we're given a "ministry of reconciliation" (2 Corinthians 5:17–20). As we become more fully aware of how God deeply desires us to reflect His covenant love in our marriages, we will persevere in the toughest of times, we will forgive, reconcile, and restore, and we will wait patiently for Him to move according to His good purpose.

Following God requires our commitment to build a marriage God's way. His way takes time, wisdom, patience, courage, and perseverance, all of which God possesses. And by His grace, so do we.

 Whether faced with everyday marital challenges or the seemingly impossible, come boldly to God's throne of grace to receive mercy and find grace to help you in your time of need (Hebrews 4:16). Take the time now to seek Jesus in your need. Draw from Him, and depend on Him and the leading of His Holy Spirit. Most important, persevere, trusting Him with your marriage one day at a time. Lamentations 3:22–24 says, *"The LORD's lovingkindnesses indeed never cease, for His compassions never fail. They are new every morning; Great is Thy faithfulness. 'The LORD is my portion,' says my soul, 'therefore I have hope in Him.'"*

LOVING GOD'S WAY

What do you think of when the word "love" comes to mind, especially as it relates to your husband? No matter how old we are, how experienced we are, or how long we've been married, we have in our minds certain preconceived notions about love—what it is and what it should be. We took our cues while growing up, observing our parents and other married relationships. We formed opinions and ideals from our personal experiences with love, whether good or bad. We're still influenced by the cultural perspective, or worldview, that surrounds us. We also take in the biblical and spiritual view as we study and grow in the Lord. Ed Wheat points out, "What you believe about love right now—true or false—is presently doing three things for you. It is (1) affecting your marriage; (2) shaping your behavior and responses to your mate; (3) helping determine your future happiness and emotional well-being. What you believe is that important. How much better to believe the truth!"[14]

What do you believe about love, and where did your beliefs come from? Without any help from your dictionary, give your definition of "love"—not what you think it ought to be but what you think it really is. Write in two- and three-word descriptions what truly embodies your concept of love.

_____

_____

Next, how is your concept of love affecting your marriage? How is it shaping your behavior toward and responses to your husband? How is it determining your future happiness and emotional well-being?

The Bible is rich in truth about love. It's the only source on which to focus if we want to enhance or restore our marriages.

"This is how God showed his love among us: He sent his one and only Son into the world that we might live through him."

1 John 4:9 (NIV)

_____

_____

_____

📖 No matter what we think about love, we have only one standard by which to measure both its correctness and its capacity. The Bible is rich in truth about love. It's the only source on which to focus if we want to enhance or restore our marriages. Read 1 John 3:16–18. How does John define love in this passage?

_____

_____

God's covenant love is *agape*—unconditional, fully accepting, sacrificial, and the same for all humanity. It's who He is. And since we were made in His image, He has chosen to love us, not with an irrational emotion but with deliberate kindness, genuine compassion, and righteous concern for our well-being. Therefore, He doesn't love us because of who we are but because of *who He is*.

📖 Now read 1 John 4:7–16. What does our love or lack of love prove (verses 7–8, 12)?

_____

_____

John defines God as "love" in verse 8. How did God show His love among us (verses 9 and 10)? For what very important purpose (verse 9)?

_____

_____

🛑 APPLY Do you believe that God loves you unconditionally, mercifully, sacrificially, justly? How easy or difficult is it for you to love your husband in the same way? If he's a Christian, how is your love enhancing his walk? If your husband is not a Christian, would he want to become one because of the persuasiveness of God's love in you? Explain.

_____

_____

_____

_____

📖 Now read 1 John 4:17–19 very carefully. If God's love is perfect and is being matured, completed, and perfected in us (verse 12), what is our confidence (verse 17)? How are we able to love with His perfect love (verse 19)? What do you think that means?

_____

_____

_____

_____

Verse 18 says there is no fear in love—fear about what or whom? How does God's perfect love drive out our fear of punishment? How can His perfect love in us help us to love our husbands faithfully and without fear?

_____

_____

_____

The perfect, *agape* love that is God, made real to us by His Son, is in us. It's unconditional, not condemning; sacrificial, not demanding; merciful, not fearful; just, not enabling. The more we understand, accept, and experience the depth and breadth of His perfect love for us, the more we're able to surrender to it without fear of punishment. Then we can love as He loves us. It's this love that enables us to confront the hard issues and sinful behaviors in marriage—our own and our husbands'. Love is the powerful force of God working within us for the good of those He brings before us.

APPLY Do you believe that God has your highest good in mind? If so, is there anything about Him or what He allows in your life that you fear or perceive as His punishment? If so, what is it? How can the perfect love of God drive out these fears? How would you respond or behave differently toward God, your husband, and your circumstances if your fears were gone?

_____

_____

_____

_____

📖 Read 1 John 4:20–21. What's John's assertion in verse 20, and what's his rationale?

_____

_____

_____

What is the believer's responsibility found in verse 21? What does this mean in a marriage? Do you think this responsibility applies even if a husband is an unbeliever? Why or why not?

_____

_____

_____

If your husband is not a Christian, would he want to become one because of the persuasiveness of God's love in you?

If you say, "I love God" and yet feel negatively toward, dislike, or even hate your husband, why do you think you have these feelings? (Yes, write your answer down.)

_____

_____

_____

📖 Read Romans 5:5. Based on this verse and all you've learned about God's love, how are you able to elevate *agape* love above any negative or "loveless" feelings?

Love is the powerful force of God working within us for the good of those He brings before us.

_____

_____

_____

Gary Thomas challenges, "If I can't love my wife, how can I love the homeless man in the library? How can I love the drug addict or the alcoholic? Yes, this spouse might be difficult to love at times, but that's what marriage is for—*to teach us how to love.*"[15]

 Understanding how much God loves us, especially in our worst moments will help us understand how to love our husbands in theirs. Ask God for that understanding and to increase in you His perfect love.

Works Cited

1. Warren Baker, ed., *The Complete Word Study Dictionary Old Testament* (Chattanooga, TN: AMG Publishers, 2003), #905, p. 118.

2. Spirios Zodhiates, Warren Baker, eds., *The Complete Word Study Old Testament* (Chattanooga, TN: AMG Publishers, 1994), #5800, p. 2348.

3. James Strong, *The Exhaustive Concordance of the Bible* (McLean, VA: MacDonald Publishing Company), #1692, 29.

4. Ed Wheat, M.D., and Gloria Okes Perkins, *Love Life for Every Married Couple* (Grand Rapids: Zondervan Publishing House, 1980), 23.

5. Fred Lowery, *Covenant Marriage* (West Monroe, La.: Howard Publishing Company, 2002), 43.

6. Malcolm Smith, *The Seven Covenants of God* (Washingtonville, NY: Malcolm Smith Ministries, 1982), Tape #MS791.

7. Kay Arthur, *Our Covenant God* (Colorado Springs: WaterBrook Press, 1999), 72.

8. "Born Again Adults Less Likely to Co-Habit, Just as Likely to Divorce," Barna Research Group, August 6, 2001, <http://www.barna.org/cgi-bin/>.

9. Robert Young, *Young's Literal Translation of the Holy Bible* (Grand Rapids: Baker Book House, 1898), 585.

10. For an excellent biblical exposition on the subject of divorce, read Spiros Zodhiates, *What About Divorce?* (Chattanooga, TN: AMG Publishers, 1984).

11. Wheat and Perkins, *Love Life for Every Married Couple,* 26–27.

12. Ibid., 40–41.

13. Gary Thomas, *Sacred Marriage* (Grand Rapids: Zondervan Publishing House, 2000), 35–36.

14. Wheat and Perkins, *Love Life for Every Married Couple,* 50.

15. Thomas, *Sacred Marriage,* 42.

6

Right Attitude – Right Love

Becoming one in marriage doesn't mean "becoming just like me." God designed a man and a woman to complement each other, to respect the other's maleness or femaleness and their gifts, talents, and differences, to fill in each other's blanks where necessary, and to be the other's strength in weakness. They were never intended to be opposites but each other's *balance*.

Gary Thomas asks a great question: "*What if God designed marriage to make us holy more than to make us happy?* If you want to become more like Jesus, I can't imagine any better thing to do than to get married. Being married forces you to face some character issues you'd never have to face otherwise."[1]

In the next five days we'll learn how our thinking defines our attitudes, what it means to love with no strings attached, to submit as to the Lord, to respect our husbands, and to respond to them rather than react. May we seek God's guidance daily as we apply His truth and wisdom to our marriages.

Becoming one in marriage doesn't mean "becoming just like me."

ENHANCING MY MARRIAGE BEGINS WITH ME

Eventually in our marriages, we have to realize that we can't change our husbands. But we can make ourselves available for God's change in us. Over time as we're becoming the wives that He designed us to be, our husbands will see, experience, and discern the credibility of Christ in our lives. Along the way, we'll still be faced with issues, both old and new, that may cause us anxiety and challenge our behavior toward our husbands. How we respond to our husbands in the midst of our problems will influence the growth and direction of our relationships with them.

📖 Read Philippians 4:4–7. What does Paul say is the remedy for our anxieties (verses 4–6)?

_____

_____

What will result when we follow Paul's instruction? What will be protected (verse 7)? Why do you think this protection is important?

_____

_____

APPLY Are there issues in your marriage relationship that cause you anxiety? If so, write them here. Does your anxiety affect how (or if) you approach the issues for resolution? In what way?

_____

_____

_____

_____

Do you believe Philippians 4:4–7 applies to every issue in your marriage? If so, how would you approach the challenges in your marriage differently?

_____

_____

_____

If you detect any doubt as you answer this question, bring it to the Lord. This may be a matter of trust that is less about you and your husband and more about you and God. Why won't you believe that you can lay every anxiety before the Lord? I ask you why you **won't** believe, not why you can't, since Philippians 4:13 says we are able to do all things through Christ who strengthens us. What is your fear? Speak it to Him. He already knows where you are and wants to hear from you. In His perfect love, He also knows where He wants you and wants to impart this to you.

📖 Let's continue with Philippians 4:8. What are we commanded to think about?

_____

_____

PHILIPPIANS 4:8 PARAPHRASED

■ whatever is true—about God and found in His Word

■ whatever is honorable—worthy of reverence

■ whatever is right—righteous and in accordance with God's standard

■ whatever is pure—that which will not soil our souls

■ whatever is lovely—loving, kind and gracious

■ whatever is admirable—of good report; respectable

■ if there is any excellence—find it

■ if there is anything worthy of praise—appreciate it

Think about such things; let your mind dwell on these things; weigh and take account of these things—fix your minds on them.

Note that verse 8 doesn't say whatever is true *or* honorable *or* just *or.* . . . What we dwell on should fit *all* the criteria listed in this verse, which puts the things we're anxious about into spiritual perspective. Spiritual perspective focuses our attention on God in our circumstances and not on the circumstances themselves. When we consider all things from a spiritual perspective, the byproduct is *right thinking*.

APPLY Are you in the habit of thinking about things (your life, your husband, your marriage) from a spiritual perspective—with God and His purposes fully at work? How would such a habit change the way you normally think on things?

_____

_____

_____

_____

What things about your husband occupy your mind? Do you dwell on the positive or the negative? Do you find the lovely or the unlovely? Do you rejoice in what is excellent or brood over the lack of excellence? Do you look for something to praise, or do you search for something to criticize? Honestly assess your thought life about your husband, and lay it out here.

_____

_____

_____

_____

Read Philippians 4:9. What is Paul's admonition and the reward for obeying it?

_____

_____

Spiritual perspective produces right *thinking*. Right thinking produces right *doing*. When we bring our entire selves—what we experience, what we feel, what we think, and what we do—under God's authority and yield to His control, He is faithful to guard us. He is our only place of peace.

I never considered myself a quarrelsome, negative wife before being convicted about my attitudes. Living in harmony meant living my way. This reality was driven home a couple of years into my Christian walk. My husband was a hard working "tanker" in the army at the time and came home after a couple of weeks of tough training. Instead of returning to a wife happy to see him, he walked in the door to my being "me" (my "You're always gone, and I'm always here alone with the kids!" mode). A look of disappointment and weariness crossed his face as he waited for me to pause, and then he gently but firmly said, "You know, Judy, you're a Christian for everybody else but me." This truth changed my life. God called me to work on my own shortcomings instead of focusing on John's. Although old habits die hard, God disciplined this "martyr spirit" out of me little by little. I repeatedly ate humble pie, seeking grace and forgiveness from both God and my husband until my attitude consistently honored them both. I'm grateful for this exercise and the maintenance that's required to keep me on His path. And so is John!

> *Spiritual perspective focuses our attention on God in our circumstances and not on the circumstances themselves. When we consider all things from a spiritual perspective, the byproduct is right thinking.*

> *Right thinking produces right doing.*

The hard truth is that if our Christian walk isn't first credible to our husbands, then our walk isn't credible.

Gary and Betsy Ricucci remark, "One of the best wedding gifts God gave you was a full-length mirror called your spouse. Had there been a card attached, it would have said, 'Here's to helping you discover what you're *really* like!' "[2] The hard truth is that if our Christian walk isn't first credible to our husbands, then our walk isn't credible.

 Read Romans 8:28–29. This is a truly burden lifting verse. God will use our marriages and our marriage partners to grow us toward holiness. What is God's promise, and what conditions are attached to this promise (verse 28)?

_____

_____

It's so easy to read verse 28 and derive comfort from it alone. But God has an even greater purpose in using anything or anyone in our lives for good. What is it (verse 29)?

_____

_____

 Romans 8:28–29 promise holiness from our circumstances. What does this mean for you in your marriage? How would applying today's scriptures change your attitudes and your behavior from the way they are now?

_____

_____

_____

_____

Seek the Holy Spirit's leading in your right thinking (spiritual perspective) and righteous responses toward your husband, no matter what your circumstances. This will honor God as you cooperate with Him in His conforming you to the image of His Son. It will also give God full permission to move in your husband's life.

Right Attitude—
Right Love

DAY TWO

LOVING MY HUSBAND, NO STRINGS ATTACHED

What makes a difficult person easier to love? What shores up the chasms in a relationship and promotes healing? What acts as a protective barrier in the face of lovelessness and rejection?

Ed Wheat answers,

> a love directed and fueled, not by the emotions, but by the will. Out of His own mighty nature, God supplies the resources for this love, and they are available to any life connected with His by faith in Jesus Christ.   This is the *agape* love of the New

Testament—unconditional, unchanging, inexhaustible, generous beyond measure, and most wonderfully kind![3]

God's *agape*, or unconditional love in us is shed abroad in our hearts by the Holy Spirit (Romans 5:5). It is not dependent on our husbands' meeting certain conditions first, but instead, it removes the heavy hand of expectation from our checklist, accepting our husbands "as is." Therefore, we can choose to work toward their best interests with no strings attached, expecting nothing in return.

Doesn't that thought just go against every feeling in us? That's because God's way is not the world's way, and we're more practiced in the world's way. Because *agape* love doesn't have to be returned in order to be effective, it enables us to release our husbands to the Lord and leave the results to Him. It stabilizes our emotions, preventing them from charting the course of events from day to day. This permits God to work in and through situations that are highly frustrating or seemingly impossible.

Dr. Wheat says it well:

> Even in the best of marriages, unlovable traits show up in both partners. . . . *Agape* is the answer for all the woundings of marriage. This love has the capacity to persist in the face of rejection and continue on when there is no response at all. . . . To the relationship of husband and wife, which would otherwise lie at the mercy of fluctuating emotions and human upheavals, *agape* imparts stability and a permanence that is rooted in the Eternal. Agape is the Divine solution for marriages populated by imperfect human beings![4]

Marriage is challenging—for some on a daily basis. Nothing else can meet the challenge but God's *agape* love in us.

Define *agape* love (unconditional love) in your own words as you have learned it thus far.

_____

_____

_____

_____

APPLY As it relates to your marriage, agape love is loving your husband "as is." What's *right* with the way your husband is? Has he always been this way?

_____

_____

_____

What's *wrong* with the way he is? Has he always been this way?

_____

_____

_____

_____

Marriage is challenging—for some on a daily basis. Nothing else can meet the challenge but God's agape love in us.

Do some of the personality traits you admired when you met your husband irritate you now? Which ones? Why do they irritate you now? Do you now see these traits as sinful, or "just the way he is"? Are you able to tell the difference? What *is* the difference? Explain.

_____

_____

_____

Do you find it difficult to accept your husband the way he is? If so, why do you think that is?

_____

_____

_____

"Love never fails."

1 Corinthians 13:8a

(NIV)

📖 Let's explore the "how to" of unconditional, *agape* love found in 1 Corinthians 13:1–8. How is this love qualified in verses 1–3?

_____

_____

Study verses 4–8 prayerfully. In the spaces below, fill in the elements of *agape* love—what it *is* and *does* and what it *is not* and *does not* do.

Love Is	Love Does	Love Is Not	Love Does Not

APPLY Now re-read aloud 1 Corinthians 13:4–8, inserting your name for the word "love" and pronouns that are associated with the word "love." What do you learn about this love in you? Does God's *agape* love differ from the love you demonstrate to your husband? If so, in what ways?

_____

_____

Which elements of *agape* in this passage are *strong points* for you? What impact do your strong points have on your husband?

_____

_____

_____

What elements of *agape* in this passage are *weak points* for you? What impact do these weak points have on your husband?

_____

_____

Thank God for your strong points of *agape* love, and ask Him to build on them. Confess your weak points, asking God to help you replace them with the love that will build up your husband and honor him. One of the most common weak points is keeping a record of wrongs. Remember how God deals with your wrongs and ask for that same grace for your husband's. May you begin to see your husband through God's eyes as *"very good"* (Genesis 1:31).

What should *agape* love look like in an ideal marriage? What should it look like in a tough marriage? What should it look like in a marriage with an unbeliever? Should the love of God in you look any different or be dependent on whether you are married to a devoted Christian who is devoted to you, or a baby Christian who doesn't "get it," or a husband who is lost, disagreeable, and resistant to the things of God? These questions are necessary to consider, especially in light of how God drew you to Himself. He drew you with His love and holds you fast by His love. And that love is in you. Are there ways in which the Lord is calling you to love your husband differently? If so, what are they?

_____

_____

_____

_____

1 Corinthians 13:8 says that love (God's love in us) never fails. What does this promise mean for you in your marriage?

_____

_____

How could loving your husband "as is" be a gift *to him*?

_____

_____

_____

Let's put that gift into action! First, *choose* to love your husband with your thoughts, attitudes, words, and conduct with no strings attached. This means you accept him as he is. To which character traits or aspects of his behavior will you apply God's *agape* love? Write them below:

Areas in Which I Will Choose to Love My Husband Unconditionally ("As Is")

_____

_____

_____

_____

Second, attune yourself to *how* and *why* you may close yourself to your husband, choosing not to accept him or respond to him physically, sexually, emotionally, intellectually, spiritually. Are issues unresolved? Is your husband just being "himself"? Are you trying to manipulate him or circumstances in order to get your own way?

I close myself to my husband

when . . .	because . . .

Third, ask your husband to write down what his three greatest needs are *from you* that help him feel secure in your love. He can write them on a separate piece of paper and slip it to you, or he can send you an e-mail if he's not comfortable "eyeball to eyeball." Decide in advance not to be offended by his answers. Be willing to accept his truth "as is." Write down below what *you* think his three top needs from you are. Compare your lists. You may be surprised!

My Husband's Needs

He says his top three needs are . . .

_____

_____

_____

_____

I think his top three needs are . . .

_____

_____

_____

_____

Fourth, begin to study your husband afresh—his unique maleness and the related differences that lend balance to your relationship. Write each of these down as they're revealed. Choose to love, accept, and appreciate who he is all over again. This is God's will for you. And He won't let you down. He promises reward and blessing!

His Unique Male Qualities

_____

_____

_____

_____

Accepting and loving your husband unconditionally is action, not just attitude. Pour yourself into this way of loving him. It doesn't require emotion, but it does require *commitment*. Ask the Holy Spirit to motivate you into action.

 Acknowledge to the Lord those areas in which you find it difficult to accept your husband unconditionally. Confess the ways in which you close yourself to him. Receive God's forgiveness, and then ask the Holy Spirit to create in you the desire to love your husband God's way, to provide you with many opportunities to practice the *right attitude* and the *right love*, to develop in you a new, enriching outlook, filling your heart with "good treasure." Love—God's love in you—never fails!

SUBMISSION—GOD'S POWERFUL CONDUIT

God's divine principle of biblical submission is not only misunderstood but is greatly maligned as well. Sadly, the biblical truth about submission has been distorted to the point that many Christian women distain the principle, thinking it means "under the husband's feet" (doormat) instead of under the husband's (and God's) love and protection. Author Nancy Leigh DeMoss writes,

> Satan has done a masterful job of convincing women that submission is a narrow, negative, and confining concept. He has taken a beautiful, holy, and powerful Truth and made it look ugly, frightening, and undesirable. Satan knows that if we could see the Truth about biblical submission—one of the most liberating principles in all of God's Word—we would joyfully embrace it. He cannot afford to let us choose the pathway of submission, for when we do, he is stripped of his authority and rendered powerless in our lives and in the lives of those we love.[5]

What picture does the word "submission" conjure up in your mind? What is your definition of it?

_____

_____

_____

Let's look at what biblical submission in marriage is not:

☞ It is not permitting a husband's physical abuse of his wife or his children. God has placed institutions of government authority to protect a family from such heinous behavior.

☞ It is not being a doormat who, out of fear, meets a husband's every demand no matter how sick or sinful. That's blind obedience.

☞ It is not putting a husband's authority above Christ's.

☞ It is not enabling a husband's addictions by covering for him in his weakness so as not to be caught.

☞ It is not being intellectually or emotionally dependent. A wife is to live out who she really is with courage and conviction, and in love.

☞ It is not being afraid to discuss problems and issues with a husband, or to express concerns and insights. A wife is free in Christ to communicate these things in love and without condemnation, because that's what a helpmeet does.

If submission is not all of these things, then what is it? I believe true biblical submission is first yielding our wills to the will of God. Only then can we yield to another's advice, admonition, or authority in the *right* way. With respect to a wife and her husband, biblical submission means "to subject oneself, place oneself in submission."[6] It does not mean "to yield under," which

> *I believe true biblical submission is first yielding our wills to the will of God. Only then can we yield to another's advice, admonition, or authority in the right way.*

denotes struggle or force. She willingly submits herself to her own husband, freely places herself under his God-ordained authority. It is a *voluntary* act.

Biblical submission is about function, not status. It's about responsibility, not rights. *The Complete Word Study Dictionary: New Testament* expounds further on this topic of submission,

> We are all equal before God and the laws of society, and yet we have varying functions and responsibilities. If we accept certain functions under a fellow-human, we must subject ourselves to that individual to accomplish a common goal. So it is with a wife placing herself in the proper and divinely-fitted position under her husband.[7]

When viewed in the context of function and responsibility, submission is morally, legally, and spiritually correct and proper.

There's nothing doormat-like about biblical submission. Whereas fear is the foundation of doormat submission, faith is the foundation of biblical submission. The former exhibits only weakness; the latter exhibits strength and dignity. We see the perfect example in Christ. His loving submission to the Father led Him to the cross. As a result, the power that was unleashed opened the way for all believers to spend eternity with Him. God's plan and purpose were carried out and completed in Christ's act of obedience. As with Jesus, submission is the conduit through which the power of God works out the will of God in and through believers.

Relational strife was God's judgment against Adam and Eve for choosing their will over His. Her desire would be for her husband; yet he would rule over her (Genesis 3:14–19). The word "desire" is not a positive one. John MacArthur states, "Sin has turned the harmonious system of God-ordained roles into distasteful struggles of self-will. Lifelong companions, husbands and wives, will need God's help in getting along as a result. The woman's desire will be to lord it over her husband, but the husband will rule by divine design."[8]

I don't know many women who haven't struggled with their husband's headship over the years. I, too, have struggled with this. The reason we struggle is rarely because our husbands are poor leaders or providers. Rather, it's an issue of control. Husbands and wives compete for control in the home, in the car, over the finances, over the kids, and so on. Control issues may vary from household to household, but they're always there.

📖 Wherever there's a decision to be made or an opinion to be had, the Garden of Eden judgment rears its ugly head. But God has given husbands and wives specific commands that can soften the judgment, approximating God's original intent for the marriage relationship. These commands are found in Ephesians 5. The husband is commanded to love his wife; the wife is commanded to submit to and respect her husband. Let's look at God's commands to the husband first in Ephesians 5:25–33. What do you think it means to *"love your wives, just as Christ loved the church and gave himself up for her"* (verse 25, NIV)?

_____

_____

_____

As with Jesus, submission is the conduit through which the power of God works out the will of God in and through believers.

"Husbands, love your wives, just as Christ loved the church and gave himself up for her."

Ephesians 5:25 (NIV)

What divine parallel is being drawn in verses 25–27? What is the husband's spiritual responsibility to his wife?

_____

_____

What personal parallel is drawn between the husband and the wife (verses 28–31)? What do you see in these verses that coincides with Genesis 2:23–24?

_____

_____

_____

How should God's command to love affect a husband's authority over his wife?

_____

_____

Although the decree of headship stands, it's *how* a husband uses his authority that Paul emphasizes in this passage. A man is born to lead, provide for, and fiercely protect what's his. That's what his maleness is all about. But loving his wife—who is part of his own body—as Christ loves those who are a part of His body does not come naturally to a man. This is why the command is necessary. Even if the husband is a Christian, it will take the conviction of and teaching by the Holy Spirit to love his wife sacrificially and with the tenderness, compassion, understanding, and affection of Christ.

APPLY Describe your husband's love for you. How does it compare with Christ's love for the Church? Does the comparison affect how you feel about your husband? If so, in what ways?

_____

_____

_____

_____

If your husband loves you as Christ loves His own, you have much to be grateful for and good reason to return much to him. If, however, you continue to wait for your husband to understand this love—either because he's an unbeliever or is a believer who has not yet grasped this teaching—you still have much to return. That's what *agape* love is all about. Continue to pray for him daily. Release him into God's hand, and remain open and teachable as the Holy Spirit shows you how to be God's woman for your man.

📖 Read Ephesians 5:22–24, 33, which lay out God's commands to wives. How are we to demonstrate our love to our husbands?

_____

_____

Why do you think Paul qualified the command to submit with the words *"in everything"* (verse 24)? Why not "in selective things" or "only when you think he's right"? Why would *"in everything"* be important to God? To your husband? To your marriage? To your children?

"Wives, submit to your husbands as to the Lord."

Ephesians 5:22 (NIV)

_____

_____

_____

Do you think this principle applies if a husband is an unbeliever? Explain your answer.

_____

_____

_____

How should God's command to submit to and respect her husband affect a wife's tendency to "lord it over him"?

_____

_____

God knows that yielding to our husbands respectfully (or otherwise) doesn't come naturally to us wives. God *commands* it because He knows our obedience to His instruction will greatly enhance the growth and health of our marriage relationship. The toughest aspect of the Ephesians 5 commands to husbands and wives is that they're non-negotiable, even if we feel we have lots of reasons why they should be.

APPLY Let's revisit your husband's leadership role in the home. Does he lead? How is his leadership apparent to you and your children?

_____

_____

_____

_____

Has your husband relinquished his leadership role to you? How is his lack of leadership apparent to you and your children?

_____

_____

Elizabeth Rice Handford maintains,

> Most men hate "scenes." They despise confusion and disorder. They will go to almost any length to have peace in their homes. They will let a woman have her way rather than argue and quarrel. But the price a man has to pay is the price of his manhood. Before you complain that your husband won't take the leadership of your home, search your heart carefully. Do you really rely on his judgment? Are you willing to commit yourself to his decisions? If not, don't complain that he will not lead. For the sake of peace, he may not fight for his authority.[9]

What is your honest response to your husband's leadership role in your home?

_____

_____

_____

Is submission to your husband's leadership an intimidating, perhaps fearful principle for you? If so, why? What makes accepting your husband's headship difficult? In which areas do you find yourself gripping the controls (parenting, finances, and so on)? Consider these questions prayerfully, since vying for control is really about fear of losing control.

_____

_____

_____

_____

Author Pam Forster writes,

> A wife's fear is probably one of the greatest reasons she chooses to not submit to her husband. She is afraid of the consequences of his decisions. She is afraid of potential pain, loss, or embarrassment to herself and to those she loves. She is afraid of what may happen when her husband neglects his role in the family. A wife's fear will tempt her to nag her husband into action or to simply assume his responsibilities herself, stepping in and doing those things for which God holds him directly accountable. In doing so, she shields her husband from the natural consequences of his decisions, actions, or inaction and the roles of husband and wife become confused.[10]

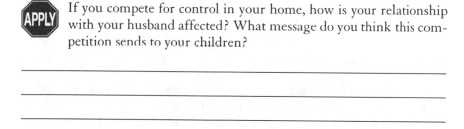 If you compete for control in your home, how is your relationship with your husband affected? What message do you think this competition sends to your children?

_____

_____

_____

_____

Adapting to our husbands' headship honors God and our husbands, and it also sends the message to our children that their father's authority is to be respected.

Parenting was an issue of control in our home. John was gone a good portion of his army career, and I knew how to raise the girls better than he did—or so I thought. When he interacted with them, I had something to say. When he disciplined them, I intervened. My interference only made him harsher in his discipline, and I compensated by being more lenient with mine. We worked against each other, and the girls bore the brunt. To some degree, John withdrew from the parenting process (remember: a man will either withdraw or fight back when his authority is challenged). I saw the damage I was doing and asked the Lord to help me turn it around. The process was difficult, but God used it to teach me to trust Him with John. I watched John foster a genuine relationship with the girls, not one that was on my terms. He and I learned to discuss, respect, support, and trust each other's parenting skills and to relax and enjoy the process.

When we place ourselves under the covering of our husbands, both God and our husbands provide protection. I can best explain this by another personal example: As my women's ministry grew, it took on an exciting yet consuming quality. I taught several mornings a week and was always available to help women apply the Word to their marriage difficulties, either face to face or by phone. My time with them spilled into evenings and weekends. One night, as John returned home from work to yet another vision of his "beloved" otherwise occupied, his "leadership" kicked in. He affirmed that he fully supported the ministry but that he would no longer compete with it. Therefore, I was to put a bookmark in it *before* he walked in the door and *close* the book on weekends! My initial (internal) reaction was indignation, which the Holy Spirit quickly quelled with "Listen to your husband." What I didn't see then I know now: John's edict was his protection over our marriage and me. Nothing was to divide us. And even though this ministry was a gift from God and being used for His purposes, I permitted it to come between John and me. God was speaking through my husband once again. I would practice what I teach.

If we fear where godly submission will lead, the problem may not be simply about trusting our husbands but trusting God with our husbands. The same Holy Spirit that drew us to God and is teaching us is able to do the same with our husbands. When we submit to our husbands, we yield to the will of God in our marriages; the will of God then yields the results of God in our marriages.

In what ways are the commands to husbands and wives in Ephesians 5:22–33 the ultimate expressions of *agape* loving? (Really think about what you've learned.)

_____

_____

_____

_____

 Ask the Holy Spirit to show you any functions or responsibilities in which you *compete* with your husband. Ask your husband too! Then submit these areas to God, and with your husband, determine whose function and responsibility they will be, or how they'll be shared. Accepting your husband's leadership in these areas will yield great reward. God's desire is to work in and through a willing and obedient heart (yours) in order to touch the heart of another (your husband's, children's, and so on) for Himself.

> When we submit to our husbands, we yield to the will of God in our marriages; the will of God then yields the results of God in our marriages.

*Right Attitude–
Right Love*

DAY FOUR

> *It's been said that respect does for a man what romance does for a woman.*

RESPECT—THE EVIDENCE OF HONOR

It's been said that respect does for a man what romance does for a woman. I had to think about that for a moment, and then the light bulb came on! It was so true. Just as romance lights up my heart, the respect I show to my man makes him stand a little taller.

Nancy Wilson writes,

> Sometimes I wonder where the church would be today if the men in it were respected as they ought to be by their wives. What power would God unleash through godly men who were respected in their homes? I am certain that lack of respect and, in some cases, overt disrespect are holding many men back.[11]

📖 What is the command to wives in Ephesians 5:33? Do you see any exceptions?

_____

_____

Ephesians 5:33 (NIV) says, *"And the wife must respect her husband."* Choosing to love our husbands unconditionally enables us to respect them, whether they've earned it or not. This is important, because God's command offers no exceptions. An attitude of respect is what enables us to submit with the right heart. And He knows we can do this because of Christ in us (Philippians 4:13).

📖 According to 1 Peter 3:1–6, what kind of respectful behavior will win a husband over to obey the Word of God? List all the traits.

_____

_____

What do you think Peter is suggesting with the phrase "without a word"?

_____

_____

This is not a directive about speaking to our husbands on issues, concerns, or decisions in general. That's *communication*, which we'll address in a later lesson. This passage is directly related to how we convey spiritual things to our husbands. Although it seems to be directed at wives wooing their unsaved husbands to Christ by their conduct, I have found that it can be practically applied to *any* husband who may be intimidated or threatened by his wife's spiritual maturity or disgusted when she flaunts it. She may beat her husband over the head with her Bible knowledge; she may self-righteously apply her knowledge to everything her husband does that she disapproves of; she may refuse to forgive him for not being a believer or, if he's a Christian, for not "getting it," "feeling it," "doing it" as she does; she may use spiritual superiority to justify treating her husband badly or withdrawing from him emotionally or sexually. All of this behavior is disrespectful and offensive to God, because it discredits *Him* in *her*. A wife's respectful behavior will make a difference in her husband's response to spiritual things, because it lends credibility to her walk.

How is a wife's beauty defined in verses 3–6? What do you think this means?

_____

_____

_____

Hers is an inner beauty, emanating a gentle and quiet spirit. Jo Berry writes, "The word *quiet*, as it is used in this passage, doesn't mean lack of noise or activity, but lack of agitation or harshness. It doesn't mean a godly woman is to be passive, complacent, or speak in a whisper. It doesn't mean she can't differ with her husband or that she has to be withdrawn or uncommunicative. It means she is to cultivate the peace of God in her life."[12] Because her hope is in God, she is able to respectfully submit to her husband without being fearful of the outcome. Her peace-filled attitude makes her beautiful to him. This inner beauty—her strength and dignity—builds a husband's trust and confidence in her, causing him to seek, welcome, and honor her positive influence.

> *"And the wife must respect her husband."*
>
> *Ephesians 5:33 (NIV)*

> *A wife's respectful behavior will make a difference in her husband's response to spiritual things, because it lends credibility to her walk.*

📖 Read Proverbs 31:10–12, 25–31. How do these verses define a woman of influence?

_____

_____

According to verse 30, why is she so successful at being the woman God has called her to be?

_____

_____

Respect speaks a husband's language. It motivates him to be for her and for their family what God calls him to be.

Can you see why respect is such an important element in the character of _every_ wife? Respect speaks a husband's language. It motivates him to be for her and for their family what God calls him to be. And if he's an unbeliever or a slow-growing believer, it paves the way to give God every opportunity to get to his heart. Like _agape_ love, respecting our husbands is a choice, an act of our will—or our "won't." Even if a husband is difficult to respect, the godly wife can choose to respect his position of authority, because that's what God calls her to do. God will take it from there!

🛑 **APPLY** How does your husband respond when you show him respect?

_____

_____

_____

How does your lack of respect affect your husband? (Have you noticed?)

_____

_____

_____

In what ways _do_ you show respect to your husband?

_____

_____

_____

_____

🙏 Thank God for your husband—all that he is and all that he does for you and for your family, even if you wish there were more. Find all that's praiseworthy and admirable, and think on those things—respect them. Have you confessed and repented of any disrespectful behavior that the Holy Spirit has brought to your attention? Ask God to enliven your mind toward your husband, to notice things about him that you hadn't noticed before, to be aware of his presence and acknowledge him, to defer to him when you know it's time to release an issue or decision, to enhance those things about him that are admirable. Above all, ask God to increase your trust in Him as you seek to be the respectful wife He calls you to be.

MY FRIEND OR MY ENEMY?

Society pounds "self" mercilessly into our heads through various forms of media—magazines, novels, television soaps, talk shows, sitcoms, and so on. It continually pushes the pursuit of "What will make *me* happy?" When we enter our marriages and something doesn't go our way—if we don't get the right feelings or get the right responses—we'll brood out of a desire for our husbands to change, withdraw until they do, or get even to hasten the process. God knows husbands won't change when wives (or anybody else) try to change them. Change is real and permanent only when urged upon us by His Holy Spirit (2 Corinthians 3:18).

 Identify any areas in which you've exerted pressure on your husband to change. What were the results?

Areas Pressured Toward Change	Results

📖 Read Matthew 7:1–5. What's the essence of this passage?

_____

_____

 Could personalizing this passage in Matthew 7 redefine your relationship with your husband? If so, how?

_____

_____

_____

_____

Trying to manipulate change in another doesn't work; it just builds fault upon fault. Therefore, criticizing or manipulating our spouses *reinforces* the very faults we would like to see disappear! And in so doing, we work against the Holy Spirit. It's His job to win a soul to Christ and to change him or her from the inside out.

📖 In John 10:10, what does Jesus say Satan's goals are?

_____

_____

Satan loves to play with the weaknesses, faults, failures, and mistakes of others. He especially loves it when a spouse makes his job easier by pointing out and driving home the mate's shortcomings. We can unwittingly assist the Enemy in his endeavor to "steal, kill, and destroy" our spouses and our marriages. He deftly camouflages his motives by asserting in our minds *our* rights and what *we* deserve. Our flesh reacts—first inwardly, then outwardly.

> *"Why do you look at the speck of sawdust in your brother's eye and pay no attention to the plank in your own eye?"*
>
> *Matthew 7:3 (NIV)*

📖 Jesus, on the other hand, is our biggest supporter (John 10:10). He loves to love us. According to the verses below, how has He proven His love?

Romans 8:31–39

_____

_____

Hebrews 7:25

_____

_____

Doesn't His response to us make it easier to love Him? We have no greater advocate! How much easier it would be for our men to love us if *we* loved as Christ—if we were our husband's greatest advocate.

Unfortunately, we're prone to *react* to our husbands and their foibles rather than *respond.* These two words are very important when exercising our free will. A reaction is a sudden, intense, sometimes out-of-control behavior fueled by emotion, with little regard for the negative thoughts preceding the emotion. It exercises self. A response is preceded by deliberate, purposeful thought, which determines the behavior. It's fueled by the Holy Spirit and exercises self-control.

📖 Although reacting and responding are frequently used interchangeably, they *are* different. How does Proverbs 15:28 spell out the difference between reacting and responding?

_____

_____

Negative thinking precedes negative feelings, which cause a reaction; right thinking precedes a response, regardless of the feelings.

Ed Wheat states, "People who constantly react are never really free. Someone else is always in control, determining how they will feel and behave."[13]

By exercising our free will, we choose to react or respond to a person or situation. We can choose to be angry or calm, hostile or forgiving, agreeable or quarrelsome, and so on. Negative thinking precedes negative feelings, which cause a reaction; right thinking precedes a response, regardless of the feelings. And we can instantly draw on the Holy Spirit at any time for an extra measure of His self-control.

📖 Read Romans 12:1–2. What is Paul urging believers to do, and why (verse 1)?

_____

_____

_____

What does it mean to be conformed to this world? What are some common behaviors in a marriage relationship that conform to the world?

_____

_____

_____

How does the renewing of our minds transform worldly behaviors we have in marriage?

_____

_____

_____

Whatever we choose to feed our minds will determine our behavior toward our husbands and in our marriages. Therefore, a mind conformed to the world will get even (reaction), and a mind transformed by renewal will put God's good, acceptable, and perfect will to the test in a marriage (response). And His will is going to pass the test—it will be *proven*—every time! How important it is to have right thinking! Our responsibility is to prove God's will, not our own, in our marriages.

APPLY List the circumstances, situations, and topics of conversation that trigger in you a react-mode or respond-mode toward your husband:

"React-mode" Situations	"Respond-mode" Situations

Over the next few days, note the situations and topics to which you react or respond to your husband. This can be an eye-opener! You may want to review your list above since these situations may come up again. It'll give you a better chance of responding.

Situation	
Reacted	Responded

How did you know you were reacting to him and not responding? What caused you to react to a situation rather than respond?

_____

_____

How did you feel after you reacted to your husband? How did you feel after you responded?

_____

_____

"And do not be conformed to this world, but be transformed by the renewing of your mind, that you may prove what the will of God is, that which is good and acceptable and perfect."

Romans 12:2

What impact did your reactions have on your husband? What impact did your responses have on him?

_____

_____

_____

In what ways can you change the reactions to responses next time?

_____

_____

_____

_____

But we'll still blow it at times, and when we do . . .

 It's sometimes difficult to remember that our husbands are *not* the enemy. God wants us to resist every temptation to cooperate with the real enemy, Satan. Ask God to show you daily how to respond rather than react to your husband, to yield to the nudgings of His Spirit in the heat of the moment, to honor Him and your husband with right responses. And thank God for what He's doing in your marriage, and for what he is going to do as He transforms you daily by the renewing of your mind.

Works Cited

1. Gary Thomas, *Sacred Marriage* (Grand Rapids: Zondervan Publishing House, 2000), 13, 21.

2. Quoted in Ibid., 89.

3. Ed Wheat, M.D., and Gloria Oakes Perkins, *Love Life for Every Married Couple* (Grand Rapids: Zondervan Publishing House, 1980), 152.

4. Ibid., 152–53.

5. Nancy Leigh DeMoss, *Lies Women Believe and the Truth That Sets Them Free* (Chicago: Moody Press, 2001), 146.

6. Spiros Zodhiates, ed., *The Complete Word Study Dictionary New Testament* (Chattanooga, TN: AMG Publishers, 1992), #5293, 1428.

7. Ibid.

8. John MacArthur, *The MacArthur Study Bible* (Nashville: Word Publishing, 1997), 21.

9. Quoted in DeMoss, *Lies Women Believe*, 154.

10. Pam Forster, *As unto the Lord*, (Gaston, OR: Doorposts, 1999), 4.

11. Nancy Wilson, *The Fruit of Her Hands* (Moscow, ID: Canon Press, 1997), 31.

12. Jo Berry, *Beloved Unbeliever* (Grand Rapids: Zondervan Publishing House, 1981), 48–49.

13. Wheat and Perkins, *Love Life for Every Married Couple,* 159

7

The Freedom to Love

The first six lessons have brought you a long way in preparation for this one. No marriage, regardless of how healthy it is, is devoid of pain. No relationship goes unhindered by offense, whether in the form of disappointment, disillusionment, or deliberate sin. This lesson will take you to those places in your marriage that require a touch of the Master's hand—and a measure of His mercy and grace.

You're also going to put your will into action as responder rather than reactor, by the power of the Holy Spirit. Remember: God wouldn't command us to do His will if it weren't possible. And He gives us wonderful assurances that hold fast on the other side of our obedience. The first is in John 14:21, which says, *"He who has My commandments and keeps them, he it is who loves Me; and he who loves Me shall be loved by My Father, and I will love him, and will disclose Myself to him."* What a powerful promise! As you walk in obedience, Jesus will reveal Himself to you; He promises to become real to you as the outcome of your obedience unfolds. He proves His truth as we walk it out.

There's a second promise that follows our obedience stated in John 15:10–11. Jesus says, *"If you keep My commandments, you will abide in My love; just as I have kept My Father's commandments, and abide in His love. These things I have spoken to you, that My joy may be in you, and that your joy may be made full."*

No marriage, regardless of how healthy it is, is devoid of pain. No relationship goes unhindered by offense, whether in the form of disappointment, disillusionment, or deliberate sin.

Living under the authority of Jesus Christ is a place of exultation and great joy. It's a place of peace. We're secure, because the parameters He draws are clear, and they are His best for us. (Contrast that with the world's best, or our perceived best. There should be no contest in our mind!) And in that security is freedom—freedom to please the only Master we'll ever require.

How important it is to get beyond *our* feelings, *our* rights—our *selves*—and understand the will of God! However, should we choose *not* to live out His commands, we won't like our dwelling place. It's called bondage. Every negative emotion will have free reign in our hearts, because we will have chosen to live outside the will of God. Paul addressed the Galatians on this very issue: *"It is for freedom that Christ has set us free. Stand firm, then, and do not let yourselves be burdened again by a yoke of slavery"* (Galatians 5:1, NIV).

Is there a yoke of slavery burdening you, one that is choking the life out of you *and* your marriage? Does it remain buried only to resurface as a consuming negative emotion or behavior? Do you perceive and understand the effect this yoke is having on you and your relationship with your husband? In this lesson you're going to examine the most common and most destructive yoke of all—unforgiveness. God's way is perfect. May you have a teachable heart so that you'll learn this week to love your husband unburdened by any yoke of slavery.

The Freedom to Love

DAY ONE

THE BURDEN

Married couples get themselves into negative habit patterns, such as nagging, complaining, criticizing, manipulating, withdrawing, and so on. Although these patterns are mostly aimed at changing a spouse, they serve only to perpetuate themselves. The more a person dwells on negatives, the more negative that person becomes. If your relationship is plagued by some of these destructive patterns, now is a good time to let God replace those patterns with godly ones. This lesson will have much application. I ask you to be diligent and faithful, as well as disciplined, in following the steps below. As you do your part, you'll realize the blessings of a faithful God—and your husband will be blessed by you. One word of caution: be diligent to reject the temptation to dwell on your husband and his part. That's the Holy Spirit's job.

 Before you begin, clean your slate with God. *Confess* your efforts to change your spouse. Confess this to God, and make no excuses for yourself, such as "If he were only this way . . ." or "If only he'd do this, I wouldn't nag or try to manipulate him the way I do," or so on. God doesn't want excuses; He wants agreement when the Holy Spirit's conviction hits the target of your heart.

Next, *repent* from any efforts to change your husband. Turn 180 degrees from this habit and toward God. Live out your repentance by rejecting future temptations to control his behavior, releasing your husband daily to the Lord. Trust the Holy Spirit to prompt you and guide you in this endeavor. The Lord will provide many opportunities to practice and perfect godly responses toward your husband. After you repent, *trust* God to protect you and your heart as you entrust your husband and your marriage to Him.

Use this page and the next to list items under the following categories: **"Husband's Shortcomings"** and **"Areas of Dissatisfaction, Disappointment, and Unmet Expectations." This page is for your eyes only and not to be shared with anyone, particularly your husband.** List everything you can think of in each category. Yes, that's right—everything. Ask God to help you think of every fault and shortcoming that plagues you, every area of dissatisfaction and disappointment, and every unmet expectation. Write each down, great and small. Do it now, *alone and undisturbed.* (Important: if you genuinely can't think of anything, please don't think you must come up with something. Praise God with thanksgiving for this blessing. However, there may be another in your life—mother, father, sibling, friend—with whom you could list items in these categories. Don't neglect this prompting.) This exercise is between you and God only and is not to be shared or discussed with anyone else, especially your husband. Please do not read beyond this point until this task is completed.

Husband's Shortcomings

_____

_____

_____

_____

Areas of Dissatisfaction, Disappointment, and Unmet Expectations

_____

_____

_____

_____

_____

_____

_____

_____

_____

_____

_____

_____

_____

_____

_____

_____

_____

_____

_____

_____

_____

_____

_____

_____

_____

_____

_____

_____

_____

_____

_____

Thank you for completing this task. I know that it has been more difficult for some than others. For now, lay this page at the feet of the Lord and walk away. You will continue to peel away the burden on Day Two.

THE UNBURDENING

I n Day One, you completed a huge and perhaps painful task. It's now time to return to this task. Right now, take time to ask the Lord for His insight as He walks you through this next study section. His insights will make all the difference in your marriage—or in any relationship.

The critical part about the list you've just finished is what you do with it. Some wives will want to embrace and caress it, using it to justify their anger and bad behavior. They live as discontents. Others will use the list to mourn a relationship that "could have been" had it not been for all the problems. They live as walking wounded—broken and defeated, hopeless that anything could change. Still others may not even complete the list because they are resigned to a lifetime of misery. After all, it's been this way for years. They live as if dead: no life, no joy, no goals—just existing.

I believe that you're taking this course because God *called you to act* by faith. He is meeting you right where you are in His perfect timing. Over the past six weeks, He has been giving you His Truth to use to tear down lies you've believed for years—lies that foment doubt and despair, anger and hopelessness. The truth is this: there is no circumstance bigger than God Almighty. *Nothing* is hopeless. Trust God. Believe Christ. Will your newfound direction change your husband? Maybe. Maybe not. But it will change *you*, so that you "*may prove what the will of God is, that which is good and acceptable and perfect.*" (Romans 12:2).

What you are about to walk through now is one of the most difficult, illogical principles in the Bible. It is also one of the most powerful, liberating, and life-changing principles. And it will demolish any yoke of slavery. It is the reason Jesus went to the cross. It is *forgiveness*.

Let's examine the principle of forgiveness:

📖 Read Matthew 6:14–15. What is God's condition for forgiving *our* sins?

_____

_____

To forgive means "to let go from one's power, possession, to let go free, let escape . . . to let go from obligation toward oneself . . . to pardon." It denotes cutting someone loose. The essence of unforgiveness is that the one who is not forgiven is symbolically roped to the back of the one who will not forgive. Unforgiveness is the means by which you bind yourself to the one who has hurt you. Most often, the greater burden is upon the one who will not forgive rather than on the one who is unforgiven. Forgiveness is the practice of cutting loose the one roped to your back. Hence, *both of you* can be freed from the burden and bondage of unforgiveness.

> **The truth is this: there is no circumstance bigger than God Almighty. Nothing is hopeless. Trust God. Believe Christ. Will your newfound direction change your husband? Maybe. Maybe not. But it will change you. . . .**

> **"For if you forgive men for their transgressions, your heavenly Father will also forgive you. But if you do not forgive men, then your Father will not forgive your transgressions."**

> **Matthew 6:14, 15**

Jesus' message of "seventy times seven" or "seventy-seven times" was that a person's requirement to forgive has no limit. This is a tough truth, since forgiveness makes no sense from a human perspective. But from a spiritual perspective, it is the power of God.

📖 In Matthew 18:21–35, the parable of the unmerciful servant describes what happens to one who refuses to forgive as he or she has been forgiven. This passage begins with pointed questions asked by Peter. What are they (verses 21–22)?

_____

_____

What was Jesus' answer, and what do you think He meant?

_____

_____

APPLY Has the same person repeatedly sinned against you? If you had just told Jesus about this person and He gave you this answer, how would you genuinely respond to Him?

_____

_____

_____

_____

Jesus' statement was in contrast to the Jewish rabbinical teaching that since God forgave Israel's enemies only three times (Amos 1:3, 6, 9, 11, 13), "it was presumptuous and unnecessary to forgive anyone more than 3 times."[2] Jesus' message of "seventy times seven" or "seventy-seven times" was that a person's requirement to forgive has no limit. This is a tough truth, since forgiveness makes no sense from a human perspective. But from a *spiritual perspective*, it is the power of God.

Please read Matthew 18:23–35 with a heart willing to receive the truth. As you do so, picture the following roles. The *king*, or *master*, who wants to settle accounts with His servants (verse 23) is God. The *servant* who owes ten thousand talents is you. The *fellow servant* who owes you one hundred denarii is your husband. Respond to the questions below based on this account in Matthew. Ready?

What was the debt you owed your Master (verses 23 and 24)?

_____

When your Master confronted you about the debt you owed Him, how did you appeal to Him (verses 25–26)?

_____

_____

What were your Master's three responses to your appeal, according to verse 27?

_____

_____

Once you left the Master's presence, what did *you* do? How much were you owed, and how did you treat your husband who "owed you" (verse 28)?

_____

_____

Did you note the word "found" in verse 28? The servant *"went out and found"*; he went looking. That struck me. It caused me to consider how we end up holding our husbands hostage. It can be easy for me to go "looking" for his faults, to pursue his offenses, even if they're not sin but just who he is or the way he does things (which can simply mean that he doesn't do things the way I do.) I can let these become an offense to me. Or maybe he really does "owe" me—the offense is legitimate. Either way, I let him know, in obvious and not-so-obvious ways, that he owes me. My deliberate intent is to inflict punishment, not to forgive.

APPLY How about you? What fills your thoughts when it comes to your husband? Are negative thoughts constantly lurking in the recesses of your mind throughout the day, feeding disappointment, magnifying disillusionment, and bemoaning unmet expectations? Do you desire to inflict punishment, to rope him to your back until the debt is paid? If so, write your thoughts and feelings here:

_____

_____

_____

_____

Continuing the role-play: What was your husband's response (verse 29)?

_____

_____

What did you do (verse 30)?

_____

_____

APPLY When your husband apologizes, or perhaps without a word he exhibits behavior toward you that says, "I'm sorry," does it help his case, or do you play out the same role as the servant? What is your typical response?

_____

_____

_____

_____

How did your approach to your debtor (your husband) differ from your Master's approach to you? Review verse 27.

_____

_____

When your Master heard of how you treated your husband, what did He do (verses 32–34)?

_____

_____

_____

In verse 35, what does Jesus say God will do if you choose not to forgive *"from your heart"*?

_____

_____

What do you think *"from your heart"* means?

_____

_____

APPLY How does the above apply to your not forgiving your husband's offenses?

_____

_____

_____

What makes forgiving your husband difficult?

_____

_____

Unforgiveness says, "You owe me, and I'm not releasing you until I get what I deserve." When we refuse to forgive, we'll get what we deserve. God will turn us over to our jailers and "torturers"—anger, bitterness, hostility, resentment, anxiety, and depression.

In this parable the master was owed ten thousand talents, the equivalent of about ten million dollars. In that time, it would take thousands of **years** of labor to pay off such a debt! In contrast, the servant was owed one hundred denarii, the equivalent of one hundred **days** of labor. What the servant really owed his forgiving master was gratitude, praise, and honor, because his debt had been so great and impossible to pay. Because the servant didn't consider the master's mercy and extend to his debtor that which he had received, he was imprisoned for his hard, merciless heart. In the same way, unforgiveness in our hearts will imprison us. Yes, we can make our debtor pay a high price, but not nearly the price we'll pay physically and emotionally for the sin of unforgiveness.

Unforgiveness says, "You owe me, and I'm not releasing you until I get what I deserve." When we refuse to forgive, we'll get what we deserve. God will turn us over to our jailers and "torturers"—anger, bitterness, hostility, resentment, anxiety, and depression. These were my jailers. Are they yours right now? I tell you in all sincerity—you'll remain in that jail and be subject to its torturers until you choose to use the key the Master has given you.

The spiritual dynamic that forgiveness releases is unsurpassed by any other. God spent His Son in order to unleash that power in the form of a healing balm—redemption, reconciliation, and restoration. What we really owe our Master for His forgiveness of *all* our debt—past, present and future—is gratitude. Only then can we forgive another from our heart.

 Prayerfully ponder what you have just learned. Ask God to show you how it applies to your own circumstances. Please don't reject its application to your own circumstance, no matter how painful or unjust it is. Your very life (in Christ) depends on it.

Understanding Forgiveness

I've known women who were so embittered by unforgiveness (I used to be among them) that their faces were haggard and their personalities peaceless. *Nothing* hides the effects of unforgiveness.

📖 Let's take a moment to reinforce this teaching about forgiveness, just in case you aren't convinced that you're able to forgive your husband. What is the reminder in John 15:5 and Philippians 4:13?

_____

_____

_____

What is forgiveness all about? What does it mean to really forgive your husband? How do you deal with all the things that make forgiving so difficult? Below are tough truths about forgiveness. As you read the scriptures and the points alongside them, the Holy Spirit will be ministering to your heart. Record any *personal insights* He gives you as well as the *personal impact* each scripture and point has on you and on your marriage.

📖 Read Galatians 5:1. Forgiveness is a **decision** in response to the command of God—a crisis of the will (or the "won't"). You may not feel like forgiving, but you know it's possible, because God requires it of you and has provided His Holy Spirit to ensure success. It's the right thing to do. It instantaneously releases your husband from your jail and frees you. Over time, feelings of forgiveness will follow the right decision to forgive.

Personal insight/impact:

_____

_____

_____

📖 Re-read Matthew 6:14–15. Forgiveness is a non-negotiable principle of God. The gospel is all about forgiveness. If we don't forgive, perhaps we don't (or won't) embrace the way we have been forgiven. Or perhaps we're too casual about the cross of Christ and the cost of Christ. I had to examine these areas in my own life, to challenge myself with this question: "Do I truly understand the message of the gospel?" Do you need to do the same?

Personal insight/impact:

_____

_____

_____

📖 Read 2 Corinthians 2:10–11 and Ephesians 4:26–27. Forgiveness avoids Satan's snare. Unforgiveness makes his job much easier. Its poison will affect your life, your husband's life, your marriage, your children, your health, your mental stability, and on and on. When relationships are fraught with hatred and bitterness, the Enemy has won.

> *Forgiveness is a decision in response to the command of God—a crisis of the will (or the "won't").*

> *When relationships are fraught with hatred and bitterness, the Enemy has won.*

Personal insight/impact:

_____

_____

_____

📖 Read Ephesians 4:31–32 and Acts 17:28. Choosing to forgive imitates Christ. It's the way we are to become.

Personal insight/impact:

_____

_____

_____

📖 Read Psalm 103:12 and Hebrews 8:12. Forgiveness means that you no longer hold your husband's offense against him. It's impossible to erase a memory; however, you can choose to quit pushing the replay button in your thinking. You may have to practice taking those thoughts captive that keep you wedded to the offense and making them obedient to Christ (2 Corinthians 10:3–5), _replacing_ them with godly thinking. God separates you from your sin and determines never to use it against you. You must do the same when your husband offends you.

Personal insight/impact:

_____

_____

_____

📖 Read 1 Peter 2:23 and Romans 12:17–21. Forgiveness says, "I will not retaliate." It's God's job to be the just Judge. When we entrust our circumstances and ourselves to the just Judge, we will have no reason to "get even."

Personal insight/impact:

_____

_____

_____

📖 Read Ephesians 4:25. Forgiveness is not pretending we weren't hurt. Pretending just buries the truth within us while we live out a lie. This verse admonishes us to be genuine and to say what's real. Here's a familiar scenario:

Husband: "What's wrong, Honey?"
Wife: "Oh…nothing."

That common response from wives is neither genuine nor speaks truth. Such a response perpetuates unforgiveness, delays resolution, gives birth to bitterness, and is manipulative. Acknowledge the hurt to the Lord and then, if He so directs, to your husband. Then forgive as you've been forgiven.

Did You Know?

HEAPING BURNING COALS

A common interpretation of Romans 12:17–21 teaches that the phrase _"heaping burning coals on his head"_ means to behave in such a stellar way as to embarrass someone into repentance or right thinking or behaving—to make them see the error of their ways—sort of a "killing them with kindness" approach. As a matter of fact, this passage depicts the epitome of _agape_ love. In the ancient Hebrew culture, homes were heated and meals cooked with a bed of coals that was kept constantly burning by daily adding more coals. A family's comfort level and survival were dependent on these burning embers. If their embers went out, or if they could not afford more coals, family members would walk in front of their neighbors' homes with a bowl on their heads, into which the neighbors would "heap burning coals." Even if there were contentions between two families, the need was met. Neighbors would sacrifice that which was dear to their livelihood for the sake of another's. There was no withholding, because life depended on their mercy.

Personal insight/impact:

_____

_____

_____

📖 Read Luke 23:34. Forgiveness is the only way to stop the agony of an offense. And where does that pain go? Into the hands of the One who understands perfectly the agony of betrayal and the anguish of rejection. Was your husband's offense deliberate? Was it sin? Was he aware of the impact of his words or actions? Do the answers to these questions matter? From the standpoint of your requirement to forgive—no, they do not. From the standpoint of communication, resolution, and restoration—yes, they do. When you've untied your husband from your back (forgiven him), you're then able to lovingly address offenses in ways that honor God.

Personal insight/impact:

_____

_____

_____

📖 Read Galatians 6:1–5. Forgiving does not ignore recurrent sin. We can forgive past sins and lovingly confront any future offenses. Tolerating sin enables the offender to continue on a destructive path. Please understand from these verses the process and the goal: This is not about condemnation but about restoration. And depending upon the offense and your husband's response to your loving confrontation of it, you may need the assistance of one or more godly men who are biblically grounded, _"responsive to and controlled by the Spirit"_ (verse 1, AMP), and not afraid to speak the truth to him in love.

Personal insight/impact:

_____

_____

_____

📖 Read 1 Corinthians 13:7. Forgiveness means that you're willing to bear the outcome of your husband's sin. This would be your sacrifice, as it is the Lord's with you. When you sin, His unconditional love for you compels Him to forgive you. Loving your husband unconditionally requires the same of you. If there are consequences associated with his sin, they'll stand whether you forgive him or not. The difference will be your dwelling place—with your jailer or with your just Judge. If you choose forgiveness, God will faithfully see you through any and all consequences as you continue to trust and cleave to Him. His promise is to cause all things to work for your good and growth (Romans 8:28–29). That's mercy followed by grace.

Personal insight/impact:

_____

_____

_____

Forgiveness is the only way to stop the agony of an offense.

> **"Now to him who is able to do immeasurably more than all we ask or imagine according to his power that is at work within us, to him be glory in the church and in Christ Jesus throughout all generations, for ever and ever! Amen."**
>
> **Ephesians 3:20–21 (NIV)**

📖 Read Ephesians 3:20–21 and 2 Corinthians 1:3–4. Forgiveness permits God to move in your circumstance. *God is able* to move through obedient forgiveness to impact the circumstances in a way that produces great good and blessing beyond what you can ask or imagine. (Note through whom the power works, according to the Ephesians passage.) He *will* supply all your needs. And when you're yielded to the Father, the door of your heart is open to receive His comfort. He will not waste one tear but later on can make you useful in the life of another who is facing a similar challenge.

Personal insight/impact:

_____

_____

_____

📖 Read 1 John 3:21–22. No matter how painful your ordeal, forgiveness opens the door to effectively pray for your husband. No feelings are necessary, because it's an act of your will in response to the will of God.

Personal insight/impact:

_____

_____

_____

📖 Read Psalm 73:21–26 and Hebrews 12:15. Forgiveness guards against the bitter root that will grow upward, shoot forth and contaminate (defile) many. If bitterness has already taken root in your heart, confess it to God—pull it up by its root, and lay it at the foot of the cross of Christ. Receive His forgiveness, and then forgive your husband.

Personal insight/impact:

_____

_____

_____

📖 Read John 12:24–26. Forgiveness is life giving (freedom); unforgiveness is life threatening (bondage)—psychologically, socially, mentally, physically, and spiritually. Everything about you will die a slow death while dwelling in the darkness of unforgiveness. Forgiveness is a profound demonstration of "death to self and my rights."

Personal insight/impact:

_____

_____

_____

📖 Read John 8:1–11. Forgiveness *restores*. That's what the cross is all about.

Personal insight/impact:

_____

_____

_____

📖 Read Matthew 18:32–35. Forgiveness changes *you*. If you keep your husband in an ongoing state of forgiveness, you'll no longer be "roping" him to yourself and reacting with bad attitudes, habits, words, or behavior. In time the pain will diminish, and you'll be able to interact with rather than react to your husband. It's a sure, supernatural dynamic of God.

Forgiveness changes you.

Personal insight/impact:

_____

_____

_____

Please remember that God never requires anything of us that He didn't first require of Himself through His Son: *"Father, forgive them"* (Luke 23:34).

 Thank the Lord for the insight He has given you in today's lesson. Ask Him to continue to work in your heart, so that His will is accomplished in your life and in your marriage.

Day Four will be one of the most important days of this exercise.

TIME TO FORGIVE

The Freedom to Love
DAY FOUR

This is a day of application. Is your husband roped to your back with the cords of unforgiveness? It's time to slice the ropes, set him free, and unburden your heart before the Lord. You can now choose to embark on one of the most freeing expressions of trust you can utter. Here's how:

Return to your completed lists in Day One, and read the first "shortcoming." Give it to the Lord. The following is a very simple, effective prayer if you need some help:

> "Father, I forgive my husband for _____." (Name it specifically and aloud.)

> "I will no longer judge my husband with regard to that fault."

> "I will no longer condemn my husband for that fault."

Do the same with each category, one item at a time. Take your time. This is an exercise of your **will**, a decision you are making right now. As you think through your decision to forgive, the freedom of having forgiven will follow over time, and God will bring healing to whatever negative emotions are attached to that offense. Remember that you're not doing this alone. You're in prayer, and the Holy Spirit is with you. Your willingness to forgive is all God needs to work with. Please be sure to verbally walk through this process. Speaking the words clarifies and solidifies the choice you are making before God to forgive. Note where there might be reluctance to forgive, and don't ignore it. Push through that resistance in faith, being assured that your heavenly Father has brought you to this point and will see you to the other side. That's where the freedom is.

Tell God that these problem areas are now His. When you have completed your lists, simply tear the sheet of paper from your book and destroy it. *It is finished!*

A word of warning: Down the road, Satan will want to convince you that you've not forgiven your husband because of the way you sometimes feel. Remember that you're not to "*let* [yourself] *be burdened again by the yoke of slavery*" (Galatians 5:1, NIV). Refute all of these thoughts and arguments that take place in your mind. They set themselves up "*against the knowledge of God*"—the Truth that you now know. Begin to "*take captive every thought to make it obedient to Christ*" (2 Corinthians 10:5, NIV). Remember: God was a witness to your decision to forgive your husband, and He is rejoicing over you. Continue to put your thought life under His authority, continually submitting it to Him and resisting the Enemy's attempts to return you to jail. Fill your mind with correct thinking (Philippians 4:8), followed by a prayer, such as the one below.

 Dear Lord, I forgave my husband for _____, and I will not take it back. I will not re-rope him to my back. I place these thoughts under your authority, Jesus, and move forward to stand firm in the forgiveness I have already granted. I will think on whatever is true, whatever is honorable, whatever is right, whatever is pure, whatever is lovely, whatever is of good repute, excellent and worthy of praise. I will dwell on these thoughts, that you might be glorified in my obedience. In Jesus' name. Amen.

Bottom Line: As we ourselves are not perfect, we would want the Lord to forgive us in the same way we have just forgiven, and will continue to forgive, our husbands. We must keep our husbands in an ongoing state of forgiveness.

> *Down the road, Satan will want to convince you that you've not forgiven your husband because of the way you sometimes feel. Remember that you're not to "let [yourself] be burdened again by the yoke of slavery."*
>
> **Galatians 5:1 (NIV)**

The Freedom to Love

THROUGH YOUR EYES, LORD

It's time to refocus on what is good. This is where the rubber meets the road—where the walk meets the talk. You've just dealt with past offenses *once for all* through forgiveness. Let's now get a godly perspective on the man God has given you.

Use the space below to list each of your husband's good qualities, special attributes, and strengths—great and small. (You don't have to have much for God to build on.)

Good Qualities, Special Attributes, and Strengths

_____

_____

_____

_____

_____

_____

_____

Go down the list right now, one item at a time, and thank God for these qualities.

Ask God to show you this man through His eyes and to reveal more good qualities to add to your list. Do so each morning and/or evening while you're in prayer. When you praise God for the good qualities in your husband, you'll begin to be *transformed by the renewing of your mind* (Romans 12:2, NIV).

☞ Tell your husband at least once a day that you love him. You don't need to feel emotional love. Loving him is a *commitment*. It says, "I'll be here for you, under any and all circumstances" (1 Corinthians 13:4–8).

☞ Tell your husband about one of his good qualities every day. He needs your love and encouragement most when he is down or when he has failed. Speak truth in love; be sincere about his good qualities, and they'll begin to grow. Rely on your list above, and add to it.

☞ At least once a week, do something for your husband that you know he'll like, such as baking his favorite cookies. This is an *act* of love (commitment). God will guide this expression of love. Record what you did below:

_____

_____

_____

☞ If you could think of all the things you would do for the "husband of the year," do them for yours. Now is a good time to develop the habit of responding to what's important to him. Does he like a tidy home or his socks folded together instead of in a pile (a great chore for the kids)? Most things are very simple. All are thoughtful. The key is action. What might some of them be?

_____

_____

_____

☞ When with friends or relatives, show and express your new commitment to your husband by being loyal (in your thoughts and words) and supportive. Don't use light sarcasm toward him. This is deadly poison with a smile! Since you've forgiven his faults, there will be no need to share them with family members. They are God's now. *Live out your loyalty* to your spouse before others, every day and under every circumstance. Re-read 1 Corinthians 13:7. This is God's love in you, and it's always available!

☞ Talk to your husband about your concerns without pointing a finger of blame at him. (Is he unsupportive of you? Sarcastic? Critical? Withdrawn?) Start your statements with "*I feel*. . . ." instead of "*You make me* feel. . . ." This way you're taking responsibility for your own feelings without being judgmental about your husband. Your goal is to try to help him understand without an overload of emotion. Lay out the facts clean and simple.

Though your husband has hurt you, he has also blessed you in many ways. "Dwell" on those ways (Philippians 4:8). Start by making a list in the space provided on the next page.

When you praise God for the good qualities in your husband, you'll begin to be "transformed by the renewing of your mind" (see Romans 12:2, NIV).

If you could think of all the things you would do for the "husband of the year," do them for yours.

Ways My Husband Has Blessed Me

_____

_____

_____

_____

_____

Remember that you and your husband are works in progress.

📖 Read Hebrews 12:15. Love ("God's love in you") never fails. People do. You and your husband are works in progress. Guard your heart against bitterness. It's Christ's nature in you that heals. Let Him heal your heart as you follow His.

🛑 **APPLY** The following questions are to be done in your quiet time with the Lord. They examine where you are in your marriage and where you want to go. Ponder these questions, taking your time, answering each question prayerfully.

What initially attracted you to want to know your husband?

_____

_____

_____

_____

What motivated you to continue dating him?

_____

_____

_____

Why did you want to marry him?

_____

_____

_____

Why didn't you stay single?

_____

_____

_____

_____

What did your wedding vows mean to you when you said them?

_____

_____

_____

_____

What do your wedding vows mean to you now?

_____

_____

_____

_____

What do you and your husband presently have in common?

_____

_____

Since a picture is worth a thousand words, what is the picture of your marriage saying to your children (or to other family members if you don't have children)?

_____

_____

_____

_____

List the ways in which you show to your husband your love for him.

_____

_____

_____

List the ways in which your husband shows his love for you.

_____

_____

_____

What does God want a marriage to be like?

_____

_____

_____

How does your marriage compare to your answer in the last question?

_____

_____

_____

_____

What would you like to see changed in your relationship?

_____

_____

_____

_____

Since a picture is worth a thousand words, what is the picture of your marriage saying to your children or to other family members?

Based on what you've learned thus far in this study, how are the changes you listed above likely to be made?

_____

_____

_____

_____

 Begin praying in earnest for your husband—faithfully and daily. Be careful not to pray for all of the changes you would like to see made. This will refocus you on all the negatives and rekindle all the things in your heart that you placed at the Lord's feet this week. Ask the Lord to show you how to pray for your husband. Ask God daily to bless him and to draw him to the Creator and Lover of his soul. That frees you from fixing your eyes on your husband and the changes you're "expecting." Instead, fix your mind and your eyes on Jesus (Hebrews 3:1; 12:2), determined that your expectations are in Him alone as the Author and Finisher of your faith—and your husband's. Trust Him.

It's time to move on to the next topic. May your heart be ready for the beauty and blessing that will be covered in Lesson 8.

Works Cited

1. Spiros Zodhiates, Warren Baker, eds., *The Complete Word Study Dictionary: New Testament* (Chattanooga, TN: AMG Publishers, 1992), #863, 299.

2. John MacArthur, *The MacArthur Study Bible* (Nashville: Word Publishing, 1997), 1426.

8

Our Sexuality: God's Ultimate Wedding Gift

When I bring up the subject of sex in my women's Bible studies, there's a hushed twitter; faces blush, and nervous giggles erupt in semi-controlled waves across the room. Yes, we're naked and still ashamed!

God gives husbands and wives the gift of sex as the ultimate act that binds their souls in oneness—with perks. Could the Creator have intended us to seek and enjoy the powerful stirring in our bodies in response to our mates? Absolutely! The sensual feelings draw us into something deeper, where a greater need is met. Sex brings more to the marriage than pleasure. It brings strength, protection, healing, and comfort. It was intended to bless a husband and wife—often.

> *Sex brings more to the marriage than pleasure. It brings strength, protection, healing, and comfort. It was intended to bless a husband and wife –often.*

THE PURPOSE AND PLEASURE OF SEXUAL INTIMACY

Have you ever finished making love with your husband and felt so satisfied, so secure, so real—and not ashamed? If you've been married many years, do you still explore all the nuances of your changing bodies? When was the last time you felt a warm comfort, that essential belonging that stirred gratitude in your soul?

God was delighted when the first couple became one flesh. Genesis 2:25 (AMP) states, *"The man and his wife were both naked and were not embarrassed or ashamed in each other's presence."* The Hebrew word translated "ashamed" (*bosh*), comes from a root word meaning "to become pale" or "to blush."[1] Adam and Eve stood naked before each other without blushing. What wonderful freedom! And God must have smiled as He watched the excitement, anticipation, and passion stir, ignite, and pour forth in purity and mutual honor. A virgin man lay with his virgin wife, naked and unashamed, ratifying a covenant that was ordained, witnessed, and blessed by God.

📖 Paul talks about this one-flesh experience, calling it a mystery (that which was hidden but now revealed). According to Ephesians 5:31–32, what is the mystery of the married sexual union?

_____

_____

Paula Rinehart says, "No matter how much our culture tries to pretend, we cannot keep ourselves from realizing that sex has both context and meaning—that in a sexual encounter, we are standing at the edge of something holy."[2] That "something holy," I believe, is the reality that our sexual relationship with our husbands is not separate from our spiritual relationship with our Lord Jesus Christ. The deep fellowship and intimacy of our marital oneness is intended to reflect the deep spiritual oneness with our Lord. Each affects the other, influences the other.

🛑 **APPLY** How does this spiritual aspect of sexuality differ from what you think about sex? Can you sense this spiritual connection in your intimacy with your husband? If so, how would you describe it?

_____

_____

_____

📖 According to Hebrews 13:4, what value does God place on marriage and on the marriage bed?

_____

_____

Because our marriages are to be considered precious and honored by all, God intends for "intimate, sexual joys to be fulfilled only within the bonds of marriage, and there without shame."[3]

> **The deep fellowship and intimacy of our marital oneness is intended to reflect the deep spiritual oneness with our Lord. Each affects the other, influences the other.**

📖 We see a beautiful expression of this sexual joy on the wedding day of King Solomon and his Shulamite bride, whom we'll call Shulamith.⁴ Read Song of Solomon 4:1–16. What do you notice about Solomon's praises of his wife (verses 1–5)?

_____

_____

What effect is Shulamith having on Solomon (verses 6–11)?

_____

_____

_____

In *The Book of Romance*, Tommy Nelson said that Solomon was kissing his bride "deeply—what we would call a French kiss although it was nineteen hundred years before France was a nation. It was a genuine Hebrew kiss, deep and penetrating."⁵ There's nothing prudish about this Song!

📖 In Song of Solomon 4:12–16, how does Shulamith respond to her husband's intimate foreplay and lovemaking?

_____

_____

King Solomon's words caress his virgin wife from top to bottom. Her previously scaled spring (of her virginity) is flowing with reciprocal passion. She gives herself fully to her bridegroom, with enthusiasm! She *responds* to his love. There isn't a bridegroom alive who doesn't appreciate a warm, wholehearted sexual response from his wife, no matter how long they've been married.

📖 What is Solomon declaring in Song of Solomon 5:1?

_____

_____

📖 Someone else speaks in the last portion of Song of Solomon 5:1. Who do you think is speaking, and what is the message?

_____

_____

_____

Many theologians agree that this last portion of Song of Solomon 5:1 is God's hearty approval of the sexual delights that Solomon and Shulamith have just experienced in their marriage bed—all night long (4:6). I believe that the Creator and His angels rejoice every time we join our bodies in oneness with our husbands.

APPLY Would you want God's stamp of approval on your sexual encounters with your husband? *Every* time? Do you realize that He is there to give it—*every* time? What do you think of that?

_____

_____

"Marriage should be honored by all, and the marriage bed kept pure, for God will judge the adulterer and all the sexually immoral."
Hebrews 13:4 (NIV)

Extra Mile
SONG OF SONGS

Take time to read the Song of Solomon, also entitled in some translations, Song of Songs. Read it slowly and note how they took care to notice each other, to praise each other's physical attributes, to honor and appreciate each other long after their wedding night.

After the Fall, God must have been grieved to see the beauty and holiness of sex turn into the Enemy's playground, to watch it earn a foul reputation, to see what was to be given and enjoyed with selfless abandon between a husband and wife either given away recklessly outside marriage or parceled out selfishly within the marriage.

Some may think that sex according to Solomon and Shulamith is unrealistic and unattainable, but God created the marriage relationship for great sex. His plan is the original, even though Satan continues subverting it. After the Fall, God must have been grieved to see the beauty and holiness of sex turn into the Enemy's playground, to watch it earn a foul reputation, to see what was to be given and enjoyed with selfless abandon between a husband and wife either given away recklessly outside marriage or parceled out selfishly within the marriage.

📖 Sex and all its pure pleasure were stolen and counterfeited by Satan. He took what was perfect and made it a snare, albeit an alluring one. King Solomon warns about this trap in Proverbs 5:1–14. In this proverb, Solomon is specifically warning young men that the allure of an adulterous or licentious woman can be captivating; yet succumbing to that temptation has dire consequences. Though the warning is specifically targeted to men, there are broader applications concerning sex and sexuality that apply to women as well. What do you think these broader applications are? What will we gain if we heed the warning not to pervert sex? What will happen if we do not heed the warning?

_____

_____

_____

The adulteress has corrupted the beautiful sensuality that God intended for the wife only. If what is forbidden by God can lure a man (or a woman) into the snare of adultery and destroy a marriage, then what is blessed by God can avoid the snare and protect a marriage.

📖 Read Proverbs 5:15–20. What is Solomon's instruction?

_____

_____

_____

Why do you think Solomon compares a wife to a "cistern" and "well"?

_____

_____

_____

How can a husband and wife delight each other over the years (verses 18–19)?

_____

_____

_____

Proverbs 5:15–19 depicts a faithful, vibrant love: A husband draws from his own well—his wife, who is like fresh running water to him, always pure, refreshing, revitalizing, and thirst-quenching. He finds pleasure and satisfaction in her body alone, and she intoxicates him with her love—always. Joy and genuine delight are welcome in their marriage bed.

Can you freely discuss your sexual likes and dislikes with your husband? Can he do the same with you? If yes, why do you think communicating is so easy? If no, why do you think communicating is difficult?

_____

_____

_____

 Most of us desire a deeply satisfying sex life with our husbands. We also desire that same fulfillment with our Lord and Savior and often pursue it. And yet for many of us, this closeness is difficult to pursue with our men. Perhaps we need to go deeper with the Lord in this area, to willingly open ourselves to His teaching about sex and let it wash over old, set attitudes and misinformation like running water. If this is the case for you, please take some time now before the Lord and examine your thoughts about sex and your own sexuality. Do you dread sex? Why? What are your fears, your attitudes? Where did they come from? Do you feel you need permission to love your husband sexually and with abandon? Why? Do you wrestle with shame or guilt? Why? How have you dealt with the shame and guilt? Ask God to reveal His truths to you over these next few days. Begin to praise Him and thank Him for the gift of sex and for the husband with whom you share this gift.

PRINCIPLES OF SELFLESS SEXUAL INTIMACY

A cute joke made its rounds a few years ago: How do you impress a wife? Take her out to dinner. Call her. Hug her. Support her. Hold her. Surprise her. Compliment her. Smile at her. Listen to her. Laugh with her. Cry with her. Romance her. Believe in her. Respect her. Cuddle with her. Shop with her. Go to the end of the earth and back for her. How do you impress a husband? Show up naked. Bring food.

I laughed out loud, because it's true! If we women had to work as hard as our men do to get a little lovin' (OK—*sex*), we would have given up long ago.

In his book *His Needs, Her Needs*, Willard Harley reports that generally the husband's number one need from his wife is sexual fulfillment, while the wife's number one need from her husband is affection.[6] He continues: "The typical wife doesn't understand her husband's deep need for sex any more than the typical husband understands his wife's deep need for affection."[7] Based on personal experience and meeting with hundreds of wives, I agree with this statement.

Read Ephesians 5:22–25, 33. How do these verses shed light on Dr. Harley's findings?

_____

_____

_____

These verses reveal a spiritual dynamic that God intended to be mutually beneficial. Here's how it works: As a wife respects and responds to her husband's need for sexual fulfillment, he gratefully returns her need for affection. She in turn is more willing to meet his sexual needs, which inspires him to treat her more lovingly, and so on. When a husband is sexually satisfied, he's a more cooperative, chipper, confident guy. And when a wife is emotionally satisfied, she's secure and at peace. However, since husbands and wives can be self-centered, God plainly mapped out His no-nonsense instruction on married sex.

📖 Read 1 Corinthians 7:3–5. In the space below, list what husbands and wives are instructed to do:

Instructions to Husband	Instructions to Wife
Verse 3	Verse 3
Verse 4	Verse 4
Verse 5	Verse 5

Did you note the mutuality of Paul's instructions? Sexual intimacy and pleasure were never intended by God to be exclusively a man's world. This passage levels the playing field by establishing three principles of married sexual intimacy. They apply to both spouses, even if one is an unbeliever.

The **Principle of Need** is established in 1 Corinthians 7:3. What do you think this principle means?

_____

_____

Husbands and wives need each other sexually, but often at different times and frequencies, and for different reasons. Our needs and desires are driven mainly by hormones but are also influenced by such factors as status of health, levels of energy or stress, unresolved marital issues, distraction, boredom, performance anxiety, how we feel about sex, and how we feel about ourselves and our spouses.

A husband's need for sexual intercourse may increase during seasons of stress, such as job insecurity or loss, physical problems, fears about his sexual performance, and so on. A sensitive wife can help counter his insecurities by affirming him sexually and emotionally. Even when situations are not earth-shattering, for a man, physical intimacy speaks love and acceptance to the deepest place of his soul.

In his book *Wild at Heart*, John Eldridge explains that a man longs to know "Do I have what it takes? Am I powerful? Until a man *knows* he's a man he will forever be trying to prove he is one, while at the same time shrink from anything that might reveal he is not. Most men live their lives haunted by the question, or crippled by the answer they've been given."[8]

From the perspective of a man's sexuality, Paula Rinehart says, "The best way I have to explain what I hear is that a man's psyche is a seamless fabric. . . . Men tend to see themselves as a whole entity. If they feel sexually inadequate, then that inadequacy seeps into every other corner of their experience. If their sexual lives are floundering, then, they reason, the rest cannot be too far behind."[9] Our husbands, although it may not show, are more vulnerable than we think.

APPLY How does your husband communicate his need for sex? Generally, what is your response? What effect do you think your response has on your relationship?

_____

_____

_____

Would you say you are meeting your husband's sexual needs? How do you think he would answer this question?

_____

_____

_____

According to Eldridge, the question "Do I have what it takes?" is a powerful, unspoken question in a man's soul. If your husband were to ask you this question, how would you answer?

_____

_____

_____

We wives may not realize it, but we're answering that question every day by how we treat our husbands. As it relates sexually, the only one God has authorized to validate a husband is his wife. And that answers his question, "Do I have what it takes?" in so many other areas.

The **Principle of Authority** is established in 1 Corinthians 7:4. What do you think this principle means?

_____

_____

_____

Having authority over each other's bodies calls us to selflessly share them, even when we don't feel like it. Sex is God's gift through us to our husbands. He wants us to satisfy and to be satisfied, to willingly give and to willingly receive. When we do the right thing, the right feelings will follow. We soon discover that when we bless our husbands, we glorify God, and _we_ are blessed!

📖 How does Colossians 3:17, 23–24 give this principle of authority spiritual perspective?

_____

_____

_____

> *Our husbands, although it may not show, are more vulnerable than we think.*

> *The wife's body does not belong to her alone but also to her husband. In the same way, the husband's body does not belong to him alone but also to his wife."*
>
> *1 Corinthians 7:4 (NIV)*

Sex is God's gift through us to our husbands.

The Bible offers no specific guidelines on the "what" and "how to's" of married sexuality; therefore, each couple is *free* to mutually agree on how to love, honor, and play. This approach leaves room for active imaginations and exploration, which should always be within the context of mutual love, respect, and consent.

I would like to take this principle of authority one step further, beyond the sexual. I believe that it should also include anything of a serious nature that would impact a husband or wife's body. Both should be in agreement on all surgeries, to include tubal ligation or vasectomy. Use of birth control pills, hormone replacement therapy, or medication for erectile dysfunction should be openly discussed. Some of these decisions have potentially serious ramifications. It's not just about sex. It's also about oneness. You belong to each other—body and soul.

APPLY What is your response to a husband and wife's God-given authority over each other's body? Will understanding this principle affect your approach to sexual intimacy from now on? In what ways?

_____

_____

_____

Extra Mile
HABIT FORMING

The **principle of habit** is established in 1 Corinthians 7:5. In this verse a husband and wife are instructed not to "*deprive*" (NIV), "*defraud*" (KJV), or "*refuse*" (AMP) each other. Read this verse and then examine dictionary definitions for these three words. Based on the definitions you find, determine what a couple's mutual responsibility is according to 1 Corinthians 7:5.

1 Corinthians 7:5 establishes the **Principle of Habit**. It tells us not to *deprive* (NIV) "*defraud*" (KJV) or "*refuse*" (AMP) each other. Read this passage and answer the questions below.

What do you think "*mutual consent*" means in this passage and why is it important?

_____

_____

_____

In what ways can Satan use sexual deprivation against a couple?

_____

_____

_____

God calls us to habitually participate in the deepest level of intimacy a husband and wife can share. We interrupt it only when we agree to enter into the deepest level of intimacy with *Him*. Afterward, our mate's sexual welfare becomes a priority again.

Many women, however, avoid their husbands when they don't want to have sex. Their body language says, "Stay away." They avoid eye contact, withdraw, or even pick a fight. And then they wonder why their husbands are grouchy, frustrated, or downright angry. God knows that this divisive scenario plays into the Enemy's hands, which is why He commands habitual fulfillment.

📖 Read Song of Solomon 5:2–6. In verse 2 Solomon expressed his desire for his wife. What was Shulamith's response? What excuses did she make? What happened when she realized her error?

_____

Shulamith desired to right her wrong, and throughout the rest of the book she shows honor and respect to Solomon, which I believe fueled her desire for him. Avoidance was not her habit.

I often receive phone calls from wives who think their husbands are "over-sexed" or even perverted because of repeated sexual advances, even after years of marriage. I give them this perspective-shaping truth: if our husbands desire us after years of marriage, this is not a problem—it's a *blessing*! Once we grasp this truth, we no longer want to avoid our men but desire to be available. We return their blessing with our *gift*, and our sex life takes on a whole new meaning. Mutual availability is what protects a marriage from the anger associated with deprivation, or from the intruder who will notice the empty place and try to fill it.

📖 Read Luke 6:38 and Proverbs 11:24–25. How can these verses apply to one's selfless sexual response?

_____

_____

APPLY How does the principle of habit speak to your current level of sexual activity? Can you see "habit" in your responsiveness? Is it the habit of giving or the habit of avoidance and deprivation? If it's a habit of giving, how has it affected your relationship?

_____

_____

_____

If you are in the habit of avoidance and deprivation, what impact do you think it's having on your relationship? What avoidance practices do you use? How do you think your husband feels when you avoid his approaches?

_____

_____

_____

Are you in the habit of withholding sex as a form of punishment? If so, under what circumstances? How does withholding sex dishonor God's principles of need, authority, and habit?

_____

_____

_____

God's protection and blessing are imbedded in the principles of need, authority, and habit. By replacing avoidance with availability, a couple's armor against Satan's temptations is further strengthened. If avoidance or withholding has been your habit, you may need to ask your husband's forgiveness; otherwise, he may not be convinced that your availability is real—he'll be waiting for the other shoe to drop. What will you do to become more available to your husband?

_____

_____

Mutual availability is what protects a marriage from the anger associated with deprivation, or from the intruder who will notice the empty place and try to fill it.

If sexual intimacy is an area of avoidance for your husband, describe what you think or know the problem to be. Have you addressed the problem? If so, how? What were the results?

_____

_____

_____

A husband's avoidance or disinterest in sex is a very painful place for an increasing number of women. Reasons for a man's avoidance behavior can include a low testosterone level resulting in low libido, prohibitions from his past resulting in inhibition and suppression, a male-bashing (emasculating) environment which fuels anger and resentment (especially if he's emasculated in his own home), and fear of sexual dysfunction or failure resulting in performance anxiety. A key question to ask is, "Has he always been this way or did a change in his behavior occur during our marriage?" Can you recall a turning point in your relationship that may have triggered a gradual pulling away? If your husband is avoiding sex, seek as much knowledge and insight concerning the problem of male sexual avoidance as possible. There are excellent Christian marriage and sex manuals available. Be proactive in your research. Also examine your own heart for anything that might be contributing to the barrier. Then ask the Lord to show you how to address the problem with your husband. Seek His guidance on how to proceed, trusting Him with the results.

 The commands in 1 Corinthians 7:3–5 are no-nonsense. Are there any areas of complacency or neglect you need to confess and repent of before the Lord? If your husband has been neglectful, will you lift him up, forgive him, and entrust him to the Lord, and then press on with your part? If you recognize that change is necessary, seek God's wisdom, guidance, and instruction on how to approach, discuss (if necessary), and resolve your difficulties. Then obey the leading of His precious Spirit. Allow Him to guide your imagination. He won't waste any time drawing you closer to your husband. He stands ready to bless, encourage, and heal.

Our Sexuality: God's Ultimate Wedding Gift

DAY THREE

MAJOR ROADBLOCKS TO OUR SEXUAL FULFILLMENT

Because our sexual intimacy with our husbands is designed to represent our intimacy with Jesus Christ, there's a profound sense of detachment when it's not up to par. In a recent conversation, Shay Roop, author of *For Women Only: God's Design for Female Sexuality & Intimacy*, said, "Sex is perfectly natural, but rarely is it naturally perfect." What's comforting about this statement is the admission that it's not unusual for a woman to experience sexual problems. There are *many* challenges to attaining and maintaining an active and healthy sex life. The good news is that all are within our scope of influence, and most are within our sphere of correction or removal.

Today, we'll be looking at what I consider to be roadblocks that have the potential to threaten our sexual fulfillment. You may have already tackled some of them or are currently on the glide path to their elimination. That's great! But if you recognize one that you haven't confronted, God is ready to start the process of influence, correction, or removal as soon as you are. You may even want to ask Him to give you the *desire* to address a particular roadblock. As we begin today's lesson, please do the following:

☞ Read each scripture reference carefully. It will give you insight into the roadblock.

☞ Address each roadblock prayerfully and purposefully.

☞ Acknowledge any that have been blocking your path to free sexual expression and fulfillment.

☞ Record the effect that a roadblock has had on your sexual response.

☞ Record any personal insight that the Lord gives you into each roadblock you've acknowledged.

📖 Read Colossians 3:12–14. One of the most common roadblocks is having *negative thoughts about our husbands* that trigger bitterness, resentment, anger, and unforgiveness. It's important that we listen to our "self-talk." What do we tell ourselves about our husbands throughout the day? Is our general attitude positive or negative? What effect are these thoughts having on our emotions? How do they affect our sexual response? One woman quipped, "There are only two things wrong with my husband: everything he says and everything he does." Needless to say, there probably wasn't much free-flowing "amore" in their marital bed. How we perceive our husbands is vital to our sexual response.

From another perspective, it's possible that your husband's behavior has "earned" your anger and negative attitude. Loving him sexually may be difficult at times. You may even be tempted to withhold sex as punishment. Be proactive about resolving conflict or anger issues with your husband while remaining sexually intimate. Depend on God's love in you to accomplish this. If necessary, seek biblically based counsel outside the home. God still desires to reach your husband, and you may be His most effective route to his heart.

APPLY If negative thoughts about your husband are a roadblock for you, what effect are they having on your sexual response to him?

_____

_____

_____

What personal insight is God giving you into removing this roadblock?

_____

_____

_____

📖 Read Colossians 3:16; John 8:31–32; and Philippians 4:13. Another roadblock is *negative or fearful thoughts about sex* leading to shyness or inhibitions. If we believe our bodies should be hidden from our husbands or that sex is shameful, dirty, disgusting, painful, unpleasant, for procreation only, for men only, to be tolerated only (and not giving ourselves permission to enjoy it), then we'll convey these attitudes even without words. Some women can't disrobe in front of their husbands; some can't have sex if the kids are still awake or the lights are on; some can't initiate sex or even talk about it. The only way these habits of the mind are

> "And so, as those who have been chosen of God, holy and beloved, put on a heart of compassion, kindness, humility, gentleness and patience"
>
> Colossians 3:12

changed is by understanding God's truth (read Proverbs 2:1–11.) Then we can do what we were afraid we couldn't. In a column entitled "CAN'T OR WON'T", radio Bible teacher Charles Swindoll quotes physicians Frank Minirth and Paul Meier: "If an individual changes all his *can'ts* to *won'ts*, he stops avoiding the truth, quits deceiving himself, and starts living in reality."[10] And the Holy Spirit is the power behind the reality. He'll move us forward in God's freedom. Healthy sexual response is learned as God's truth seeps into the soul and takes root.

APPLY If negative or fearful thoughts about sex are a roadblock for you, what effect are they having on your sexual intimacy with your husband?

_____

_____

_____

What personal insight is God giving you into removing this roadblock?

_____

_____

_____

Read 1 John 1:9 and Zephaniah 3:14–17. Today, many Christian women have *a history of premarital or extramarital sexual sin* that has set up a roadblock of guilt and shame. In the book *Intimate Issues*, Lorraine Pintus recounts a conversation with a troubled young woman, asking her, "Do you believe sex with your husband can be exciting and wonderful, but don't give yourself permission to enjoy it because you feel guilty about things you did in the past?"[11] Many of us could answer "Yes" to that question. Many of us still have lingering shame over our sexual sin—feeling unworthy of the white gowns worn at our weddings; disappointed that the wedding night was "business as usual"; angry with our husbands and ourselves for ignoring God's standard; kicking ourselves for even *thinking* about another man and then risking our marriage for the exhilaration of his attention. And so, we **won't** give ourselves permission to enjoy sex with our husbands. But God's grace woos us into the arms of our Savior so that we can become whiter than our wedding gowns, purer than our wedding nights.

Lorraine has a wonderful, cleansing analogy for our sexual sin. She explains that

> cleansing ourselves from past sexual sin is much like taking a shower. First we get rid of the old, like we remove dirty clothes before showering. Next we step under the water and allow God's forgiveness to pour over us and wash our past down the drain. Finally, we put on new, clean garments, which the Bible calls clothing ourselves in the righteousness of Christ (2 Corinthians 5:21; Galatians 3:27).[12]

What a beautiful word picture! I tell you truthfully—it works. Guilt from premarital sexual sin affected me for years. It was hidden in the depths of my soul, and I knew I wouldn't be free to truly enjoy my husband sexually until *I permitted* God's forgiveness to pour all over me, cleanse me, wash my past away, and make me *"holy in his sight, without blemish and free from accusation"* (Colossians 1:22, NIV). For me, a shower is a frequent reminder of God's grace.

Healthy sexual response is learned as God's truth seeps into the soul and takes root.

"The Lord your God is in your midst, a victorious warrior. He will exult over you with you, He will be quiet in His love, He will rejoice over you with shouts of joy."

Zephaniah 3:17

APPLY If premarital or extramarital sin is a roadblock for you, what effect is it having on your ability to enjoy sex?

_____

_____

_____

Have you renounced past sexual activity, receiving God's forgiveness? If not, why not do so now? What personal insight is God giving you into removing this roadblock?

_____

_____

_____

📖 Read Isaiah 61:1–3 and Luke 4:17–21. Another potential roadblock to our sexual fulfillment is past *sexual abuse or violation*. In her book *Romancing Your Husband*, Debra White Smith, a victim of sexual abuse, advises that the "deeper the heart is wounded, the deeper the love of God must go." She continues:

> Allow God's love to plunge to the depths of your sorrow. Don't hold Him at arm's length. Begin the healing process. . . . I'm living proof that God wants to heal and is eager to heal all those who *will ask* and *take the time to embrace the healing*. You don't have to stay a prisoner of the past. You can stand victorious in Christ—a new creature empowered to impact your world, your marriage, and your household for the Lord. Your husband needs you to be his lover. You cannot fully meet that need until you recover from the past. Let the recovery begin today.[13]

APPLY If past sexual abuse or violation is a roadblock for you, what effect is it having on your ability to freely respond to your husband?

_____

_____

_____

How are you moving forward toward healing? How is your husband a part of your healing process?

_____

_____

_____

📖 Read Proverbs 25:11 and Ephesians 4:15, 25. *Poor communication* is one of the biggest boulders blocking the road. Shay Roop asserts, "The worst enemy of good sex is silence."[14] If you don't speak up about your desires, your concerns, your fears, and what does and doesn't make you more open to sex, and if you're unwilling to receive the same information from your husband, then your sex life will remain stagnant. Perhaps your husband doesn't even know he's doing something you find annoying. He might think it's pleasurable, perhaps because it once was. But if you haven't *told* him that your preferences have changed, then it's likely he doesn't know. He'll continue doing the same things, and you'll continue being annoyed. How fun is that? If you ask Him,

> "The worst enemy of good sex is silence."
> —Dr. Shay Roop

the Lord will create moments that allow communication to be natural, simple, and positive. Communicating a desire may be as simple as gently placing your husband's hand elsewhere during lovemaking. In some cases, you might not have to tell him what you don't like but what you *would* like, keeping the atmosphere light and positive. I know how deeply a husband can be hurt when an approach is insensitive. It assaults him as a lover. Communicating with kindness is key.

APPLY If communicating about sex is a roadblock for you, what's keeping you from opening up? What effect is silence having on your sex life?

_____

_____

_____

What would you like your husband to know about your sexual relationship that you've been afraid to communicate? Write it here. Will you ask God to show you *when* and *how* to communicate it?

_____

_____

_____

Read Song of Solomon 4:16 and 5:1. Having *difficulty reaching orgasm* can thwart healthy sexual fulfillment. One physiological factor that can hinder a person from reaching orgasm is low levels of estrogen or testosterone. Getting your levels checked by your doctor is a good first step to resolving this difficulty. Another factor is too little stimulation during foreplay. Dr. Roop says,

> If I had to identify one problem for which I counsel couples the most, it's this: *Not allowing enough time in foreplay for the female to become truly aroused and enter into the excitement phase.* Most women whom I have seen require at least fifteen to forty minutes of foreplay before they are fully aroused. When a woman is rushed, she is less likely to have an orgasm…There is a direct correlation between how long a couple spends in foreplay and how frequently a woman has an orgasm. There is also a direct correlation between how frequently a woman reaches orgasm and how sexually satisfied she reports that she is.[15]

Communicate Shay's comments regarding foreplay to your husband. Learn to take the time to love each other more deliberately. This will greatly enhance your potential for orgasm. However, we can become preoccupied, even obsessed, with making orgasm the goal of lovemaking. If we make *oneness* the goal, focusing on our soul connection with our husbands, we can get past the pressure and into the pleasure of our union.

There's another saboteur to achieving orgasm. Check any medications you're on to see how they may affect your sexual responsiveness. Dr. Roop explains: "Antidepressants, blood pressure medication, tranquilizers, narcotics, and even anticholesterol agents can cause low desire, arousal difficulties, diminished genital sensitivity, and can hinder orgasm."[16] Talk with your doctor. There are often ways to diminish the negative effect of medications on your libido, such as adjusting both the timing and dosage.

Read for knowledge about your body and its sexual response. Dr. Roop's book leaves no stone unturned. Make your research an adventure with your husband!

APPLY What fresh perspective can you have on reaching orgasm? How can this perspective affect your attitude about sex in general?

_____

_____

_____

What can you do to enhance your orgasmic response? How will you include your husband in this process?

_____

_____

_____

📖 Read Matthew 5:27–28; Colossians 3:1–5; and 1 Thessalonians 4:7. *Inappropriate fantasizing* (usually about someone else) or *use of pornography* is a roadblock that interferes with loving our husbands openly and freely. Even though "mental movies" may be used to stimulate sexual feelings toward our husbands, these images are a form of mental adultery since they invite another into our sexual experience. Pornography also fits into this category, whether viewed or read. Today's best-selling novels can be "porn on a page." They fill our minds with questions like "Why doesn't my husband make me feel like that?" "What's wrong with him?" "What's wrong with *me?*" Beth Moore maintains that couples

> who are physically monogamous may be far from emotionally and mentally monogamous. . . . Alarming numbers of believing couples have unhealthy marriages because sexual perversion and pornography entered the home under the guise of "spicing things up." *God* can spice things up. And His choice of spice brings edification, healing, and the kind of romance that lasts.[17]

The antidotes to this roadblock are repentance, and renewing our minds by praising and thanking God for our husbands. Set your sights on your man alone **every day,** and ask God to spice things up with healthy fantasy.

If your husband is addicted to pornography, spend your energy in prayer for him rather than on anger or worry. Become well informed about this addiction so that you'll understand how to help him. Please fight the temptation to reject him sexually, remembering that your husband is not the enemy. The Enemy is the enemy, and his goal is to separate you. Steve Arterburn and Fred Stoeker, authors of *Every Man's Battle,* lend insight: "Though you know you should pray for [your husband] and fulfill him sexually, sometimes you won't want to. Talk to each other openly and honestly, then do the right thing."[18] Remaining lovingly committed and sexually connected will strengthen your bond and weaken the Enemy's hold. Read biblically-based books on this topic, and pray about finding a biblically-grounded Christian sister who can share this burden with you in confidence, pray with you, and help you stay accountable for your behavior toward your husband. Don't give up. Persevere, wait patiently, and believe that you'll see the goodness of the Lord in this situation (see Psalm 27:13–14).

Today's best-selling novels can be "porn on a page." They fill our minds with questions like: "Why doesn't my husband make me feel like that? What's wrong with him? What's wrong with me?"

APPLY If inappropriate fantasizing or pornography is a roadblock for you, what effect is it having on your sexual response? How do you feel after you use improper fantasy or pornography?

_____

_____

_____

What personal insight is God giving you into removing this roadblock from your life or addressing it in your husband's?

_____

_____

_____

Read Jeremiah 17:14 and Galatians 6:2. Making love when you or your mate has a _health problem or physical disability_ can be a painful physical and emotional roadblock. Such problems can include effects from a physical injury, debilitating arthritis, effects from long- and short-term illnesses, age-related health issues such as menopause or sexual dysfunction, and so on. With the right information and proper communication, health challenges can draw a couple closer than ever. It is wise to be lovingly proactive about researching and confronting the difficulty, preferably together. Dr. Roop's book covers this topic well.

APPLY If a health problem or physical disability is a roadblock for you or your husband, how is it affecting your sexual intimacy?

_____

_____

_____

How can you and your husband address this problem?

_____

_____

_____

 If you've identified any of the roadblocks as your own, go back to each one now and ask God to show you His will. Trust Him with your whole heart as He directs your path. Confess where necessary, receiving His forgiveness. Fix your eyes on Him, and wait on His timing with praise and thanksgiving. Respond to His counsel with faithful obedience, and watch Him work.

Our Sexuality: God's
Ultimate Wedding Gift
DAY FOUR

COMMON OBSTACLES ALONG THE WAY

Major roadblocks such as those covered in Day Three can deaden or halt sexual response (even though we may engage in the "act" of sex) and thwart sexual fulfillment. There are less traumatic, more commonly experienced obstacles that can hinder sexual enrichment. We'll use the same approach to today's lesson as we used on Day Three.

☞ Read each scripture reference carefully for insight into an obstacle.

☞ Approach each obstacle prayerfully and purposefully.

☞ Acknowledge the obstacles that interfere with your sex life.

☞ Record the effect that the identified obstacles have on you.

☞ Record any personal insight that the Lord gives you into addressing each obstacle.

📖 Read Romans 15:7; Matthew 10:29–31; Ephesians 2:10. A hindrance to our sexual fulfillment can be *negative thoughts about ourselves*. If we've spent a portion of our lifetime feeling unworthy, unacceptable, or unattractive, where did this message come from? The world pushes its criteria for acceptance with every magazine we read and every television program we watch. It poisons the truth of God with the lie that unless we're beautiful, popular, skinny, and buff, there's something wrong with us. Preoccupation with our feelings, our body, ourselves is the Enemy's perfect ploy that keeps us from surrendering totally to our heavenly Bridegroom. This preoccupation can also keep us from surrendering totally to our earthly bridegroom. When we understand who we are in Christ and what we're really worth to Him, we can offer it all back to Him daily for His use in our relationships. The New Testament describes believers as salt of the earth (Matthew 5:13), light of the world (Matthew 5:14), friends of Christ (John 15:15), temples of God in whom the Holy Spirit dwells (1 Corinthians 3:16), and so much more. Begin to look for and embrace God's descriptions of you as you read His Word daily. We're children of the King, precious enough for God to keep a running tab of the numbers of hairs on our head.

🛑 APPLY If negative thoughts about yourself are an obstacle, what effect are they having on your ability to respond to your husband sexually?

_____

_____

_____

What personal insight is God giving you into removing this obstacle?

_____

_____

_____

📖 Read Ephesians 6:1–3. It's tough for us moms to admit, but we can permit our *children* to hinder our intimate interludes with Dad. We can be so sensitized to our children's presence in the home or to the proximity of their delicate ears that our distraction level is off the charts! The message we may send to their fathers is that the kids' antennas have priority over their parents. It's necessary to teach our children early in life to respect the high value we place on our marriage and that our "quiet time" is precious together and needed. When our girls were little, John and I took quiet times when they were down for naps. As they got older, we taught them not to interrupt when our bedroom door was closed but to honor our privacy. (Emergencies were the only exception!) We had a lock on our bedroom door, and we used it. This sent a necessary message to our children over the years that continued to take shape as we modeled the traits of a strong marriage relationship. As teens, they got over the embarrassment of Mom and Dad "disappearing." And as adults, they now have a deep

Preoccupation with our feelings, our body, ourselves is the Enemy's perfect ploy that keeps us from surrendering totally to our heavenly Bridegroom. This preoccupation can also keep us from surrendering totally to our earthly bridegroom.

"Children obey your parents in the Lord, for this is right."

Ephesians 6:1

respect and appreciation for married sex and a healthy attitude about it. They were "trained up" for their own marriages, and we were building and strengthening ours for the empty-nest years.

APPLY Are you permitting your children to hinder your sex life? What effect is this having on your sexual intimacy? What is your husband's opinion on the topic?

_____

_____

What personal insight is God giving you into addressing this obstacle to your "quiet times"?

_____

_____

_____

📖 Read James 4:13–17. If we're *too busy or too tired* to think about sex, it's surely not going to make it on our list of things to do. But our husbands still think about it—more often than we realize. We can fill up our schedules, run ourselves ragged with the kids, and have nothing left for our men. Praying about and prioritizing how and where God wants us to spend our time is critical to making time for our husbands. Praying about our children's activities is as critical, since after-school and weekend activities can consume huge chunks of time and wear out the whole family. A meaning in Christian circles for the acronym BUSY is "Being Under Satan's Yoke." Our husbands need time with us. And many of them are willing to do what is necessary in the home and with the kids to help their wives create that time. (No, it's not intuitive to most husbands when we need help. So *ask* yours.) *We* need time with them too. We may simply be too busy or too tired to notice.

A meaning in Christian circles for the acronym BUSY is "Being Under Satan's Yoke."

APPLY If busyness and fatigue are obstacles, what effect are they having on your sex life?

_____

_____

_____

Consider those things that demand your time. Are you truly called to them, or are you doing them for the wrong reasons? Prayer is key to reducing busyness, stress, and associated fatigue. It will show you how to prioritize the essentials and eliminate the nonessentials. It's important to know where you belong and why. It's just as important to know where you *don't* belong and why. What personal insight is God giving you into your busyness and fatigue?

_____

_____

_____

📖 Read Colossians 3:9–10. *Feigning orgasm* keeps us from enjoying genuine sexual response and disrupts mutual sexual fulfillment, because it deceives our husbands, keeps us keyed-up, and sabotages our growth as a sexual couple. However, this "little secret" isn't hidden. God knows, and perhaps so do our husbands. Our sexual relationship must be built on honesty. Linda Dillow talks about Mona, who was caught up in this deception: "Finally, she got up her nerve and told her husband that while she enjoyed the warmth of lovemaking, she'd never had an orgasm—and she wanted to learn. Together they read books, prayed, and went on a treasure hunt of discovery."[19] The more honest we are with our men, the freer we'll be to "let go" and enjoy all the sensations of lovemaking.

If, however, you generally reach orgasm when you make love, yet feign orgasm occasionally because you're distracted by kids, or things to do, or the time it takes to reach orgasm, it's still a deception. And it can become your habit. Confess it to the Lord and ask Him to help you become *fully* engaged in your sexual intimacy. *Nothing* is more important at that moment in time. Take your distracting thoughts captive and make them obedient to Christ (2 Corinthians 10:5). This is a great exercise in mental discipline. And both you and your husband will reap the benefits.

 If feigning orgasm is an obstacle, what effect is it having on your sex life?

_____

_____

_____

What personal insight is God giving you into removing this obstacle?

_____

_____

_____

Ponder what the Lord has shown you today. Lift up every obstacle you've acknowledged, and pray that each would be replaced with the response that would honor your husband and glorify Him. He will lovingly guide you toward His holiness in each area. Embrace the initiative, by the grace and power of God, to do what He calls you to do. Trust that you can rely on the Holy Spirit to begin to effect change where change is needed.

ON THE ROAD TO SEXUAL FULFILLMENT

Our Sexuality: God's Ultimate Wedding Gift
DAY FIVE

There's more to having a fulfilling sex life than saying, "God ordains it." God designed a man and a woman's body, inside and out, to be the perfect "fit" for sexual fulfillment.

Read Psalm 139:14. What does this scripture say about our bodies? How can this verse apply to the design and function of our sexual selves?

_____

_____

_____

_____

> *"I praise you because I am fearfully and wonderfully made; your works are wonderful, I know that full well."*
>
> **Psalm 139:14 (NIV)**

God designed many intricacies into our bodies that accommodate, enhance, and electrify the sex act. There are excellent Christian resources on the topic, such as Shay Roop's *For Women Only: God's Design for Female Sexuality & Intimacy* and Douglas E. Rosenau's *A Celebration of Sex*. Please make the time to "read up" and get to know your body and your husband's body better.

I want to share two facts that had a huge impact on how I viewed my sexuality:

Fact #1: A woman's body is designed by God to enjoy sex. Did you know that the *only* function of the clitoris—that little nub at the base of your pubic bone just above your urethra and vagina—is to receive and transmit pleasurable sexual stimuli? When gently and properly stimulated, the woman's entire body is programmed to respond.

Fact #2: The human body is designed by God to go from arousal to orgasm automatically. It is a *reflex response*, like our heartbeats, eyeblinks, and breathing. When our brain perceives sexual stimuli—something we see, hear, smell, touch, taste—arousal is the involuntary response. As a matter of fact, our bodies can physiologically respond to arousal before we're emotionally awakened to the *feeling* of arousal. Our vaginas begin to lubricate "within the first minute or two of arousal."[20] This fact should have a significant impact on our sexual psyche, because it reveals to us that if we stop "trying" to reach orgasm, orgasm will be easier to reach. If we relax and pay attention to our bodies and enjoy the physiological sensations that they naturally produce during *unrushed* foreplay and intercourse, the natural (orgasm) is more likely to happen.

 What do these two facts say *to you* about God's intent for a woman's sexual experience?

_____

_____

Can this knowledge change your response to lovemaking? In what ways?

_____

_____

Despite all those wonderful organs that churn out the right stuff to prepare our bodies for sexual intercourse, one organ can thwart the mission: the *brain*. It can take us down the right road with glorious imaginings and creative fantasies about our husbands, or it can head us down the wrong road with thoughts like *We just did it last Tuesday. I can't believe he wants to do it again* or *Why do I have to subject myself to this? I'm still not going to have an orgasm.* We must "Philippians 4:8" those thoughts! Our brains will sabotage us every time we let them, leaving us unfulfilled emotionally *and* physically, despite our husbands' loving efforts. Disciplining our thinking before and during sex, and focusing instead on the pleasurable sensations God designed into the sex act, will help us reject negative attitudes and self-talk, outside distractions, and unrelated mental meanderings (2 Corinthians 10:5).

 What thoughts tend to distract you before and during sexual intimacy? Do you entertain them? If they're not thoughts that edify your sexual experience, what will you replace them with?

_____

_____

Good sex is a matter of getting out of your brain and into your body—feeling those sensations deep in the pit of your abdomen; feeling your husband's hands on your body as if you had never felt them before; being aware of each other's bodies; feeling skin on skin; being aware of the sensations in your genitalia—sensations that have been deadened by busyness, complacency, or the disbelief that nothing about your sexual response can change. **Choose** to feel. Ask God to help you discover or rediscover your sexual self and to reawaken your heart and soul to your husband's sexuality. Desire to please your husband. And permit yourself to be pleased by him. If necessary, lovingly speak up about your need for longer foreplay or different foreplay. Most important, *enjoy* your two bodies becoming one—again and again and again. Linda Dillow says, "If you have not experienced an orgasm, or do so rarely, release this as the ultimate goal of your sexual union. Instead, love your husband and enjoy learning what pleases you sexually. God will take care of the results!"[21] Amen.

 Finally, fix your thoughts on your husband *as your lover*. How does Shulamith do this in Song of Solomon 5:10–16; 6:2–3? What similarity do you see between this passage and Song of Solomon 4:1–5, which we looked at on Day One?

_____

_____

_____

Shulamith praised her husband in the same way he praised her in chapter 4. Keeping our husbands alive in our hearts and minds will enhance every aspect of our marital relationship, most notably our sexual response.

 In what ways do you keep your husband alive in your heart and mind throughout the day? What specific attributes of his can you focus on?

_____

_____

_____

Begin to thank and praise God for the splendor He designed into lovemaking. Thank Him for your husband as your partner in sexual intimacy, and ask Him to show you how to rediscover him sexually all over again; to give you the courage to explore his body; to touch him and taste him; to enjoy his responses and permit them to excite you. Ask Him to reawaken and heighten your sexual sensations; to give you the courage to permit *yourself* to move freely, breathe freely, verbalize freely while in your husband's embrace; to help you stop "trying" to have an orgasm but to help you fully engage in the experience of oneness with your husband—loving him, enjoying him, pleasing him, all the while letting your body be loved by him, enjoyed by him, pleased by him; to let your body *go* and do what it was designed to do—*respond*! Ask Him. I did.

In Lesson 9 we'll discover how the beauty of romance can enhance every aspect of your relationship.

The Marriage Dance

In the dance of marital love,
Intimate bonds of covenant are forged
Deep and strong before God.
Vows are not to be broken.

A sacred seal is impressed on two hearts,
Binding them together as one
Till death doth part.

From the beginning,
God's special plan for husband and wife.
A marriage consummated
By both body and soul as spirits unite.

Bone of my bones
Flesh of my flesh.
They are naked and unashamed
As God intends.
Two hearts beating as one.
A passionate embrace
Without guilt,
Without shame.

This is the dance to be cherished.
Each lover's thought is for the other's pleasure;
Their bodies no longer their own
As the music begins.

A gentle caress
Hands intertwined
A taste like sweet wine
Is the kiss of tenderness.
Love is given, love is received.
Hearts overflow with the joy of fulfillment.

Love has been shared.
Their marriage bed is deemed sacred
By God Most High,
And undefiled.

This couple is simply blessed!
They bask in the freedom of being fully known,
Accepted and treasured.

Completeness floods their hearts
Prompting them to pray.
They give thanks to God.

Floating on a sigh of contentment,
They drift to sleep with a whispered "I love you"
As the curtain closes.

Their Heavenly Father is pleased.

True love, so beautifully expressed, will continue
As they dance yet again and again…

Works Cited

1. Spiros Zodhiates, Warren Baker, eds., *The Complete Word Study Old Testament* (Chattanooga, Tenn: AMG Publishers, 1994), #954, 2304.

2. Paula Rinehart, *Strong Women, Soft Hearts* (Nashville: W Publishing Group, 2001), 128-129.

3. Zodhiates, Baker, *The Complete Word Study Old Testament*, 8.

4. This is the name ascribed to Solomon's feminine counterpart in Ed Wheat and Gloria Oaks Perkin's book *Love Life for Every Married Couple* (Grand Rapids: Zondervan Publishing House, 1980), 210.

5. Tommy Nelson, *The Book of Romance* (Nashville: Thomas Nelson Publishers, 1998), 100.

6. Willard Harley, *His Needs, Her Needs* (Grand Rapids: Fleming H. Revell, 1994), 12-13.

7. Ibid., 43.

8. John Eldridge, *Wild at Heart* (Nashville: Thomas Nelson Publishers, 2001), 62.

9. Rinehart, *Strong Women, Soft Hearts*, 136.

10. Quoted in Wheat and Perkins, *Love Life for Every Married Couple*, 333.

11. Linda Dillow and Lorraine Pintus, *Intimate Issues* (Colorado Springs: WaterBrook Press, 1999), 82.

12. Ibid., 82-83.

13. Debra White Smith, *Romancing Your Husband* (Eugene, OR: Harvest House Publishers, 2002), 234.

14. Shay Roop, *For Women Only: God's Design for Female Sexuality & Intimacy* (Chattanooga, TN: AMG Publishers/Living Ink Books, 2004), 171.

15. Ibid., 78

16. Ibid., 131.

17. Beth Moore, *Praying God's Word* (Nashville: Broadman and Holman Publishers, 2000), 274.

18. Stephen Arterburn and Fred Stoeker, *Every Man's Battle* (Colorado Springs: Water Brook Press), 35.

19. Dillow and Pintus, *Intimate Issues,* 193.

20. Douglas E. Rosenau, *A Celebration of Sex* (Nashville: Thomas Nelson Publishers, 1994), 50.

21. Linda Dillow, *Creative Counterpart* (Nashville: Thomas Nelson Publishers, 1986), 187.

9

Let the Romance Begin

God knows what it's like to woo someone, to win over a heart, to stir a fire that leads to an all-consuming communion with Himself. That's how He won us. He knows how to pursue us, and, when He captures our hearts, His love is sublime. And we keep this loving relationship alive by fervently pursuing Him and reciprocating His blessings upon us by showering Him with our love, honor, gratitude, and time. Are you getting a picture of what earthly romance can be like?

If we're not experiencing this dynamic of romantic love with our husbands, we're missing a key element of enjoyment in the continual, relationship-building process. Romancing our husbands requires us to engage our hearts, to practice our commitment in fun and unique ways. To do so revitalizes us toward them and vice-versa.

In the next five days, let God show you how to build romance in your marriage, to stir in your husband what He stirs in you.

RETURNING TO "FIRST LOVE"

Think back to when you first met your husband. Take a few minutes to probe that part of your history—the very beginning of your relationship. Do you remember when you first laid eyes on him? Do you remember what attracted you to him, the feelings that stirred you when his face popped into your mind? Or when he first held your hand? What was it about him that made you feel giddy and weak all over? Do you remember pulling his picture from your wallet and talking about him to your friends? Can you perceive the light in your own eyes and hear the lilt in your voice? And what about the letters you wrote and the cards you sent? Do you remember what you wrote and how you expressed it? Do you remember?

It wouldn't be healthy to live "back there," but it is healthy to revisit the beginning every so often, just to see how our love has evolved over the years and to take stock of where it appears to be headed.

📖 Jesus charged His bride to assess her love for Him when He addressed the Ephesian church. Read Revelation 2:1–5. Why did Jesus commend the Ephesian Christians? What good were they doing, and for what purpose (verses 2–3)?

_____

_____

_____

Why were their works, their patience, even their intolerance for evil and false prophets not good enough? What did Jesus say was missing (verse 4)?

_____

_____

_____

What do you think Jesus meant when He said the church had left or abandoned its "first love"?

_____

_____

"First love" is betrothal love—the love of Christ and the Church, and the love of a man and a woman—that compels lifelong commitment. It is simple, pure, and passionate. Jesus admonished the believers of Ephesus about abandoning their love for Him, permitting religious convention to take His place. The church was dead to its former, first-love passion for Christ, and all that they did for His name's sake was no substitute for loving Him intimately. "It had become like a loveless marriage, with all the routine but none of the romance."

First love leads a man and woman to their wedding day. If they're not diligent about keeping the marriage fire stoked, the flames will slowly die out, just like the heart embers of the Ephesian believers. My guess is that the church wasn't even aware that their love for Christ had grown cold.

> "Yet I hold this against you: You have forsaken your first love."
>
> **Revelation 2:4 (NIV)**

> "First love" is betrothal love—the love of Christ and the Church, and the love of a man and a woman—that compels lifelong commitment. It is simple, pure, and passionate.

As Christians, we may be doing all the right things, but if Jesus took our spiritual temperature, what would it read? And as wives, we may be pretty good at doing all the "wifely" things, but if our husbands measured our heat index, would it read "flame" or "flicker"? Like the Church in Ephesus, we might not even be aware that the flame of our first love is dim or almost out.

In order to return to the first love relationship, Jesus told the church to do three things. What were they (verse 5)?

_____

_____

What would happen if they didn't repent?

_____

_____

Jesus called the Ephesians to *remember*, *repent*, and *return*. And if they chose not to repent, He would come back to judge them, removing their testimony.

At the point of salvation, Jesus raises up all new believers to a heavenly place in Himself (Ephesians 2:6). We're alive with new vision, new motivation to love and serve our Savior. What insight does this give you into Jesus' command that the Ephesians remember the height from which they had fallen?

_____

_____

_____

How can repentance and returning rekindle the Ephesians' love for their Savior?

_____

_____

_____

APPLY Now apply the scriptural example of the Ephesians' relationship with Christ from two perspectives: (1) your own relationship with Jesus Christ and (2) your relationship with your husband. Compare the two, noting the similarities of how they began, where they are now, and where they're going. Place your husband's name in each blank space.

My Relationship with Jesus: Do you remember when you first met Jesus? Describe how you felt about Him.

_____

_____

_____

My Relationship with _____: Do you remember when you first met your husband? Describe how you felt about him.

_____

_____

_____

In Their Shoes
RESURRECTION

Read Ephesians 1:18–21 and 2:4–7. Compare Christ's experience after His resurrection with a believer's experience after his conversion. Where are we placed as a result of our salvation?

My Relationship with Jesus: If you know that your love for Christ is not what it used to be, if mediocrity has replaced your vibrant, first-love zeal for Him, what would you have to repent of and return to?

_____

_____

_____

My Relationship with _____: If your love for your husband is not what it used to be, if mediocrity has replaced your vibrant, first-love zeal for him, what would you have to repent of and return to?

_____

_____

_____

From your first-love experience until now, in what ways does your relationship with Jesus Christ compare to your relationship with your husband?

_____

_____

_____

Remember + Repent + Return = Rekindled Romance
If we pour ourselves into our relationship with Jesus Christ (Mark 12:30), it remains strong and vibrant, and we'll always have a testimony. To seek Him, worship Him, praise Him, read His love letters—His Word—and enjoy intimacy with Him in prayer is to be in a romantic relationship with our Savior. Our love relationship with Him sets the stage for romancing our husbands.

 If you see a chasm between your betrothal love and your current love for your Savior and your husband, you can fix that right now. The formula Christ gave in Revelation 2 is His perfect combination for reviving your romance with Him and with your man. You need only _remember_ how far you have fallen and acknowledge this to Him. Then _repent_ from whatever has taken the place of your first love. (Is it "busyness," children, ministry, weariness, or apathy?) Next, _return_ to the things you used to do so that our gracious Savior can _revive_ newness in your soul for Him. When you ask, He will ignite newness in your heart for your husband. Let the _romance_ begin.

> **If we pour ourselves into our relationship with Jesus Christ (Mark 12:30), it remains strong and vibrant, and we'll always have a testimony.**

Let the Romance Begin

DAY TWO

THE OBJECT OF MY LOVE

When God blessed the first couple and commanded them to be fruitful, multiply, and fill the earth (Genesis 1:28), He supplied a healthy number of sexual hotspots on and in the human body that He intended us to delight in, both as giver and receiver. Since these hotspots are not in a constant state of "burn," God provided the right kind of loving that prepares the heart, mind, and body for lovemaking. It's called romantic love, or _romance,_ and God designed it into a relationship to ignite the flame of our sexual response.

What is your concept of romance or romantic love? What does it mean to you?

_____

_____

_____

Look up the word "romance" in your dictionary. (You may be surprised at what you find!) Define it here.

_____

_____

_____

I was surprised to discover that "romance" is primarily defined as a medieval tale or story of a chivalrous hero involved in an extraordinary adventure. We might think of fairy tales, or the Knights of the Roundtable in King Arthur's court. Over time, the word evolved to mean a love affair. When we met our husbands, *our* extraordinary adventure began. Has anyone ever asked you how you and your husband met? Did you tell them your story? Was yours a "fairy tale romance?" Was the hero chivalrous? Was he your knight in shining armor? Even retelling the story is fun, energizing, and uplifting. We remember that our romantic adventure solidified our feelings toward the other and drove us to the altar. And the flame of love burned brightly—until at some point in time on the other side of the altar, the fairy tale romance collided with the realities of life and became overshadowed by higher priorities.

Clearly, there's not much of a romantic story to coming home dog-tired from our workplace to a pile of dirty dishes from the night before, madly shuffling kids to multiple events after school and on weekends, or bathing our chicken pox-covered youngster numerous times a day for *days*, trying to sooth her in her agony, only to have our next little one burst out all over. The often-harsh realities of our marital and parental responsibilities frequently distract us from the first love romance that brought us to this place. This is why we must breathe romantic love back into our marriages, to do the things we did at first.

We all need a regular dose of good, healthy, imaginative adventure in our marriages, because:

☞ Romance inclines our hearts toward each other, setting the stage for emotional intimacy.

☞ Romance energizes us toward lovemaking, adding more fun and spark to the mix.

☞ Romance stimulates creativity, keeping the marriage lively so that apathy doesn't set in.

☞ Romance pours a sense of well-being into the relationship, causing us to fall in love over and over again with the same person.

None of us is born romantic. But perhaps because women are the more relational of the two sexes, romance comes more naturally to us. A man's nature tends to be more practical and less relational. Men work hard to win their mates, drawing from whatever reservoir will accomplish the mission. Romantically speaking, the pre-engagement period may be their finest hour, for we then marry our "heroes," who have proven their chivalrous devotion. Their trophy is won and wedded, and then they move on to the next mission. Many a wife wonders what happened, and months to years later she's still waiting to be romanced. The husband's way is not wrong—it's just different. But when neither spouse does anything to keep the embers

The flame of love burned brightly— until at some point in time on the other side of the altar, the fairy tale romance collided with the realities of life and became overshadowed by higher priorities.

of romantic love burning, they begin to fall from the heights of their first love into the depths of complacency, boredom, and for some, indifference.

There's good news for women whose marriages are romantically challenged.

There's good news for women whose marriages are romantically challenged. Romance is learned, and for many of us wives who may be out of practice, *relearned*, only this time with maturity and solid biblical principles as the foundation. And what about our men? Who's going to teach them? *We'll* teach them—by doing.

📖 There is no better illustration of romantic love than in the Song of Solomon. In Lesson 8, we saw Solomon and his new wife (we're calling her Shulamith[2]) abandoned to their sexual passion on their wedding day. Let's look at the romance that led to this surrender. Read Song of Solomon 1:1—3:5. Shulamith does most of the talking. She has an active imagination about her husband-to-be. What does she reveal about the man she loves?

_____

_____

_____

Shulamith's thoughts were full of good things about Solomon. Even when she spoke to the daughters of Jerusalem in chapters one and two, her honor was evident. And when her desire for him heightened, she declared her commitment to chastity until her wedding day (Song of Solomon 2:7), after which all barriers would be removed. John MacArthur comments, "This refrain [in 2:7], which is repeated before the wedding (3:5) and also afterward (8:4), explicitly expresses her commitment to a chaste life before and during marriage. She invites accountability to the daughters of Jerusalem."[3]

🛑 **APPLY** Were your thoughts toward your husband and your words about him similar to Shulamith's or different? In what ways?

_____

_____

_____

_____

📖 On their wedding day, Solomon praises his wife from her head down (Song of Solomon 4:1–7). After their wedding day, Shulamith lauds her husband in the same way (5:10–16). Years later, Solomon continues praising his wife. Read Song of Solomon 7:1–9. What is unique about his praises this time?

_____

_____

_____

Solomon praised his wife's feet, and then worked his way up. Typically, feet aren't very attractive, and Shulamith's feet weren't among the specific features he praised earlier in Chapter 4. However, there's a tenderness, devotion, and beauty to his praise in Chapter 7, as if he were conveying to her that his love had continued to mature and gain depth over the years, well beyond her still-obvious beauty.

📖 Read Song of Solomon 7:10-13. How does Shulamith respond to her husband's "toe-to-head" praises?

_____

_____

_____

🛑 **APPLY** In what ways does your husband praise you? How do you respond to his praises? Do you receive them well? Do you return them? In what ways?

_____

_____

_____

📖 Read Song of Solomon 8:6–7. Think about married love. Shulamith uses metaphors to qualify their love. What do you think she's saying?

_____

_____

_____

Faithful commitment is Shulamith's theme. She desires to be an inner seal (of ownership) over Solomon's heart for his remembrance, and an outer seal of possession for all others to note (verse 6a). She declares love as irreversible as death (verse 6b), as intense and consuming as the flames of fire (verse 6c), unshakable in its perseverance through adversity (verse 7a), as priceless as the most valued possession (verse 7b). Shulamith declares fidelity, regardless of the cost.

📖 Compare Song of Solomon 2:16 (betrothal period) and 6:3 (newlyweds) with 7:10 ("oldie-weds"). How would you describe the progression of their love and commitment?

_____

_____

_____

📖 Finally, read Song of Solomon 8:10. What has Shulamith become to her husband over the years? How does this verse compare to Proverbs 5:18–19?

_____

_____

_____

After you've read these passages from this powerful book on married love, what would you conclude about how to keep first love alive in a marriage?

_____

_____

_____

Solomon and Shulamith kept their _hearts_ turned toward each other, elevating each other in their own thoughts. They spoke _of_ the other and _to_ the

> _"Place me like a seal over your heart, like a seal on your arm; for love is as strong as death, its jealousy unyielding as the grave. It burns like blazing fire, like a mighty flame. Many waters cannot quench love; rivers cannot wash it away. If one were to give all the wealth of his house for love, it would be utterly scorned."_
>
> **Song of Solomon 8:6 and 7 (NIV)**

other with genuine praise and gratitude. They generously displayed their affection. No wonder their passion was still alive. Their words and actions spoke *life* (Proverbs 10:11)!

APPLY Assess your romantic love quotient with the questions that follow:

Describe the last time your heart really "squeezed" when you looked at your man.

_____

_____

_____

What physical attributes attracted you to your husband in the beginning?

_____

_____

_____

What physical attributes attract you to him now?

_____

_____

_____

What character traits attracted you to him in the beginning?

_____

_____

_____

What character traits attract you to him now?

_____

_____

_____

Look at your husband through the eyes of another woman. What can she appreciate about his physical appearance? What can she admire about his character?

_____

_____

_____

Do you take your husband for granted? If so, in what ways?

_____

_____

_____

_____

How often do you tell your husband you love him? Why is it important to tell him often, even if he doesn't tell you as often? How do your actions back up your declaration of love?

_____

_____

_____

Is your husband more sentimental than you are, or less so? How do you know?

_____

_____

_____

In your early marriage, what were some of the ways you romanced your husband? What made your love thrilling, exciting, and emotionally intimate (not to be confused with sexual intimacy)? What are you doing *now* to add romance to your marriage? Be honest.

Romance Then (in Early Marriage)	Romance Now

In what ways has your romantic love gotten *stronger*? To what do you attribute that strengthening?

_____

_____

_____

In what ways has your romantic love gotten *weaker*? To what do you attribute the weakening?

_____

_____

_____

Do you believe that God's love in you can change the quality of your love for your husband? Do you think he would benefit from this change? If your answers to these questions are yes, your heart is open to God's teaching. Ask God to awaken and revitalize your desire to love your husband—to give you a sentimental, romantic, renewed, stimulating love for your husband. God will show you what to do and how to do it. And *"as a bridegroom rejoices over his bride, so will your God rejoice over you."* (Isaiah 62:5, NIV).

BUILDING ROMANCE—HOW DO I LOVE THEE?

The Song of Solomon instructs us well on how to keep our hearts and minds attentive to the object of our love. Shulamith thought about her husband, deliberately bringing him to mind. Her focus was on his good qualities, and over the years she found more good qualities. She gave voice to her love of him and to her desire for him. We'll continue to focus on scriptures from the Song of Solomon, as well as eight points that will help us develop this frame of mind, this attitude of romantic *thinking* that lays the foundation for *doing* the things of romance.

📖 Read Song of Solomon 5:10–16. Shulamith says Solomon is beyond rival. There's no other like him. And she's not afraid to express exactly what he means to her. Like Shulamith, build your husband up in your thoughts. See him as "the best," and be quick to tell others.

"My lover is dazzling and ruddy, outstanding among ten thousand."

Song of Solomon 5:10

What does your husband mean to you? Express it here, remembering that God will build on what you give Him.

_____

_____

_____

_____

📖 Read Song of Solomon 5:9. Don't criticize your husband in your own mind or with your mouth. And don't permit others (parents, in-laws, children, friends, coworkers) to criticize him. This builds trust in your marriage, and that's a wonderful foundation for romance.

Who tends to criticize your husband? How will you influence this behavior?

_____

_____

_____

_____

📖 Read Song of Solomon 6:3; 8:6–7. Be unswervingly devoted to your man, making him your top priority.

How do you convey your devotion to your husband? How does he know that he's top priority for you, second only to Jesus Christ?

_____

_____

_____

_____

📖 Read Song of Solomon 2:4. Desire your husband's banner of love and protection over you. This speaks that he's still your hero, your knight in shining armor.

How do you convey to your husband that his love and protection are important to you?

_____

_____

_____

📖 Read Song of Solomon 2:15. Be willing to resolve areas of contention or conflict when they occur so that they don't ruin the vineyards of your love.

What unresolved issues may be influencing your romantic response to your husband? What action are you taking to resolve them?

_____

_____

_____

📖 Read Song of Solomon 3:6–11. Develop renewed appreciation for who your husband is and what he does. Express it to him daily. He'll love you for it!

What *do* you appreciate about your husband? How do or will you show him your gratitude?

_____

_____

_____

_____

📖 Read Song of Solomon 2:14; 4:9. Engage your eyes and ears when speaking with your husband. Let him see attentiveness and love in your eyes. Hold him with your gaze, and steal his heart!

How do you convey your interest in what your husband has to say?

_____

_____

_____

📖 Read Song of Solomon 1:5–7, 9–11; 2:1; 7:1–6. Look good for your man. Generally, men are visually oriented, so they'll notice when we look good *for them*. And so we should ask ourselves: "Do I look as good for my husband as I do for others, or do I greet him at the door in sweats and scary hair?" Freshly combed hair, a little lipstick, and a warm smile say a lot to a man. In today's age of health and fitness, we have everything we need to do the best we can with what God gave us. Whatever was attractive to your husband in your "beginning" can still be attractive to him now, even with a few more wrinkles and a few more pounds. But if weight is a constant battle, for your health and your wellbeing, fight the good fight! Judy and Arthur Halliday's book *Thin Within* is a great tool. Their focus is on "godly goal setting," which gives you a healthy, balanced approach to lasting weight loss.[4]

I want to mention another kind of beauty that goes beyond the physical. Early in their relationship, Shulamith seemed insecure about her sun-darkened skin (1:5–7). Her daily work in the vineyard caused her to neglect her own vineyard, her body. And yet Solomon thought she was altogether lovely (verses 1:9–11). Did you note how Solomon described her body later in their marriage (verse 7:2)? I visualize it as a little more "mature" with age. Solomon saw the perfect inner beauty of her love, which charmed and delighted him (verse 7:6). She was beautiful *to him* inside and out. Inner beauty with outer care is an appealing combination.

 Does your inner beauty match your outer care? What can you do in the short term to enhance your appearance? Write your answer here.

_____

_____

_____

What long-term goals have you been considering but just haven't started? Write them here. Stormie Omartian says, "Caring for our body is not something we can do successfully independent of God."[5] So make a plan with Him, and go for it! He'll happily guide your steps (Proverbs 16:9).

_____

_____

_____

 Ask God to help you view your man as the best. Renew your appreciation of him and increase your devotion to him. Willingly receive his banner of love and protection. Resolve conflict between you quickly. Defend your husband when he's criticized. Be attentive to him. Resurrect and bask in good memories. Honor your body in ways that honor your relationship with Him and with your husband. Then praise and thank God for the ability to do what's pleasing in His sight, and ask Him to build on it.

If we don't breathe new life into our romantic love every so often, it will fade away or disintegrate altogether.

BUILDING ROMANCE— LET ME COUNT THE WAYS

If we don't breathe new life into our romantic love every so often, it will fade away or disintegrate altogether. You may ask, "What about my husband's responsibility to romance *me*?" This is an excellent question. Don't we want to be the ones romanced? Isn't this the way it's supposed to be? But after the wedding day, men don't often differentiate romance and sex. We women see romance as a means through which to establish emotional intimacy, thereby preparing our hearts for the sexual experience. Men, on the other hand, find that *sex* prepares them for emotional intimacy. The ideals of romance we find essential often do not enter their picture. (Remember—we're different.) So what's a wife to do? She *becomes* the picture by modeling romance for him. As she makes her husband the object of her romantic love (Day Two) and is deliberate about how she conveys her love (Day Three), over time he'll get the picture. In today's discussion we're going to learn seven ways of romantic loving—what we can *do* to enhance a romantic experience.

📖 Read Song of Solomon 6:2–3; 8:14. *Think* romance! God gave us a powerful resource called "imagination," which can be used to stimulate and intensify romantic feelings toward our husbands if we put it to use. Think of a past romantic experience with your husband, and allow its memory to stir your feelings. Then let your imagination go as you think about and plan another romantic occasion. We can fantasize lavishly about our husbands and not have to confess!

What past experiences with your husband make you smile (or perhaps blush)? Write your favorites here. What feelings do they stir in you? How can you use imaginative fantasizing to build romantic love for your man?

_____

_____

_____

_____

📖 Read Song of Solomon 5:16. Create a positive, warm, emotional atmosphere between you and your husband that's consistent. We do this when we give him a warm send-off to work and a warm greeting upon return every day, slip an occasional love note into his pocket, briefcase or lunchbox, send a romantic greeting card or e-mail to his workplace, go for a walk together hand in hand, make his favorite meal, and so on. When this atmosphere between you is consistent, transition into romance is much easier for both of you.

What are you presently doing that warms the atmosphere between you, keeping you both in a state of readiness for romance?

_____

_____

_____

📖 Read Song of Solomon 1:16. Lovemaking takes place most often in the bedroom. Take a look at yours to see if it speaks rest and romantic recreation—or litter, laundry, and little ones. This room should speak "haven" to you and your husband.

What message does your bedroom send to you and your man? Is it a haven for two lovers or a holding tank for whatever doesn't have a place? What can you do to improve the atmosphere of your bedroom?

_____

_____

_____

📖 Read Song of Solomon 5:1. Reminisce with your husband. Warm recollections are powerful tools to apply to the present. Memories bring warmth to our hearts and a smile to our faces. They illuminate where we've been, where we are, and where we want to be and are useful for retooling a relationship. Romance is built on a foundation of pleasurable

"How handsome you are, my beloved, and so pleasant! Indeed, our couch is luxuriant!"

Song of Solomon 1:16

feelings and experiences and is sustained when we actively keep those feelings awakened by creating more memories of our lovemaking.

What memories can you reminisce about that will help to create emotional warmth between you and provide light moments of love and laughter? Focus on those that are exciting, fun, tender, or humorous. (Avoid those that would poke fun at your husband.)

_____

_____

📖 Read Song of Solomon 7:11–13. Fight boredom! Create romantic scenarios for you and your husband that lead to a much-anticipated sexual experience for both of you, such as a quiet dinner for two in front of the fireplace, a trail of rose petals to follow when he returns from work, an overnight away, or a pair of your pretty panties in his carryon when he travels, with a promise attached for his return. These little "jolts" will remind him that he's the object of your love. They'll also serve to recalibrate his attention toward you. So use your imagination, and be innovative! In *The Book of Romance*, Tommy Nelson explains that Shulamith "had some pleasures for [Solomon] both 'new and old.' She was still willing to experiment in the bedroom. She had some surprises remaining in her storehouse of creativity for Solomon."[6] He then exhorts wives to "never lose sight of the fact that you can still be even more creative in your lovemaking. Your husband will delight in the fantasies you create and the innovations you bring to sexual intimacy. Lay up some 'new treasures' for your husband to enjoy."[7] Our Creator gave us the capacity to love our husbands in this way. Pick His brain! (*Lord, show me . . .*)

Describe a past romantic scenario that you designed for you and your husband. What was fun about it? Did it enhance your sexual intimacy? In what way? How did your husband respond to it? What would you do differently?

_____

_____

_____

📖 Read Song of Solomon 8:1–3. Touch your husband every day—tenderly. If touching is foreign or uncomfortable for you (or for him), start with a gentle caress of your hand across his back as you pass by, or rest your hand on his shoulder as you lean over him. Kiss him goodbye in the morning and hello in the evening. Snuggle on the couch. Lay in his arms before getting out of bed in the morning. Hold hands as often as possible. Touching speaks the language of caring and oneness, and of possessing the object of one's love. It communicates affection. You might have to *think* about touching your guy if you're out of this habit (and it should be a habit). Be deliberate about making the opportunities. It will soon come naturally and pay big dividends.

How would you describe the physical display of affection (touching) in your relationship? Do you touch more or less than when you were first married? If less, why?

Memories bring warmth to our hearts and a smile to our faces. They illuminate where we've been, where we are, and where we want to be and are useful for retooling a relationship.

Touch your husband every day—tenderly.

_____

_____

_____

_____

_____

 Read Song of Solomon 7:10. Buy something uniquely lovely for yourself that's for his eyes only—something feminine that will make you both feel good. And check out your underwear. One evening John and I were dressing for a social function when I noticed that he was staring at me—intently. Since I was scantily dressed, I wasn't sure what effect I was having on him, so I asked, "What?" In his typical tender but firm style (from which instruction comes), he said, "I don't care how much it costs—do something about that underwear." I had to smile, since my cotton briefs and whalebone bras had been my habit for a long time. But I was happy to accommodate him! A few days later, I traipsed around in my new, *matching* bra and panties. He loved the sets I bought. What surprised me is how much lovelier and more feminine *I* felt. So, I'll ask you: How's your underwear? You, too, may want to consider ditching the cotton briefs and enjoying the lovely stuff. You'll both reap the benefits.

Has your husband ever commented on your nightwear or underwear? If so, how have you responded? If not, are you curious about what he thinks? What do you wear to make his eyes bug out?

_____

_____

_____

Ask the Lord to help you breathe new life into your love life. Think romantically so that you can maintain an atmosphere of warmth and readiness. Keep your bedroom a haven for rest and recreation. Reminisce with love and laughter. Enjoy each other's touch as a natural display of your affection. Oh, yes—and remember the things of feminine sensuality. Ask Him to show you what would appeal to your husband's eye and to his heart.

BUILDING ROMANCE— PUTTING IT ALL TOGETHER

There's a term we use in the military called "OJT." It stands for on-the-job training. The trainee takes what he or she has learned and *does* it—puts hands and feet to it. So today we're going to create several romantic encounters, from simple to more elaborate, drawing on what you've learned thus far. Debra White Smith gives this encouragement:

> The more energy you put into seducing your husband, the more exciting it becomes for you. The more exciting it becomes for you, the more thrilled he will become. The more thrilled he is, the more exhilarated you will be. Soon, the two

"I am my beloved's, and his desire is for me."

Song of Solomon 7:10

Let the Romance Begin

DAY FIVE

of you will become true lovers—not just two people living under the same roof—and every glance, every word will be laden with the nuance of expectancy. Your marriage will become a fulfillment of the Song of Songs. I am convinced this is God's perfect will for *every* Christian marriage.[8]

Depending on the level of romance that currently exists in your marriage, you may need to build slowly. You'll want to capitalize on smaller successes at first, observing your husband's responses and develop your romantic settings from there. (You don't want to hit him with romantic overload!)

Over the next few days, move toward a romantic evening that will end with your sexual intimacy. (This doesn't mean you wait until then for sex! That evening will just be a different approach.) Ask God to help you elevate your husband throughout the week as the object of your love, to help you foster an attitude of romance toward him, and to show you how to be creative in planning your romantic encounter. We'll work on three levels of romance: The "Simply Romantic Evening" Plan, which you can implement any time and as often as you like; the "Extended Romance" Plan, which takes a little more planning but gives you much-needed time together every quarter or so; and the "Elaborate Overnight or Weekend for Lovers" Plan, which every marriage needs at least twice a year. You'll select a favorite verse or passage in Song of Solomon that sets God's romantic tone in your heart and build on it. Take the time to create each plan today, let the ideas "cook," and then follow through.

The **Simply Romantic Evening Plan** has the following benefits:

☞ It adds joy and spice to your sexual intimacy.
☞ Planning time is minimal.
☞ Preparation time is minimal.
☞ It is relatively non-intimidating for you and your husband.
☞ It is generally inexpensive.
☞ It can take place after the kids are in bed.
☞ It can take place anywhere in the house.

First, select a favorite verse from Song of Solomon and write it here. Meditate on it while you make your simple plan.

_____
_____
_____

Second, decide **where** you would like your lovemaking to take place. (Remember—keep the place simple and familiar at first, such as your bedroom, in front of the fireplace, and so on.) You can prepare this place for lovemaking by putting fresh sheets on your bed, or building a lover's "nest" in front of the fireplace, for example. Where will your "bed" be, and what will you do to make it comfortable and ready?

_____
_____
_____

Third, select a simple accessory to enhance your evening. Some examples: a particular candle fragrance that fits your mood but is also pleasant to a male

Ask God to help you elevate your husband throughout the week as the object of your love, to help you foster an attitude of romance toward him, and to show you how to be creative in planning your romantic encounter.

nostril; gently discernable music that invites two lovers to love freely; fresh rose petals that adorn your fresh, clean sheets. Choose only one accessory to start. In later romantic evenings you can add a second, then a third. Consider several options of your own, and write them here. What accessory will you use? Why did you choose this accessory?

_____

_____

_____

Fourth, prepare yourself for the evening. As you read Song of Solomon, note how often Solomon refers to the things of Shulamith that make his senses reel. What will you wear? How will you wear your hair and do your make-up? What message will you want your body fragrance to send (Song of Solomon 4:10–11)? Tommy Nelson encourages, "All senses delight him. . . . Use the whole arsenal at your disposal!"[9] What do you want him to see, hear, taste, smell, and touch? (So don't forget to shave your legs!)

_____

_____

_____

Fifth, prepare your husband. You might want to send him a note at work that day, planting a little erotic anticipation. But mum's the word. The beauty of romance is the state of expectancy it arouses. How will you prepare your husband for your "Simply Romantic Evening"?

_____

_____

_____

Last, have fun! It might be helpful afterward to note here what you would do differently next time.

_____

_____

_____

The **Extended Romance Plan** has the following benefits:

☞ It gives you the day together to anticipate late afternoon or early evening "delight."

☞ It gives you a day of one-on-one with your husband.

☞ You can plan an activity you've wanted to share for a long time.

☞ It's relatively non-intimidating for you both.

☞ Its expense is activity-dependent, but you can compensate in other ways.

☞ The kids can have fun spending the day with their buddies or grandparents.

First, select a favorite verse from Song of Solomon, and write it here. Meditate on it while you make your plan.

_____

_____

_____

The beauty of romance is the state of expectancy it arouses.

Second, a month beforehand, secretly select an activity that you and your husband have talked about doing together but haven't made the time to do, such as: golfing, biking, dinner and a movie, hiking, picnicking, canoeing, time at home alone together ending with a quiet candlelight dinner that you prepare together. This is a great time to brainstorm with the Lord. These activities aren't to wear you out but are intended to energize you toward each other. How will you prepare for this activity? Do you need to rent special equipment or wear special attire? Give yourself the time you need to arrange the particulars and budget for their expense. Make a list of things to do:

_____

_____

_____

Third, decide where the children will go for that day. This is important, since you'll want the freedom of your home for lovemaking. Make a "trade agreement" with a friend, or treat Grandma and Grandpa to a day with the grandkids. Write where they'll go, when and how they'll get there:

_____

_____

_____

If you have an active day planned, have fresh towels in place for when you shower together, or warm massage oil for those muscles you haven't used in awhile. But then, you don't need an outdoor sport to enjoy these two suggestions.

Fourth, where will your sexual encounter take place? (You can be creative about this too.) Try not to plan *when* it's going to happen. What preparation will you have to make for your sexual activity? Example: If you have an active day planned, have fresh towels in place for when you shower together, or warm massage oil for those muscles you haven't used in awhile. But then, you don't *need* an outdoor sport to enjoy these two suggestions.

_____

_____

_____

Fifth, prepare yourself for your planned activity. Will you need special attire? How will you fix your hair and don your makeup? This is not a problem if you're going scuba diving on Saturday, but if you're planning a surprise candlelight dinner on Friday evening, consider *his* five senses.

_____

_____

_____

Sixth, take time to prepare your husband for this activity without giving it away, especially if he needs to clear his calendar for it. To ensure success, be specific about the date and time you "need" him all to yourself. Then drop written or verbal hints during the week. Build his anticipation. You'll find the anticipation is heightened for you too! What will you have to do to prepare your husband for your **Extended Romance Plan**?

_____

_____

_____

Seventh, enjoy each other! Then make a note of what you might have done differently.

_____

_____

_____

The **Elaborate Overnight** or **Weekend for Lovers Plan** has the following benefits:

☞ Planning and preparation time are worth the smiles on your faces.

☞ It gives you an overnight or weekend to catch up with each other.

☞ You can sleep in without the interruption of little voices or panting pets.

☞ It's a respite for you both.

☞ Its expense is accommodations-dependent, but you can compensate in other ways.

☞ The kids are spoiled by friends or by Grandma and Grandpa.

First, select a favorite verse from Song of Solomon, and write it here. Meditate on it while you make your plan.

_____

_____

_____

Second, several months beforehand, consider where and how you want to spend a weekend with your husband. Pray about what you both would enjoy doing together. Will it be sightseeing? Camping? Museum-hopping? A combination? Don't cram it too full of activities, since leisurely sexual activity is top priority. If your budget is limited, these activities range from free to minimal cost and may be close enough to home to enjoy your own bed afterward. Nonetheless, budget wisely so that you can assure your husband that the weekend is paid for. If you travel, make arrangements early for accommodations and equipment, if necessary. How would you like to spend a weekend with your husband? What arrangements would you have to make in advance?

_____

_____

_____

Third, secretly prepare your husband by making sure that weekend is on his calendar. Use your active imagination for building anticipation closer in. Kidnap him from work, so plan in advance what he'll need in his suitcase. In what ways can you build romantic suspense around your weekend?

_____

_____

_____

Fourth, once your weekend date is set, make whatever arrangements are necessary for your children (without guilt, please). Build "trade" opportunities with friends, or give grandparents time with their grandkids. Who can you leave your children with for an overnight or weekend? What transportation arrangements will you have to make for them?

_____

_____

_____

Fifth, prepare yourself for the weekend. Be deliberate about your attire (daytime and nighttime), your fragrance and what accessories you bring for sexual intimacy. What will enhance the romantic mood?

_____

_____

_____

Hold hands, reminisce, touch each other affectionately—often. Steer clear of emotional issues. Instead, lose yourselves in each other.

Sixth, enjoy each other! Hold hands, reminisce, touch each other affectionately—often. Steer clear of emotional issues. Instead, lose yourselves in each other. And enjoy each other sexually as often as possible. When your weekend is over, write here what you would do differently next time.

_____

_____

_____

 May the beauty of the emotional and sexual bond that's forged by romantic love pour all over your marriage like a revitalizing, medicinal balm. May you return to the things you did before—loving, honoring, and valuing your husband. And may you cherish your intimacy with him as a priceless gift from God, the Father. *"Eat, O friends, and drink; drink your fill, O lovers"* (Song of Solomon 5:1, NIV).

Works Cited

1. Bill Bright, *First Love: Renewing Your Passion for God* (Peachtree City, GA: New *Life* Publications, 2004), 73.

2. This is the name ascribed to Solomon's feminine counterpart in Ed Wheat and Gloria Oaks Perkin's book *Love Life for Every Married Couple* (Grand Rapids: Zondervan Publishing House, 1980), 210.

3. John MacArthur, *The MacArthur Study Bible* (Nashville: Word Publishing, 1997), 943–944.

4. Judy Halliday, R.N. and Arthur Halliday, M.D., *Thin Within: A Grace-Oriented Approach to Lasting Weight Loss* (Nashville: Word Publishing Group, 2002), 31.

5. Stormie Omartian, *The Power of a Praying Woman* (Eugene, OR: Harvest House Publishers), 203.

6. Tommy Nelson, *The Book of Romance* (Nashville: Thomas Nelson Publishers, 1998), 177.

7. Ibid., 178.

8. Debra White Smith, *Romancing Your Husband: Enjoying a Passionate Life Together* (Eugene, OR: Harvest House Publishers, 2002), 155.

9. Nelson, *The Book of Romance,* 178.

10

Words Are Not Enough: The Art of Communicating

It's been said that anybody can talk, but not everybody can communicate. Effective communication is the bedrock of a healthy marriage. It establishes rapport, fosters understanding, and expands a couple's knowledge of each other, paving the way for greater physical, emotional, intellectual, and spiritual intimacy. Good communication builds up, clears up, shapes up, and shores up a relationship. The ability to communicate well is learned, and we have no better teacher than the Holy Spirit within.

Over the next five days we'll study **1)** the general communication differences between men and women, **2)** how the tongue can set the course of life, **3)** God's guidelines for meaningful communication, **4)** the saboteurs of good communication, and **5)** how to disagree without being disagreeable (or downright ugly).

Let's get started.

It's been said that anybody can talk, but not everybody can communicate.

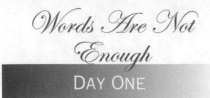

MEN AND WOMEN—VIVE LA DIFFERENCE!

I f you've ever traveled to a foreign country and tried to speak the language, you know how difficult it was at times to get your point across. Using your hands, intensifying your facial expressions, and even speaking louder didn't quite close the loop on what you were trying to communicate. Perhaps it was not only frustrating but potentially embarrassing if what you said wasn't what the local resident heard. Sometimes being in a marriage is like being in a foreign country, because communicating with our husbands requires us to be bilingual, to learn their language.

What is it that makes communicating between a husband and wife so difficult at times? Women have little trouble conversing with each other. We can discuss a topic, issue, relationship, person, or circumstance. We can also embellish it, emote over it, analyze it, speculate about it, and literally exhaust it. Men, on the other hand, have a tendency to say what they *need* to say to each other and to their wives and move on.

Is a woman's way of communicating right and a man's way wrong? Not at all! Both sexes communicate *differently*. And their differences are real, substantiated by scientifically measured brain differences. Marriage and family therapist H. Norman Wright states, "If people really knew the differences between male and female styles of thinking and communicating, they would honor the differences and respond to each other in an appropriate and accepting way."[1] I think it's important to understand these basic brain differences so that we can connect the dots in our own communication habits and better understand our husbands' habits.

Basically, the brain is divided into two hemispheres, the left brain and the right brain. The segment that connects the two sides is made up of nerve bundles. Females have up to forty percent more nerve bundles than males, which means that they can use both sides of their brain simultaneously. Males, however, can use only one side at a time, depending on the requirement. Now before you get puffed up, neither brain difference is better than the other. *Both* are necessary to lend balance to the relationship. Here's how the *general* differences break down in terms of thought processes and taskings (keeping in mind that there are always varying degrees of exception):

Male	Female
Later language skills	Earlier language skills
Later reading skills	Earlier reading skills
Well-developed spatial skills—he *acts* (makes a good warrior)	Better developed expressive/verbal skills—she *talks* (makes a good nurturer)
Singularly focused, task-oriented	Multi-tasker
Oriented to the physical; (competitive)	Oriented to the emotional (compassionate)
Excludes what's going on around him until task is completed	Includes all around her in her tasks

Male	Female
Interruption is energy drain	Energized by change must refocus
Structured, orderly, organized, likes rules	Can function "all over the map"
"Fixer"—wants to *do* something about a problem	"Feeler"—wants to talk through a problem
Thinks through feelings, then shares (maybe)	Talks through feelings while thinking
Fixes problem while thinking	Solves problems out loud
Talks to exchange information; factual, bottom-line talk	Talks for connection, emotional intimacy, relationship; more detail, plus feelings[2]

Generally, because men are "do-ers," they are open and ready to engage in the *physical*, with undivided attention—washing the car, conquering the wilderness, running the race, winning the contract—or the girl, the game, the match, and so on. Activities such as these define a man's sense of self-worth. What he does validates him in his family and in his world. He remains undistracted until his mission is completed. He then moves on to the next thing. (Does this remind you of the day after the wedding?)

On the other hand, since women tend to be "feelers," they're more open and ready to engage in the *relational,* which draws from their emotional and spiritual pools, not from the physical. A woman wants to share "thoughts, feelings, goals, and dreams. . . . And her desire for deep relationships usually exceeds what the average man desires."[3] As a result, two distinctive approaches to communication emerge and define the differences between them. A man's communication traits tend to coincide with his mission-oriented, "conqueror" nature, while a woman's traits tend to coincide with her capacity to nurture. A man can converse like a "bullet" on a briefing slide, making each point in seven words or less. A woman can converse like a full-blown novel, using many pages to express every nuance. He communicates *facts*. She communicates *feelings*. He goes for the bottom line. She just goes.

Gary Smalley found that men "primarily relate to their wives using what we call a *language of the head* while women tend to speak a *language of the heart*" and that men "tend to be logical, factual, and detail-oriented. In general, when a man runs out of facts to talk about in a conversation, he often stops talking!"[4]

The bottom line is that a wife's relational nature is intended to complement her husband's more physical nature. She has what he doesn't, and vice versa. They're supposed to "dovetail" into each other's strengths and weaknesses, even in the area of communication. As both the husband and the wife learn to bridge both worlds—the language of the head and the language of the heart—they're able to close the gap between them so that their differences become enhancers rather than destroyers.

> **The bottom line is that a wife's relational nature is intended to complement her husband's more physical nature. She has what he doesn't, and vice versa. They're supposed to "dovetail" into each other's strengths and weaknesses, even in the area of communication.**

 Describe how your husband communicates with you. Does he match the general description above? If so, in what ways? If not, how is he different?

_____

_____

_____

Describe how you communicate with your husband. Do you fit the general mold? In what ways? If not, how are you different?

_____

_____

_____

What are some of the difficulties and frustrations you have in communicating with your husband?

_____

_____

_____

What changes would you like to see in *his* communication style?

_____

_____

_____

What changes would you like to see in *your* communication style?

_____

_____

_____

 As you continue this week's lesson, ask the Lord to give you the wisdom to recognize and understand your own communication skills and habits and how they blend or don't blend with your husband's. Ask Him to help you observe and understand how your husband communicates with you and to respect his differences. Most important, ask Him to help you be teachable and willing to modify or change where necessary in order to communicate more effectively with your man.

Words Are Not Enough

DAY TWO

CHARTING THE COURSE

Sticks and stones can break my bones, but words can never hurt me!" Do you remember that little jingle? I said it as a kid—often. Only half of it is true: Sticks and stones *can* break our bones; but, oh, those words—their damage is far worse. They can break our spirits. Christian author Mike Mason writes, "For the tongue is a pen, which pressing deeply enough (and whether for good or for evil) will write upon the heart."[5]

We know the powerful, long-lasting effect our parents' tongues (or siblings', teachers', and so on) had on our growing up. If the effect was positive, we're hopefully modeling it to our husbands and our own children today. If the effect was negative, we may be faced with the challenge of releasing some of the verbal habits we've acquired. Until we purposefully attune our own ears to the words of our mouths and the sound of our voices, we may be desensitized to the potential damage we're doing with our tongues.

📖 Scripture depicts the tongue as a powerful tool that can be used for good or evil. Read James 3:1–12. How is the perfect man portrayed in verses 1–2?

_____

_____

_____

To what is the tongue compared and why (verses 3–6)?

_____

_____

_____

What indictment does James make about our ability to tame the tongue? How does he describe the tongue (verses 7–8)?

_____

_____

_____

What contrasts are used in verses 9–12? What point is James making?

_____

_____

_____

📖 What does James 1:26 say about our talk matching our walk?

_____

_____

_____

📖 How does Matthew 12:34–37 drive home what James says? There is also a sobering consequence for words carelessly spoken. What is it (verses 36–37)?

_____

_____

_____

As Christians, only the words that reflect Christ's presence in our lives should exit our lips. This verifies our walk (Matthew 12:34). But our old habits die hard, and we'll give account for every irresponsible and useless word we speak (Matthew 12:37). Nonetheless, once the Holy Spirit convicts us of careless or inappropriate speaking practices, we can be on the road to change.

Sticks and stones can break our bones; but, oh, those words—their damage is far worse. They can break our spirits.

"But no one can tame the tongue; it is a restless evil and full of deadly poison."

James 3:8

Once the Holy Spirit convicts us of careless or inappropriate speaking practices, we can be on the road to change.

📖 Let's take a look some scriptures about the tongue from Proverbs, God's book of wisdom. How does each scripture say the tongue can impact a relationship?

Proverbs 10:21

_____

_____

_____

Proverbs 12:18, 25

_____

_____

_____

Proverbs 15:1

_____

_____

_____

Proverbs 15:4

_____

_____

_____

Proverbs 16:24

_____

_____

_____

Proverbs 18:21

_____

_____

"Death and life are in the power of the tongue, and those who love it will eat its fruit."

Proverbs 18:21

Yes, our tongues can set a course toward life or toward death. Tim and Joy Downs claim, "If Proverbs is correct about the power of the tongue, then we all carry a concealed weapon—without a permit, without training, and without restraint."[6]

Proverbs 31:26 says of a woman who reveres the Lord, _"She opens her mouth in skillful and godly Wisdom, and on her tongue is the law of kindness"_ (AMP). This wife is wise, positive, and nurturing. Her words promote life. Her children call her blessed, as does her husband, who also praises her. What a great legacy for any wife!

APPLY What course did your parents' tongues chart for you throughout your childhood?

_____

_____

_____

_____

_____

What course did your parents' tongues chart for each other in their marriage?

_____

_____

What course would you say your tongue has charted throughout your marriage? Is it similar to or different from your folks' course?

_____

_____

In what ways is your tongue a nourishing source of life to your husband?

_____

_____

Are there times when your tongue can be characterized as *"a restless evil, full of deadly poison"* (James 3:8, NIV)? Who would agree with you? When is it most difficult to keep your tongue in check? What impact does your unbridled tongue have on your husband? On your other family members?

_____

_____

In what ways would you like to change the course your tongue has been on?

_____

_____

 If you've recognized yourself in any of today's scriptures, prayerfully offer your speaking habits to the Lord for change. Ask Him to keep your tongue from uttering reckless words, to help you use pleasant words that bring healing and life to the hearts of those who hear them, and to speak *"as one speaking the very words of God . . . so that in all things God may be praised through Jesus Christ"* (1 Peter 4:11, NIV). Amen.

GOD'S GUIDELINES FOR GOOD COMMUNICATION

Talking with (not *to*) our husbands can be a scary proposition, especially if we don't speak their language. We may be particularly gun-shy about broaching sensitive subjects if past efforts were uncomfortable or outcomes were unsuccessful. But when we learn and practice God's guidelines on communicating, we're able to talk with *anyone* about *anything*. Does that mean that all of our issues will be resolved? Not always, but communicating God's way will significantly increase the probability of resolution. When we communicate in accordance with His will, we're able to leave the results with Him. We remain in His peace while He works out the details.

When we learn and practice God's guidelines on communicating, we're able to talk with anyone about anything.

📖 Good communication requires three things: *speaking correctly, listening carefully,* and *understanding clearly*. Read Luke 6:31. How can this scripture be applied to these three elements of communication?

_____

_____

_____

We all want to be spoken to correctly, to be carefully heard, and to be clearly understood. Modeling these skills is the best way to receive them in return.

📖 Let's take a look at how we're to *speak correctly*. Read Ephesians 4:15. How do you think *"speaking the truth in love"* benefits the speaker? How do you think speaking the truth in love benefits the hearer? Looking at the latter part of this verse, what do you think the spiritual value is for both when the truth is spoken in love?

_____

_____

_____

Love is the key to speech that honors God and our husbands. It's the quality that continually rises to the surface as foundational to all we think, say, and do. Someone once said, "Truth without love is cruel." I'm sure all of us have taken a hit from someone who "gave it to us straight," without love and kindness. The truth (what we say) can hit God's mark more effectively when bathed in love (how we say it).

Good communication requires three things: speaking correctly, listening carefully, and understanding clearly.

The other half to the saying "Truth without love is cruel" is "Love without truth is license." When we exhibit only love because we are afraid to speak the truth, we may be enabling a behavior to continue unrestrained by the truth of God. That's a responsibility that, if neglected, can have painful or frightening consequences later on for both the speaker and the hearer.

📖 What do the following verses in Proverbs say about truthful lips and lying lips? How do these verses apply to communicating in marriage?

Proverbs 12:19

_____

_____

Proverbs 12:22

_____

_____

"An honest answer is like a kiss on the lips."

Proverbs 24:26 (NIV)

Proverbs 24:26

_____

_____

Proverbs 26:28

_____

_____

📖 Read Ephesians 4:25. Since there's no neighbor closer than our husbands, how are we supposed to interact with them?

_____

_____

_____

In verse 25, God commands us to *"put off falsehood and speak truthfully"* (NIV). This means we're to be genuine and say what's real. The reality is that any other way is *not* real. And when I follow God's command to speak in accordance with His will, the *genuine* me is talking, and the *real* message is being conveyed in love. This gives God a lot to work with in a marriage, even if the other spouse is resistant or uncooperative. He will honor our doing our part.

📖 In Ephesians 4:29 are several essential elements that lay out godly communication in a nutshell. What are they?

_____

_____

_____

This strong instruction decries bad, rotten, or "putrid" words, because they're destructive, not instructive; they tear down rather than build up; they ignore a husband's need rather than speak to it; they work to his detriment rather than to his benefit. Following this one simple guideline could profoundly influence a number of struggling marriages.

APPLY How would adhering to Ephesians 4:15, 25, 29 affect your day-to-day communication with your husband? How would that prepare you for tougher discussions?

_____

_____

_____

_____

Careful listening is the second key to good communication. Listening with intent takes discipline, just as speaking with purpose does. We may find ourselves looking at our husbands while they're speaking but hearing nothing because we're busy in our minds with other things and therefore distracted. Maybe we're busy forming our own thoughts and not hearing theirs, or judging what they're saying rather than hearing their hearts. Or perhaps we're focused only on the opportune time to interrupt.

📖 How do Psalms 34:15; 116:1–2 characterize *God's* listening skills? What response did God's careful listening evoke from the psalmist?

_____

_____

_____

When someone is truly listening to our hearts, we draw closer, we trust more, and we're inclined to listen in the same way we've been heard. God knows how important it is to be heard. Careful listening is a skill that He

> *When I follow God's command to speak in accordance with His will, the genuine me is talking, and the real message is being conveyed in love. This gives God a lot to work with in a marriage, even if the other spouse is resistant or uncooperative.*

> *"Do not let any unwholesome talk come out of your mouths, but only what is helpful for building others up according to their needs, that it may benefit those who listen."*
>
> **Ephesians 4:29 (NIV)**

will reward. As you apply God's instruction to your own listening habits, you might be surprised to see your husband's listening skills sharpen as well.

📖 What insights do you derive from the following proverbs on listening?

Proverbs 1:5

_____

_____

Proverbs 12:15

_____

_____

Proverbs 18:13

_____

_____

When someone is truly listening to our hearts, we draw closer, we trust more, and we're inclined to listen in the same way we've been heard.

"He who answers before listening – that is his folly and his shame."

Proverbs 18:13 (NIV)

Often when my grown daughter, Leslie, and I discuss certain matters of a sensitive sort, she'll get a gleam in her eye, stick her forefingers in her ears, and with a sing-song voice warble, "I'm not listening!" We both laugh and move on to the next subject. We wives can do the same with our mates, only not with plugged ears and the humorous warning but just by mentally or emotionally "checking out." We're really *not* listening.

Listening requires discipline, and disciplined listening requires humility—raising our husbands above ourselves and regarding what they have to say as more important than what we have to say (Philippians 2:3–4). If we're poor listeners, then we've raised ourselves above our husbands. We sharpen our listening skills when we intentionally look at our husbands as they speak; when we nod or utter a verbal acknowledgment; when we put down the temptation to interrupt them or finish their sentences. We assure them that we're "all ears."

If our husbands are poor listeners, it helps to make sure that our speaking skills are in order. Are we conversing in a way they can receive? Do we take too long to get to the point? If our way of communicating isn't working, we should assess our methods and ask God *and* our husbands how we can communicate more effectively. Saying more isn't necessarily better, even if it's our nature. When we see their eyes glaze over, the bottom line may not have come soon enough!

APPLY How would you assess your listening skills? What can distract you from being a careful listener? What do you/can you do to assure your husband that you're listening? (Eye contact? Touching? A nod of your head? A verbal acknowledgment in appropriate places?)

_____

_____

_____

_____

_____

If you're prone to interrupting your husband or finishing his sentences, what will you do to change this behavior?

_____

_____

_____

How would you assess your husband's listening skills? How do you know when you're losing his attention? What can you do to keep your husband engaged in a discussion?

_____

_____

_____

Get your husband's attention *before* you begin talking. You can begin with, "Honey, I need your attention for a few minutes" or "I could really use some wise counsel. Is now a good time to talk?" This will help him fix his mind on the conversation, especially if he's distracted or his attention has been directed elsewhere. Eye contact and an occasional touch during the conversation will help keep any listener engaged. It works for our husbands, too. If "now" is not a good time for him to talk, let him tell you when is best. You're more likely to get his undivided attention when he's no longer focused on the competition.

Speaking correctly and listening carefully promote *clear understanding* of messages given and received. The loop of good communication closes when clear understanding takes place, even if the understanding is to agree to disagree.

📖 Jesus complained about hearts that weren't inclined toward understanding. Read Matthew 13:10–17. What insight do these verses give you into one's willingness to hear and understand?

_____

_____

_____

Before understanding can take place, we've got to *want* to understand what our husbands are trying to convey, not with an attitude of "What's in it for me?" but with an attitude of "What's in it for *us*?" No amount of words can clarify their point or position if our hearts are closed to understanding.

📖 Read the following verses from Proverbs. What will gaining understanding add to the marriage relationship?

Proverbs 2:1–6

_____

_____

Proverbs 13:15

_____

_____

> *The loop of good communication closes when clear understanding takes place, even if the understanding is to agree to disagree.*

Proverbs 15:21

_____

_____

Proverbs 16:22

_____

_____

Proverbs 17:27

_____

_____

Proverbs 18:2

_____

_____

Proverbs 24:3

_____

_____

"By wisdom a house is built, and through understanding it is established."

Proverbs 24:3 (NIV)

APPLY What do you currently do if you don't understand what your husband is telling you? Is there anything you can do differently?

_____

_____

_____

_____

What do you do if your husband doesn't understand what you're telling him? What can you do to help him understand you better?

_____

_____

_____

When we speak correctly and listen carefully, more than likely we'll understand our husbands and their messages more clearly, and they'll understand ours. This is the essence of good communication, which can transform every area of our marriages.

 Ask the Lord to help you send clear messages to your husband—to say what you mean, and to mean what you say; to always tell him the truth, and to tell him in love; to show you how to improve your listening skills, especially if you're prone to "wander," to interrupt, or to finish his sentences; to give you ears that can hear and understand your husband's heart when he speaks, especially if he's not a man of many words. And then ask Him to tenderize your husband's tongue, his ears, and his heart so that he can respond to you with the same sensitivity that you've now learned.

COMMUNICATION—BEWARE THE SABOTEURS!

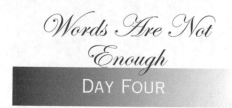
As we apply God's guidelines for good communication, we'll become more fluent in speaking and understanding our husbands' language. We'll also become more accomplished at handling issues that have caused concern or conflict in the past. However, it helps to address a few things that tend to sabotage successful communication and conflict resolution: (1) anger, (2) fear, and (3) pride and selfishness.

Anger

📖 Read James 1:19–20. What three instructions is God giving in verse 19? According to verse 20, why is He giving these instructions? How can applying them help to improve communication and resolve conflict?

_____

_____

_____

Being quick to listen and slow to speak takes practice. Being slow to *anger* takes self-control. We're all going to get angry at times. It's what we *do* with anger—how we act on it or let it "cook"—that can steer us off God's path of righteousness.

📖 Read Ephesians 4:26–27. Notice that Paul doesn't say, "Don't get angry." What is his instruction on anger, and what do you think he means (verse 26)? Why (verse 27)?

_____

_____

_____

If we won't wrestle with our anger before the Lord first, so that we'll know what to do with it, we unwittingly *give* (permit, allow, offer) the devil access to our relationship. That's why we're commanded to deal with our anger as soon as possible. Many women choose to run from, ignore, or "stuff" their anger, and in so doing, they allow the Enemy his silent impact on their marriages. Unknowingly, their marriages become his territory.

📖 What do the following scriptures say about anger, and how do they apply to marriage?

Psalm 37:8

_____

_____

Proverbs 16:32

_____

_____

> **"My dear brothers, take note of this: Everyone should be quick to listen, slow to speak and slow to become angry, for man's anger does not bring about the righteous life that God desires."**
>
> **James 1:19–20 (NIV)**

Proverbs 20:22

_____

_____

Proverbs 29:11

_____

_____

Ecclesiastes 7:9

_____

_____

📖 Read Proverbs 29:22 and Ephesians 4:31–32. What are we _commanded_ to do with our anger (verse 31)? What are we commanded to replace it with (verse 32)?

_____

_____

> **If we suppress anger and let it fester like an untreated wound, its infection will course through our being and poison us with long-lasting resentment and bitterness.**

Anger is often a response to the more primary emotions of hurt, fear, or frustration. If we choose to feed it or "stuff" it rather than deal with it in a timely fashion, angry emotions can explode into emotional or physical rage. If we suppress anger and let it fester like an untreated wound, its infection will course through our being and poison us with long-lasting resentment and bitterness. Either way, we find ourselves cooperating with the Enemy. Les and Leslie Parrot comment, "Anger in marriage, especially when we nurse it, motivates us to wound and perhaps even despise our spouse. We cannot love under these conditions, and everything we stand for is in danger of being destroyed when we allow anger to be transformed into hostile words and actions."[7]

When anger is stirring or building within—stop long enough to ask God to show you why it's there. Psalm 4:4 says, _"In your anger do not sin; when you are on your beds, search your hearts and be silent"_ (NIV). God will reveal. Then you can deal with its cause.

The good news is that since anger is a learned reaction, it can be unlearned. It was freeing for me to understand that nobody or nothing _makes_ me angry. Anger is my choice. I can respond with Holy Spirit self-control and banish my anger. Then I don't have to worry about it when the sun sets.

🛑 **APPLY** When was the last time you were angry with your husband? Why were you angry? How did you display your anger? What impact did your anger have on resolving the issue? How would you modify or change your response next time?

_____

_____

_____

_____

Fear

If we're afraid to prayerfully, lovingly and forthrightly confront our husbands with an issue, then conflict over that issue will continue indefinitely. What are we afraid of? Who are we afraid of? Who should we be afraid of?

📖 How do the following verses give spiritual perspective to the fear associated with confrontation? How does each verse apply to the marriage relationship?

Proverbs 27:5

_____

_____

Proverbs 27:6

_____

_____

Proverbs 27:17

_____

_____

Fear of conflict adds nothing to a marriage relationship. It actually impedes the growth and maturity of both marriage partners. If we ask the Lord to reveal who or what we're afraid of and why, every time we're afraid, His answer will help us discern the right approach to the concerns or conflicts we must confront and resolve. And He'll keep us safe in the process as we trust in Him.

APPLY Are you afraid of confrontation with your husband? Prayerfully and honestly consider what's behind the fear, and write your answer here:

_____

_____

_____

_____

Has there been an issue between you and your husband that continues to lie dormant or resurfaces periodically but remains unresolved because you're afraid to address it with him? How is God calling you to confront your fear? How do you think God would want you to deal with this issue?

_____

_____

_____

Pride and Selfishness

Two more saboteurs of effective communication, pride and selfishness, cannot be separated. Oswald Chambers gives sobering insight: "Pride is the sin of making 'self' our god."[8] Leslie Vernick adds to this insight: "The very center of pride is _I_."[9]

When John and I would have a spat, my heels searched for a place to dig in, and my resistance level hunkered down for the long haul. Why? Because I didn't want to lose.

> *Fear of conflict adds nothing to a marriage relationship. It actually impedes the growth and maturity of both marriage partners.*

> *"Fear of man will prove to be a snare, but whoever trusts in the Lord is kept safe."*
>
> **Proverbs 29:25 (NIV)**

> ## "Pride only breeds quarrels, but wisdom is found in those who take advice."
> ### Proverbs 13:10 (NIV)

📖 Scripture talks about the high price of pride in conflict. In each of the following passages, what point is made about pride, and how does it relate to marital conflict?

Proverbs 11:2

_____

_____

Proverbs 13:10

_____

_____

Proverbs 16:18

_____

_____

Proverbs 18:19

_____

_____

James 4:1–10

_____

_____

Even when pride keeps the quarrel alive until we "win," there's an inexplicable emptiness associated with the victory. Perhaps it's because we know that a little more life has just been drained from our relationship.

> ## Even when pride keeps the quarrel alive until we "win," there's an inexplicable emptiness associated with the victory. Perhaps it's because we know that a little more life has just been drained from our relationship.

APPLY Does your pride keep your disagreements or arguments from being resolved? Please give a recent example. How could a humble heart change the outcome of this example?

_____

_____

Can you be unyielding over an issue when appropriate compromise can help to resolve it (Proverbs 18:19)? If so, why do you think that is?

_____

_____

What steps can you take to draw humility and compromise into resolving your differences (James 4:1–10)?

_____

_____

Obeying God's commands, having ears that can hear the prompting of the Spirit, and adhering to God's guidelines will work together to enable you to speak truthfully and lovingly to your husband. Cynthia Heald uses Galatians 5:22–23 as a further scriptural guideline for communicating with our husbands: "The bottom line in communication is simply the willingness to minister unconditionally. This ministry can be defined by . . .

- speaking the truth with him in love and kindness;
- listening to him sacrificially with patience and gentleness;
- guarding what he says with faithfulness;
- responding to him with goodness and self-control;
- communing with him in joy;
- being silent with him in peace."[10]

 Conflict is tough on a marriage when we give in to our emotions. But God can add long life to a marriage when we work out our differences with patience, courage, and humility. Has God shown you habits that you resort to when in conflict with your husband? Which ones need His touch? Give them to Him now, and ask Him to mature you in a way that brings health through conflict and not destruction.

Conflicts—Handle with "Fair"

Words Are Not Enough
DAY FIVE

Conflict—you *can* live with it, because you *won't* live without it. Conflict is normal. It might sound a little strange to say, "Embrace it!" but from a spiritual perspective your marriage will win when you learn to fight a good fight. Conflict handled fairly and righteously will mature you, enhance your relationship with your husband, and strengthen your marriage. If you avoid or run from conflict, it will only chase you, and your issues will loom larger than ever, leaving your marriage limping through life.

Remember that communicating God's way requires that we speak correctly, listen carefully, and understand clearly. And we persevere until the goal of understanding is met. Below are techniques we can use to prepare us for those inevitable times of conflict. Please don't breeze past any of the scriptures. Read each one along with the accompanying guideline. Then record any insight God gives you into how it speaks directly to your habit of handling conflict.

📖 Read Psalm 141:3. *Remember to protect your husband and your relationship* when in conflict. Insights?

_____

_____

📖 Read Matthew 5:23–24. *Follow scriptural principles* when there's something between you and your husband. Insights?

_____

_____

📖 Read Proverbs 15:28. *Respond rather than react* during conflict:

☞ with your mind (2 Corinthians 10:5)
☞ with your lips (Psalm 141:3)
☞ with your facial expressions or body language (Proverbs 6:16–19)

Conflict—you can live with it, because you won't live without it.

Insights?

_____

_____

📖 Read Luke 6:37. *Resist the temptation* to question his motives, to accuse, to blame, to judge, or to condemn. Insights?

_____

_____

📖 Read Proverbs 21:23. *Refrain from using damaging words and trigger phrases*, such as "You always/never. . . . " "You could have/should have. . . ." "Why did/didn't you. . . ?" The use of "you" can be aggressive and confrontational. Stick with "I" statements: "I'm unhappy about. . . ." "I feel hurt/threatened/frustrated when. . . . " Insights?

_____

_____

📖 Read Proverbs 26:27. *Refuse to leave the room or the house when the tide is not in your favor* (in other words, when you're losing). This is a manipulative power play and a control strategy. God brings good out of fair play. Insights?

_____

_____

📖 Read Proverbs 10:32; 25:15 and Ephesians 4:29; 5:4. *Attack the problem, not your husband.* Even if what we say is necessary yet painful to hear, in many cases, it's not what we say but how we say it. Sarcasm, "witty" humor, and cynicism are often veiled attacks. The biblical bottom line is: the tougher the message, the gentler the delivery. Words kindly spoken can be edifying, even when they hurt. What is said must be *"good and beneficial to the spiritual progress of others"* and *"fitting to the need and the occasion, that it may be a blessing"* (Ephesians 4:29, AMP). It's not beneficial to his spiritual progress if he's sworn at or berated during confrontation. It's not fitting to his need if the discussion ventures beyond that which caused the confrontation. It's not fitting to the occasion if hurts of the past are dredged up and thrown at him—again. If we neglected to address a past offense, then we've missed the opportunity. And if we're supposed to address a past offense, God will ensure that it's resurrected so that we can approach it His way. Insights?

_____

_____

📖 Read Proverbs 16:2 and Matthew 7:1-5. *Honestly evaluate your own attitudes and motives*, without assuming you know his. Insights?

_____

_____

📖 Read Psalm 141:5; Proverbs 19:20; 24:26; 25:11. *Be willing to correct and be corrected.* Any behavior that threatens your relationship becomes an "us" responsibility that the two of you can approach in partnership. As your husband's helpmeet, you can lovingly express your concerns about

> *It's not beneficial to his spiritual progress if he's sworn at or berated during confrontation. It's not fitting to his need if the discussion ventures beyond that which caused the confrontation. It's not fitting to the occasion if hurts of the past are dredged up and thrown at him—again.*

an issue or behavior of his that's affecting your relationship. No, this is not permission to nag or criticize. Confront him once with the truth said in love, and then entrust him and the results to God. In the same way, be willing to receive your husband's correction for a behavior or your contribution to a problem. We create a non-threatening climate of cooperation and mutual concern when our husbands are free to be honest with us without fear of retaliation, intimidation, coercion, or defensiveness. Humility guards against defensiveness (pride), and honesty guards against the temptation to play the victim or the martyr. We're then able to accept responsibility with dignity. Insights?

_____

_____

📖 Read Proverbs 8:1–21. *Ask questions to clarify the issue; then listen, listen, listen.* Remember that the goal of communication is to understand each other clearly. This is difficult if our attentions are focused on controlling the outcome of the conversation by interrupting, finishing sentences, or pouting and becoming silent. Insights?

_____

_____

📖 Read Proverbs 18:19 and Ecclesiastes 4:9–12. *Discover together the things you do agree on.* Compromise where appropriate, and build. Stick together, and defend your relationship against the Enemy's attempt to drive the wedge of separation between you. Never lose sight of his goal. Insights?

_____

_____

📖 Read Proverbs 15:1 and Ecclesiastes 3:1, 7. *If emotions do get out of hand, and either or both of you are losing objectivity, agree to revisit the issue at another time.* You can suggest that you take a breather from the issue and come back to it when you're both fresher and can discuss it more fairly. Then follow through. Timing is always key in any discussion. Resurrecting an issue at bedtime, in public, or when he walks in the door from work is capitalizing on his vulnerability. This is not fair play. Seek God's timing. He'll unfold the timing perfectly. This will give you both time to think and pray about the next interaction—not how you're going to win the argument, but how you're going to understand each other so that you'll better understand how to resolve the issue. Insights?

_____

_____

📖 Read Proverbs 19:11. *Be willing to forgive and to ask forgiveness.* Revisit Lesson 7 if this is a problem area for you. Insights?

_____

_____

 Now is the time for some practical application. On Day One, you identified some difficulties and frustrations you had communicating with your husband. Rewrite them in the space provided on the next page. What have you learned in Days One through Five that, over time, may ease or correct the difficulties you identified?

We create a non-threatening climate of cooperation and mutual concern when our husbands are free to be honest with us without fear of retaliation, intimidation, coercion, or defensiveness.

> *There is a time for everything, and a season for every activity under heaven: a time to tear and a time to mend, a time to be silent and a time to speak..."*
>
> *Ecclesiastes 3:1, 7 (NIV)*

Communication Difficulties & Frustrations	Corrections

Next, let's look at topics or issues that have been difficult to discuss or that create conflict. Based on what you've learned this week, how would you approach them differently?

Topics & Issues That Create Conflict	More Effective Approach to Handling Topics/Issues

 Start at the top of your list of "Communication Difficulties and Frustrations" and work down, giving each item to God. Ask Him for His guidance and power as you're given opportunities to work out the "Corrections." Then proceed to the list of "Topics & Issues That Create Conflict," asking Him to bless you with His wisdom as you're given occasions to practice what He's teaching you. May you anticipate with *joy* what He's going to do in each area. Trust Him to work with you *and* with your husband as you remain faithful to what's true, right, and fair. Amen.

Works Cited

1. H. Normal Wright, *Communication: Key to Your Marriage* (Ventura, CA: Regal Books/Gospel Light, 2000), 125.

2. Ibid., 128–144.

3. Gary Smalley, *Love Is a Decision* (Dallas: Word Publishing, 1989), 45.

4. Ibid., 44.

5. Mike Mason, *The Mystery of Marriage* (Sisters, OR: Multnomah Books, 1985), 84, 85.

6. Tim and Joy Downs, *Fight Fair! Winning at Conflict without Losing at Love* (Chicago: Moody Publishers, 2003), 75.

7. Les and Leslie Parrott, *Meditations on Proverbs for Couples* (Grand Rapids, MI: Zondervan Publishing House, 1997), 70.

8. James Reimann, ed., *My Utmost for His Highest: The Golden Book of Oswald Chambers* (Grand Rapids, MI: Discovery House, 1992), June 12 devotional reading.

9. Leslie Vernick, *How to Act Right When Your Spouse Acts Wrong* (Colorado Springs, CO: WaterBrook Press, 2003), 89.

10. Cynthia Heald, *Loving Your Husband* (Colorado Springs, CO: NavPress, 1989), 89.

11

My Husband, My Friend

What is a friend? What do you look for in a friend? Is your husband your friend? Are you his? My husband's not just someone I spend time with—but someone I want to spend time with. I want to enhance our bond of intimacy physically, emotionally, intellectually, and spiritually. In our thirty years together, God has been building our friendship. Construction has been tough at times, but out of the "tough" has come the resolute assurance that we belong together no matter what. That makes the tough times worthwhile.

Couples often begin their marriages as close friends or best friends, but the camaraderie can change over the years. Life's events, hardships, and disappointments come along, and with each one their spirits can close to the other a little more. Gradual, almost imperceptible separation builds instead of oneness, and one day they realize that they're little more than strangers sharing the same house.

This week we'll concentrate on building a friendship with our husbands. Personal assessment is woven throughout the lesson. Take time before the Lord to answer all the questions forthrightly. Most important, because God designed friendship and companionship into a marriage relationship, ask Him to enhance, revive, create, or restore it in yours. Then commit your way to the Lord; trust Him, and anticipate His results.

What do you look for in a friend?

BUILDING TRUST

Trust is the foundation of every close friendship.

The more we know Jesus Christ, the more we understand that He responds to us and our every need out of His perfection. Even so, trusting Him can be a day-to-day challenge for many Christians. It's even tougher trusting our spouses, who are not perfect. Trusting them with our innermost thoughts, personal needs, and desires can be risky business, even if they've proven themselves trustworthy! We wives aren't perfect either, but are we trustworthy? Are our husbands able to trust us with who they are?

Trust is the foundation of every close friendship. In a marriage, trust thrives when we secure each other with our loyalty, when we affirm the other's behavior with respect and admiration, and when we're a source of emotional strength for the other in a time of need. Let's take a look at these three key elements that establish trust in a relationship.

Loyalty

We've all had opportunities to demonstrate loyalty to others and to be on the receiving end of another's loyalty. How would you define loyalty? What are some of the basics of loyalty that make it such an essential element of trust?

_____

_____

_____

📖 Faithfulness, devotion, allegiance, trustworthiness, constancy, reliability, dependability, steadfastness, commitment, dedication, responsibility, credibility—these elements of loyalty remind us of everything that God is for us. Romans 8:28–39 crafts a profound picture of His loyalty. Read through this passage, and list the ways God has exhibited His loyalty to us.

_____

_____

_____

_____

"If God is for us, who can be against us?"

Romans 8:31 (NIV)

Paul asks in verse 31 (NIV), *"If God is for us, who can be against us?"* That's how secure we are in our relationship with our heavenly Bridegroom, Jesus Christ. Let's apply this query to our marriages: when I insert my name and my husband's name, it reads, "If Judy is for John, who can be against him?" Now insert your names, and think about the question for a while. The answer to the question should be "It doesn't matter who's against him, because I'm for him." This thought is pretty sobering, isn't it? Are we really for our husbands in a way that enhances in them the Romans 8:31 kind of inner security?

📖 First Corinthians 13:7 is what I call the loyalty verse: *"Love bears up under anything and everything that comes, is ever ready to believe the best of every person, its hopes are fadeless under all circumstances and it endures everything"* (AMP). According to this verse, there are four characteristics that God's love in us can exhibit. What are they, and how do you think each applies to the marriage relationship?

Write your answers in the spaces provided below.

Characteristic #1:
Application to marriage:

_____

_____

_____

_____

Characteristic #2:
Application to marriage:

_____

_____

_____

_____

Characteristic #3:
Application to marriage:

_____

_____

_____

_____

Characteristic #4:
Application to marriage:

_____

_____

_____

_____

To "bear up under" means to protect. Love "hides the faults of others or covers them up."[1] Is that the same as pretending they don't exist, or ignoring them rather than confronting them when necessary? No. I believe it means we don't broadcast them outside the marriage. All too often, relational discomforts or rifts occur between husbands and in-laws or others when wives freely share their marital difficulties or their husbands' shortcomings. Husbands are no longer secure but vulnerable to outside judgment, ridicule, or rejection. Even if intended in jest, when we expose our husbands' quirks or idiosyncrasies, we leave them open to ridicule. When a husband's trust is breached, he'll take the initiative to protect who he is, closing the door to his more vulnerable self.

Believing the best about our husbands is always a challenge in a society that tears down the male while elevating the female. Commercials and sitcoms frequently portray men as incompetent, clueless couch potatoes. As Christian wives, we can continually filter out the disrespectful messages out there by choosing to focus on and believe the best of our mates and encouraging other wives to do the same. Fadeless hope is based on anticipating the work of God in our lives and in our marriages. This is particularly necessary for those whose husbands give them reason to give up hope. It's at times like this that

When a husband's trust is breached, he'll take the initiative to protect who he is, closing the door to his more vulnerable self.

we can look to the Lord for grace and guidance and whatever measure of courage and strength it takes to endure without weakening.

In her book *How to Act Right When Your Spouse Acts Wrong,* Leslie Vernick writes,

> Normal feelings such as hurt, sadness, anger, and disappointment occur in every marriage. . . . God does not expect us to endure our marital difficulties with cheerfulness. That would be silly. Yet within these difficult and painful emotions, God *does* want us to guard our heart against the hardness of heart, bitterness, vengeance, or hopelessness that can result from being in a difficult marriage.

The characteristics of love in 1 Corinthians 13:7 seem like an impossible foursome, especially in a more challenging marriage. But we have to remember the Source of this love. Jesus bore up under all, believed, hoped, and endured everything for our sakes. Apart from Him, none of us is capable of loving like this. It's His love in us that takes over when one of these four pearls of loyalty needs more cultivating.

 Can your husband trust that you don't talk about him behind his back, or even worse, while he's standing there? That he can count on your support, especially in the tough times? That your confidence in him doesn't waver even when his does? That you'll stand your ground on his behalf, especially to relatives? You may need to ask your husband these next two questions: Where in your marriage is your loyalty evident to him? Where do you need to establish loyalty?

_____

_____

_____

_____

Are you and your husband in a challenging place that requires you to exercise the four traits in 1 Corinthians 13:7 more purposefully? What is your challenge, and how will exercising these elements of loyalty help you through this time?

_____

_____

_____

As our loyalty continues to build trust and security in our marriages, the door to our husbands' hearts will gradually open to us more and more. They'll be more comfortable in seeking our encouragement and counsel and more open to receiving our suggestions.

 We can be in the habit of emotional or verbal disloyalty and not even know it. Listen to your self-talk about your husband, your spoken words, and the sound of your voice when speaking to others about him. Prayerfully consider where you must shore up your loyalty to your husband. Then commit to protecting him in this way, drawing on the Holy Spirit's wisdom and guidance. Let God establish in you this powerful ingredient of friendship and oneness.

Affirmation

📖 Although I've talked in a previous lesson about affirming our husbands, the importance of this trust-building element cannot be overemphasized. Read the following verses from Proverbs, and describe the value of a wife to her husband.

Proverbs 12:4

_____

_____

Proverbs 18:22

_____

_____

Proverbs 19:14

_____

_____

📖 Read Proverbs 31:10–12, 23, 28, 29. What is it about this wife that earns her husband's trust?

_____

_____

What does the public think of this man (verse 23)?

_____

_____

She is fully the helper, the complement to her husband, providing the affirmation and admiration he needs, in private and in public. And others take notice! According to verses 28–29, how does her husband respond to her? How does affirmation build trust in a man?

_____

_____

Linda Dillow says,

> Admiration is one major thing a wife can do to build up her husband's self-image. Even if your husband already has a healthy view of himself, *God can use your admiration to build him into more of the man God wants him to be* and into the husband you want him to be! Your husband's self-image is directly connected to your private and public admiration and praise.[3]

APPLY Let's assess your "affirmation quotient" by answering the questions below:

Yes	No	Questions
☐	☐	Do I really listen to my husband?
☐	☐	Do I respectfully attempt to understand him?
☐	☐	When he has problems, do I sympathize with him, encourage him, offer wise counsel when asked (not try to fix him or the problem)?

"Her husband is respected at the city gate, where he takes his seat among the elders of the land."

Proverbs 31:23 (NIV)

Yes	No	Questions
❏	❏	Do I appreciate his provision for our family?
❏	❏	Do I appreciate who he is?
❏	❏	Do I give him credit for the things he does well?
❏	❏	Do I show confidence in his ability to solve problems?
❏	❏	Do I show confidence in his ability to provide for our family?
❏	❏	Do I show confidence in his ability to make final decisions?
❏	❏	Do I show confidence in his ability to do jobs around the house?
❏	❏	Do I show confidence in his ability to raise and discipline our children?
❏	❏	Do I admire my husband?
❏	❏	**Bottom Line:** Do I affirm him? (Do I demonstrate that I trust my husband?)

Based on your answers, how would you assess your "affirmation quotient?" In what ways do you show your husband admiration privately and publicly?

_____

_____

_____

If you have difficulty affirming your man, why is it difficult?

_____

_____

_____

List the areas in which it's difficult to affirm your husband. Look for ways in which you can begin to build trust through affirmation. Even the smallest, genuine encouragement can make a difference in how he performs a task or responds to you. An example is provided for you.

Areas in Which To Build Trust	Ways to Build Trust Through Affirmation
Parenting	I can listen to his concerns, receive his counsel, and act on it.

Our husbands don't need us to be their mothers or their critics. They need us to be reassuring wives who see them as capable of handling what's going on around them. When we're not sure if our husbands are capable, we should give them the opportunity to prove themselves. We lovingly affirm them with our trust, pray for them, and trust God with the outcome, no matter what it is. If they fail, then they need our affirmation more than ever. God will honor our restraint from an "I-told-you-so" response. He will work good out of all things—especially the hard things (Romans 8:28).

 Affirming your husband is one of your greatest demonstrations of trust. Ask God to give you opportunities to admire and encourage your husband. If there's anything getting in the way of your using this powerful element of relationship-building, ask God to show you what it is (pride, anger, rebellion, and so on), so that you and He can work though it. Then genuine affirmation will come from His heart through yours.

Strength

Is there emotional strength in your marriage? Ed Wheat states, "If you feel you must hide your hurts from your partner, something is wrong in your relationship."[4] His point hit home. I really didn't trust my husband with my emotional needs and concerns. I would ignore the Holy Spirit's promptings to talk to John. Instead, my pride kept me from sharing any needs and drawing from his strength and encouragement. I realized that I was being dishonest, pretending to have it all together so as not to disappoint my husband (a reaction I assumed he would have), which only magnified the problem. There were times when I truly needed his input, his support, and his protection, but I was afraid to expose this "weaker" side of myself. Ah—pride!

It's equally dishonest if a wife takes advantage of her husband's emotional strength. She can place too much dependence on him as a haven. This is suffocating for any mate.

📖 Read Psalm 73:25–26. How does this passage depict the Source of our strength? How can a wife's dependence on this Source of strength benefit her husband?

_____

_____

_____

God wants us to use what He gives us. There will be times when we need to offer our husbands emotional strength and support. That's when we'll need to draw from God's supply. We're still our men's completer, even when they're running at only 50 of their 100 percent. By giving our 150 percent at times when it's necessary, we can see our husbands through challenging seasons, building a bulwark of trust that will see us through the next challenge, when we might need their 150 percent.

 Think of a time when your husband has been "a strong place" for you. How did this build your trust in him?

_____

_____

_____

_____

> *Our husbands don't need us to be their mothers or their critics. They need us to be reassuring wives who see them as capable of handling what's going on around them.*

> *"My flesh and my heart may fail, but God is the strength of my heart and my portion forever."*
>
> *Psalm 73:26*

When have you been a "strong place" for your husband? What effect did it have on your relationship?

_____

_____

_____

_____

 Loyalty, affirmation, and strength are beautiful attributes that build and shore up trust in any marriage. Ask God to dim any negative effects of trust that have been breached in the past. Because the Lord is for you, ask Him to show you how to be for your husband. Because the Lord affirms you daily, ask Him to show you how to affirm your husband daily and in what areas. Because the Lord is your firm strength, ask Him to prepare your strength for when your husband needs it.

BUILDING KNOWLEDGE

Jesus put a premium on our knowing God and Himself, because relationship with Him is a priority. A real relationship doesn't happen apart from the genuine knowledge and understanding of the friend we spend time with. I discovered a beautiful pattern to acquiring knowledge about Christ. See if you detect the same in your walk with Him:

☞ The more you know Christ, the more you trust Him.

☞ The more you trust Him, the more you yield to Him.

☞ The more you yield to Him, the more He reveals Himself to you.

☞ The more He reveals Himself to you, the more you know Him.

📖 According to Jeremiah 9:23–24, how important is it to know God?

_____

_____

_____

Leslie Vernick states, "Many of us don't realize that the thing we need _most_ in this life, after forgiveness, is to know God. He is our only true source of love and life. . . . God yearns for us to know him. He longs for us to _want_ to know him."[5] Do we strive to know Him with a determined purpose? Are we becoming more intimately acquainted with Him, recognizing and understanding more clearly the wonders of who He is? That's how He wants us to pursue knowing Him. And I believe we can learn to know our husbands in the same rich way.

 On the next page are some important questions that will help to determine how well you know your mate. Take your time answering them. If you can't answer some questions, be sure to ask your husband. You might also want to run questions by him that you've answered. You may be surprised by what you think you know about him.

Do we strive to know Him with a determined purpose? Are we becoming more intimately acquainted with Him, recognizing and understanding more clearly the wonders of who He is? That's how He wants us to pursue knowing Him. And I believe we can learn to know our husbands in the same rich way.

What are some of his likes and dislikes (foods, colors, songs, sports teams, political candidates, and so on)? How have they changed over the years?

_____

_____

_____

What is his dream or life's goal? Has it changed over the years? How? Why?

_____

_____

_____

What are his greatest fears? How do you know?

_____

_____

_____

What are his spiritual challenges?

_____

_____

_____

What is it about you that he loves and appreciates the most?

_____

_____

_____

What would he like to see changed in you?

_____

_____

_____

If answering these questions has been a tough exercise, then you might ask, "How do I get to know my husband more deeply?" (or all over again, if building a friendship has taken a backseat to other things, such as children, job, ministry, and so on). We do it in the same way we get to know our Lord:

■ Study him and his ways with determined purpose, with new eyes, and a new heart. You might be surprised at whom you see. Today observe him and his ways, and write something about him here that you didn't detect or notice previously (believe me—there's something!):

_____

_____

_____

■ Ask him questions about himself. We often guess or assume we know why our husbands respond to us or to circumstances the way they do. If there's something we don't understand, it's good to just ask—straight forward and with respect. In most cases, they'll give us the straight answer, unless they're concerned about retaliation. So be prepared to graciously receive the answer to your question. What are some things you'd like to know or understand about your husband but have been afraid to ask? There are probably a few things. Write them here.

_____

_____

_____

■ Fully accept his answers without being critical. Do this with everything he says. You'll make an impression in his heart, especially if he's used to being doubted, judged, or criticized. Trusting his answers may encourage him to be even more honest with you over time. Will accepting his answers be a challenge for you? If so, why? How will you meet the challenge?

_____

_____

_____

■ Accept him with no strings attached (agape loving—remember?). As you do, you'll see who he really is. And that's a good thing! In what areas is it still difficult to love your husband unconditionally? What expectations are you still firmly grasping? What will you do about these areas and expectations?

_____

_____

_____

■ Trust him. You could very well be surprised by his trustworthiness. Do you have a recent example of his trustworthiness? Write it here.

_____

_____

_____

■ Serve him. You'll unveil his softer side, and perhaps your own. In what ways do you currently serve your husband? In what areas do you resist serving him? What insights do you gain from your answer to these two questions?

_____

_____

_____

■ Spend time with him. That's how you get to know someone better, especially if you're both able to be real and say what's real, and still feel safe with each other. If you're not there yet, that's OK. Spending more time together will give you many opportunities to practice transparency and honest communication. How can the time you spend with your husband be different from the way you spend it now?

_____

_____

Ask God for the desire to know your husband more deeply; to seek to know him as you seek to know your Lord. Ask Him to help you see your husband through fresh eyes and to reveal fresh insights about your man. And may you marvel at your discoveries!

BUILDING FRIENDSHIP

In the Song of Solomon, there's no doubt that Solomon and his bride know they belong to one another (Song of Solomon 2:16; 6:3; 7:10), and enjoy being together. Their ease reveals that they're not only lovers but close friends—they like each other. Annie Chapman says, "People get married because they love each other. But I believe they stay married because they *like* each other."[6]

Does your marriage have this "close friends" or "best friends" phenomenon? Do you even consider your husband to be a friend? If so, you're truly blessed to share this camaraderie with the most important person in your life. If not, trust God to work as you build toward friendship.

Think about friendship. What are the qualities that make a good friendship?

_____

_____

_____

Today, true friendship in a marriage is hard to come by. Why?

_____

_____

_____

We choose friends who engender in us a sense of acceptance and comfort—in other words of belonging. Our preference is to be with them. We can tell them anything, and receive tough truth from them because our mutual trust goes deep. We serve them with a heart of selflessness and receive service from them with a heart of gratitude. They're safe with us because we love them "as is," and vice versa. When we share our pain, it eases. When we share our joy, it increases. There's nothing like a true friend.

What a blessing it would be if each of us had this true friend in our husbands! If you do, your friendship can be strengthened. If you don't, your friendship can be created and established by God. To tweak an old adage, "If you want a friend in your husband, be a friend to him."

In his book *What Makes a Man Feel Loved,* Bob Barnes encourages us in building friendship with our men: "Take the initial step and see how he responds. If you have tried before and not been well received, ask God to guide and bless your efforts and then risk reaching out again."[7]

📖 Read the following scriptures on friendship. What does each teach about being a friend? How can each be applied to marriage?

Proverbs 17:9

_____

_____

Proverbs 17:17

_____

_____

Proverbs 18:24

_____

_____

Proverbs 27:9, 17

_____

_____

John 15:13

_____

_____

Friendship is forgiving, protective, balancing, and sacrificial. These are not qualities that come naturally to anyone, let alone those bound by marriage.

📖 Read Titus 2:3–5. What are the older women supposed to teach the younger women (verse 4) and why (verse 5)?

_____

_____

In verse 4 Paul uses the Greek word *philandros* for "love," meaning loving "a friend or loving as a friend, and . . . a husband. . . . [or] Loving one's husband."[8] Teaching younger women how to love their husbands as friends is still our responsibility today. We teach it—perhaps unknowingly—as we interact with our husbands in front of our daughters, their friends, our friends, our neighbors, and so on. Do they see us laying our lives down every day for our husbands? Modeling is still the best teaching tool.

APPLY Below are some questions that assess your camaraderie with your husband. Your answers will give you a sense of where you are in your friendship:

Yes	No	Questions
❑	❑	Are you relaxed in your husband's company?
❑	❑	Do you enjoy being with your husband?
❑	❑	Do you make a plan to spend time each evening just to talk about your day?
❑	❑	Do you make a regular plan to spend time together away from the children?
❑	❑	Is spending time with him fulfilling?
❑	❑	Do you like your husband?

> *"Greater love has no one than this, that one lay down his life for his friends."*
>
> *John 15:13*

Yes	No	Questions
❑	❑	Can you look him in the eye and smile at him?
❑	❑	Can you laugh easily around him?
❑	❑	Can you cry in his presence?
❑	❑	Can you talk things over with ease, without feeling intimidated or defensive?
❑	❑	Can you turn to him for help on anything?
❑	❑	Do you work well together on projects, chores, and so on without criticism or frustration?
❑	❑	Are you willing to try new things with him?
❑	❑	Do you confide in your husband?
❑	❑	Does he confide in you?
❑	❑	Do you keep his confidence?
❑	❑	Does he keep your confidence?

Take a look at each question to which you answered "No," and ask yourself why you gave that answer. Write the reason in a few words in the margin next to each "No." When you're finished, revisit your reasons. Do you see a common thread that weaves through each? If so, what is it, and what might it reveal about your relationship?

_____

_____

_____

Building a friendship requires a willingness to love unconditionally, a willingness to communicate freely, a willingness to adapt wisely, and time. Be encouraged. You're learning the first three. Trust God with the time. Your friendship is worth whatever time He takes. Let's continue.

Does your husband know that you and he are friends? How do you show him?

_____

_____

_____

Describe what it's like to be with your husband. Be candid:

_____

_____

_____

_____

_____

Describe what you think it's like for him to be with you.

_____

_____

_____

This next question may take some calculating: in any given week, how much of your waking time would you estimate that you and your husband spend together alone? Do you consider it too much time together or not enough? Why? What would it take to change the amount of time you spend together? (What would you have to do and/or what would your husband have to do to make it happen?)

_____

_____

Falling in love was the easy part of our relationship with our husbands. Liking our husbands and living as friends, especially during the mundane routines of life, are the hard parts. Here are a few pointers to help you build on what you have:

☞ Make your friendship with your husband your top priority. Treasure what you have, and build on it.

☞ Look out for his interests—and join him there! You might rediscover what you once enjoyed or find something new you can share (Philippians 2:3–4).

☞ When with your husband, think like a friend. Let your face, your eyes, and your voice reflect appreciation for who he is. Be glad you're with him.

☞ Hold him close—loosely. Friends don't smother each other or try to control the other. So give your man the freedom to be himself.

☞ Don't share only your burdens. The beauty and joy of friendship is sharing the beauty and joy of life. Make sure he knows how he's contributing to your life.

☞ Be willing to serve him (1 Peter 4:10). Selfless service demonstrates our friendship with Christ. An act of service is a wonderful surprise when he's not expecting it!

☞ Speak his language: What makes him feel loved is probably not the same for you. A dinner date makes you feel warm and fuzzy; he might have the same response when he comes home to find the lawn mowed. (I know—that's a terrible example. But it's my husband's love language!) This is why it's important to study your man. Find out what's important to him. Accept and respect it. Then make it happen.

 If there's anything impeding your friendship with your husband, now's the time to ask for God's wisdom on how to identify and remove it. Allow God to take you where you need to be, trusting that He'll also work in your husband. Ask Him for the courage to reach out as your husband's friend, to touch his heart with the heart of the true Friend.

BUILDING UNITY

In their book *Intimate Allies,* authors Dan Allender and Tremper Longman III assert, "Life is war, and marriage provides us with a close and intimate ally with whom we may wage this war."[9]

📖 We all have faced or will face various battles in life. How do the following passages attest to this, and why do they say we face these battles?

Sidebar

Falling in love was the easy part of our relationship with our husbands. Liking our husbands and living as friends, especially during the mundane routines of life, are the hard parts.

My Husband, My Friend

James 1:2–4

_____

_____

1 Peter 5:8–9

_____

_____

1 Peter 1:3–7

_____

_____

Romans 5:3–5

_____

_____

God's purposes for our lives are woven throughout each battle. Some are clear to us, and some are not, but all are intended by God to mature us in Christ and to prepare us for the bigger battles. How battles are fought within and for our marriages will determine the survival of our marriages.

APPLY In what ways has your marriage matured you?

_____

_____

_____

From the beginning, the Enemy's goal was to separate humanity from God. His target then was the marriage, and that tactic hasn't changed in millennia. In Luke 11:17, what does Jesus say about a house divided?

_____

_____

According to Psalm 127:1, under what conditions should a house be built?

_____

_____

"Divide and conquer" is Satan's strategy. Letting the Lord build our homes gives God every opportunity to advance His kingdom and thwarts the Enemy's efforts to drive a stake through the heart of our marriages.

Read Ephesians 6:10–12. What is Paul's exhortation, and why?

_____

_____

_____

What insight does this passage give us into the need to be and stay in alliance with our husbands at all times?

> God's purposes for our lives are woven throughout each battle. Some are clear to us, and some are not, but all are intended by God to mature us in Christ and to prepare us for the bigger battles. How battles are fought within and for our marriages will determine the survival of our marriages.

> _"Finally, be strong in the Lord, and in the strength of His might. Put on the full armor of God, that you may be able to stand firm against the schemes of the devil."_
>
> **Ephesians 6:10–11**

_____

_____

_____

Christians and their marriages are on Satan's hit list—whether our husbands are believers or not. A marriage of two unbelievers is already in enemy hands. But ours are in his crosshairs! He also knows that one of the easiest ways to steal, kill, or destroy our kids is through marital strife and division. If we're not aware of how the Enemy can influence our lives and our marriages, he'll play us to his advantage.

📖 James 3:13–18 talks about two kinds of wisdom. The first is not from above. How is it described, what are its effects, and how can it influence a marriage (verses 14–16)?

_____

_____

_____

The second kind of wisdom is from above. What are its characteristics, and how can this wisdom influence a marriage (verses 17–18)?

_____

_____

_____

> _If we're not aware of how the Enemy can influence our lives and our marriages, he'll play us to his advantage._

Allender and Longman say,

> _Marriage is the soil_ for growing glory. We must see our spouses in light of what they are meant to become, without turning bitter or complacent about who they are. Marriage requires a radical commitment to love our spouses as they are, while longing for them to become what they are not yet. Every marriage moves either toward enhancing one another's glory or toward degrading each other.[10]

📖 Read Ecclesiastes 4:9–12. Based on these verses, in what ways can a friendship protect a marriage?

_____

_____

_____

Ed Wheat states, "Husband and wife develop a couple viewpoint. What hurts one hurts the other. What diminishes one harms the other."[11] When we develop, maintain, and protect our united front, we won't want to shy away from tackling whatever seeks to divide us.

 Identify any issues, opinions, and values in which you and your husband are not united, where instead of comfort there exists an underlying, ever-present tension. What impact do they have on your marriage and family relationships? Keeping James 3:13–18 in mind, what can you do to neutralize these areas?

Areas of Tension	Impact on Marriage/Family	Ways to Ease the Tensions (James 3:13–18)

📖 Read Philippians 3:10–16. Ponder these verses with regard to where you and your husband are spiritually (as individuals). Now consider these verses as they relate to those points on which you and your husband think differently. How can verses 15–16 help put your mind at ease with regard to your differences and strengthen your unity?

_____

_____

_____

This passage had a profound impact on me. I don't let differences divide John and me anymore. The beauty of the Holy Spirit's teaching role is that if there's something I need to learn, He's going to see that I "get it" eventually. And He has been faithful repeatedly. I choose to trust that He'll do the same with my husband. If in anything he has a different attitude or opinion that needs to change, God will reveal it—He'll make it clear to him in His timing. *"Only let us hold true to what we have already attained and walk and order our lives by that"* (verse 16, AMP).

 Pray for unity with your husband. Ask God to show you how to build toward it, maintain what you establish, and keep on building. Ask Him to help you address when necessary those areas that seek to divide you; to help you to resist fretting over those areas in which you're not in agreement. Ask for the courage to accept God's role in making His way clear to your husband, and with grace focus on the common ground you two have. Praise God for every inch of that common ground, trusting Him to add to it over time.

> **When we develop, maintain, and protect our united front, we won't want to shy away from tackling whatever seeks to divide us.**

My Husband, My Friend
DAY FIVE

BUILDING MEMORIES

Do you enjoy your husband? The more intimately you know him, the easier it is to enjoy who he is and who you both can become together. If you recall from Lesson 9, on romance, reminiscing is a beautiful tool to recalibrate our thinking and keep us moving forward on the right relational track. What do you and he do together that fills your memory bank? What reservoir of pleasant recollections can you draw from to satisfy your soul and fill your heart with peace, joy, and laughter when you need it? Someone once said, "God gives you memories so that you have roses in winter."

Some wives bemoan the fact that they live as "married singles" because they don't do anything with their husbands. Perhaps they don't share the same interests anymore. At some point in their marriage their activities ceased to be inclusive, and they began to slowly separate on all levels of marriage.

Building memories is a great way to build friendship. And it's important no matter what stage of marriage we're in. Our early "couple" years, our mid "with kids" years, and our "empty nest" years all offer opportunities to build sustaining memories and add depth to our friendship. Those of you who are young in your marriages are investing in your later years. You're also investing in your children's futures, building legacy and tradition for them to take into their marriages. But you should also be strengthening the bond between you and your husband. And long after the kids are grown and gone, you two can still be adding to your memory banks.

 Take some time now to assess how you and your husband spend your time together. The next series of questions are especially important at this stage in the marriage study. Since you've been learning and building on God's truth for weeks, you now have what you need to understand how to be effective in keeping your marriage alive and vital before the Lord. Answer the following questions as honestly and thoroughly as you can.

What do you enjoy about your husband? What enhances this enjoyment?

_____

_____

If you don't enjoy your husband, why not? What has changed? What do you think is impeding your enjoyment? In what way can you positively affect this impediment? What can you put to prayer for God's influence and change?

_____

_____

_____

List things you and your husband have in common (likes, dislikes, music, food, hobbies, and so on). Think of everything. Nothing is too insignificant. How can you build camaraderie around these commonalities?

_____

_____

_____

_____

In Day Three you calculated how much time you spent together alone. How would you change the quality of time spent together?

_____

_____

_____

If you and your husband are empty-nesters, how is the time you spend together different from when your children were in the home? What might you like to see change in terms of the quality of time you spend together?

_____

_____

_____

A few years ago, as empty-nesters, John and I were challenged to come up with a list of fifty things we would each like to do after age fifty, to compare lists, and then start implementing. I got to only ten items, but John had no difficulty filling his page. When I saw that whitewater rafting was listed among his top five, my first response was, "Oh, puh-lease!" But now, a few years later, I'm ready, and we'll make it happen. If you and your husband were challenged to come up with five things to do after fifty (or forty or thirty), what would they be? Yes, you'll have to ask him to write down his thoughts, too, and then compare notes.

_____

_____

_____

Even if you've got years before reaching the empty-nest stage, once you begin to think about it, you can create a very positive and lively attitude about building "couple" memories toward your future. Let's use the analogy of investing financially for retirement. We start investing early and save small amounts consistently. As compound interest kicks in, the value of our investment over time builds to the point of sustaining us in our later years. As this analogy relates to our marriages, we can also experience a good return at empty-nest time when we invest in our husbands throughout the years and trust God to compound the interest. However, if we invest heavily or exclusively in our children while neglecting to invest in our husbands, then the relationship that needs to yield the most at empty-nest time yields the least. And the marriage is as empty as the nest. To avoid this outcome, invest now in your husband and in your life together, and include your children, not the other way around. One wise husband of thirty-two years said, "Ask the question, 'Who is my best friend?' If it is your mate, there will be no problem with the empty nest."[12] Build and protect your marital friendship now, and you'll not only look forward to the empty nest, but you'll also look forward to it for all the right reasons.

You and your husband should seriously consider activities to cultivate together, perhaps some to which you've been resistant. Start simple. Whitewater rafting doesn't have to be at the top of the list. Write these activities here. Then make a plan! Keep in mind that your willingness to participate in things he would like to do could open the door to his willingness to participate in the things you would like to do.

_____

_____

_____

Build and protect your marital friendship now, and you'll not only look forward to the empty nest, but you'll look forward to it for all the right reasons.

Creating wonderful memories takes time. Here are a few suggestions on how to get started:

- Start small. In what little ways can you spend more time together?
- Be open to new things that you and your husband can enjoy together.
- Find ways now to spend a monthly date night away from your little ones, and protect this habit over the years. Don't let complacency set in. Its byproduct is boredom. Pick a night that works best for the two of you.

What do you have to do to make this happen (find a regular babysitter, rework schedules, and so on)?

■ Take photos of the two of you together on each anniversary. Cameras aren't just for kid shots! Build photo memories of you and your husband, and reminisce later during one of your "simply romantic" evenings (Lesson 9).

 Since our God is adept at building from scratch, He'll take whatever you offer and create a masterpiece of memories, no matter where you are in your marriage. Ask God to create in you a joy about your future with your husband; to prepare your heart and his for your later years together as you plan for and invest in them now.

In Lesson 12 we'll see how praying for our husbands can accomplish God's purposes—in them and in us.

Works Cited

1. Spiros Zodhiates, Warren Baker, eds., *The Complete Word Study Dictionary New Testament* (Chattanooga, TN: AMG Publishers, 1992), #4722, 1310.

2. Leslie Vernick, *How to Act Right When Your Spouse Acts Wrong* (Colorado Springs, CO: WaterBrook Press, 2003), 78.

3. Linda Dillow, *Creative Counterparts* (Nashville, TN: Thomas Nelson Publishers, 1986), 107.

4. Ed Wheat and Gloria Okes Perkins, *Love Life for Every Married Couple* (Grand Rapids, MI: Zondervan Publishing House, 1980), 127.

5. Vernick, 95–96.

6. Steve and Annie Chapman, *Married Lovers, Married Friends* (Minneapolis: Bethany House, 1989), 93.

7. Bob Barnes, *What Makes a Man Feel Loved* (Eugene, OR: Harvest House Publishers, 1998), 139–40.

8. Zodhiates, Baker, #5362, 1444.

9. Dan B. Allender and Tremper Longman III, *Intimate Allies* (Wheaton, IL: Tyndale House Publishers, 1995), 113.

10. Ibid., 11.

11. Wheat and Perkins, 124.

12. Quoted in David and Claudia Arp, *The Second Half of Marriage* (Grand Rapids: Zondervan Publishing House, 1996), 120.

12

Praying for Your Husband

I've learned that the old adage "When all else fails, pray" should be "Pray so all else won't fail!" Christian marriages are failing today more than any other time in history, or they're limping along defeated, broken, bleeding, and dying a slow death. I believe it's because we've fallen victim to the lie from the Enemy that if a marriage is broken, then nothing can fix it, so we just have to live with it or pitch it. The Enemy has turned up the heat, and we don't even know we're in the pot!

Hopefully this study has given you a biblical and practical foundation for working toward and maintaining a strong marriage. God is working in you and through you to achieve His purposes in your relationship with your husband. Has it been tough? Does it seem to be an uphill battle? Does it seem impossible that there could be any change in your husband, any improvement in your marriage? Do you want to throw in the proverbial towel at times and walk away? I understand where you are. So let me assure you that God has a bigger plan, and He wants you to learn it on your knees.

Do you pray *for* your husband or *about* your husband? Why do you pray? For what do you pray? How do you pray? What do you expect from God when you do pray? How long are you willing to wait for your prayer to be answered? What happens when you grow weary of waiting? If you're already

> **I've learned that the old adage "When all else fails, pray" should be "Pray so all else won't fail!"**

in the habit of praying for your husband, my hope is that the Holy Spirit will give you a fresh perspective from this week's lesson, taking you deeper with the Lord on your husband's behalf. If you're not in the habit of praying for him, my prayer is that it will only be a short time before the burden to do this will become so great that you'll be incapable of neglecting to pray for him. May God use this week's lesson to get our God-centered prayer lives off the ground and soaring heavenward, where all life-changing activity takes place.

Praying for Your Husband

DAY ONE

GOD'S PURPOSE FOR OUR PRAYER

My approach to my problems used to be—do what I can (whining, pouting, cajoling, demanding, debating, and so on) as best I can (I got pretty good at it!) for as long as it takes (I never wore out) until it worked out (I got my way). And if it didn't work out, well, I guess I would just have to pray about it (whining, pouting, cajoling, demanding, and debating before God). This was my tactic for whatever and whoever needed to change. You can only guess how well it worked in my life and marriage.

Stormie Omartian said that the "power of a praying wife is not a means of gaining control over your husband, so don't get your hopes up! In fact, it is quite the opposite. It's laying down all claim to power in and of yourself, and relying on *God's* power to transform you, your husband, your circumstances, and your marriage."[1]

Perhaps we don't often consider our motives when we pray for our husbands. Below are a few thoughts that can motivate our prayers when we want to see change. We might pray:

☞ **so that life would be easier.** If life is tough and we petition God for a break, we're focused on the "Why?" of our circumstance and the "When?" of its end. These two questions are distracters and can impede our hearing the will of God, because we're more focused on our needs than on the One who can meet our needs.

☞ **so that we'll feel better.** "Lord, if my husband [circumstances, life] were only this way, then I wouldn't feel anger, disappointment, impatience, or bitterness." We're desperate for change, usually in our circumstances or in someone else. This attitude can embitter us toward God, closing our ears to His counsel about us.

☞ **because we know we're supposed to.** Indifference, frustration, or defeat is usually associated with this motive. We also might resign ourselves to the lie that if we pray for our husbands dutifully, the rest is up to God and we can kick back and relax. What's missing is an earnest heart. Our prayers may be lifeless because our hearts are cold.

📖 According to the following Scriptures, what is God's purpose for our prayer?

Jeremiah 29:11–13

_____

_____

Jeremiah 33:3

_____

_____

Matthew 7:7–8

_____

_____

Luke 22:42

_____

_____

John 14:13

_____

_____

Ephesians 3:20–21

_____

_____

_____

> *"Call to Me, and I will answer you, and I will tell you great and mighty things, which you do not know."*
>
> *Jeremiah 33:3*

Let's take a look at God's purposes for our prayer:

☞ Primarily, God calls us to prayer! He wants us to come to Him first, to acknowledge who He is, and to anticipate what He's capable of doing in response to our prayers. He encourages us to seek Him so that He can reveal Himself, His will, and His glory.

☞ Prayer is the means by which we can know God intimately. As we spend quiet, top-quality time with God, being genuine with Him, He shares Himself with us. But we must first see Him as more than just a "need meeter." Hank Hanegraaff writes,

> We hurry into God's presence with a laundry list of prayer requests. And before our knees have even touched the ground we are already thinking about getting back to our frenzied lifestyles. Often we treat our heavenly Father no better than we treat our families. We want a relationship without the discipline of investing quality time.[2]

☞ Prayer releases the power of God to carry out the plans of God. He uses prayer to position us so that He can begin to work. When we relinquish control, God's power takes over, and things happen. We don't see or perhaps even understand, but the spiritual realm moves on behalf of the heartfelt prayers of a righteous child of God (James 5:16). Jesus' battle in the Garden of Gethsemane is an excellent example of this spiritual dynamic (Luke 22:39–44). Prayer prepared Him for what was ahead and brought a ministering angel to strengthen Him so that He could pray even more fervently. The war that Jesus fought on His knees brought Him to His resolute *"Not My will, but Yours be done"* (Luke 22:42), which changed eternity for all of us who believe and brought glory to God. As a result, we're now experiencing in the temporal what God accomplished in the spiritual realm—oneness with Him forever. When we ask the Holy Spirit to teach us to pray for our husbands with spiritual perspective, He'll do it.

Prayer reveals the real "me" so that change in me can generate change through me.

We have a ruthless, heartless, cruel adversary who wants to keep us too busy to be on our knees.

☞ Prayer builds our trust in who God is and in His capability. He's the only one who knows our future, and He desires to unfold it before us. He's also the only one who holds the balm for our fears and our heart's wounds. Prayer is where He meets us when we're fearful, angry, hurt, worried, frustrated, and tempted to control or manipulate our men and our circumstances. Will we trust God with our futures? Will we trust Him with our hearts? Will we trust Him with our husbands?

☞ Prayer reveals the real "me" so that change in me can generate change through me. Oswald Chambers explains this dynamic:

> To say that "prayer changes things" is not as close to the truth as saying, "Prayer changes *me* and then I change things." God has established things so that prayer, on the basis of redemption, changes the way a person looks at things. Prayer is not a matter of changing things externally, but one of working miracles in a person's inner nature.[3]

☞ Prayer protects us from the Enemy's plan. We have a ruthless, heartless, cruel adversary who wants to keep us too busy to be on our knees. We also have a world clamoring for our time and attention. And we have a human nature that's distracted by and sometimes cooperating with both our adversary and the world. But none of these is as great as the Spirit of God within us (1 John 4:4). When we pray as He prompts and guides, the powers on the outside are impotent. Stormie Omartian says,

> Walking with God doesn't mean there won't be obstacles. Satan will see to it that there are. While God has a plan for your future that is good, the devil has one too and it's not good. But the devil's plan for your life cannot succeed as long as you are walking with God, living in obedience to His ways, worshiping only Him, standing strong in His Word, and praying without ceasing.[4]

APPLY Take a minute to answer a few questions about prayer in your life: Generally, why do you pray?

_____

_____

_____

_____

How would you assess your prayer life? What are its strengths? Where is it lacking?

_____

_____

_____

What do you expect from God when you pray? How long are you willing to wait for your prayer to be answered? What happens when you grow tired of waiting?

_____

_____

_____

Do you pray for your husband? If so, why? If not, why not?

_____

_____

_____

 Does your prayer life need tweaking? I know mine does on a regular basis. Like our intimacy with our husbands, prayer is our intimacy with God, and if that relationship is to grow, it must be purposefully cultivated and consistently nurtured. Has God placed anything on your heart with regard to your prayer life? Does anything need to change? Ask Him now to change whatever is necessary to create in you a vital prayer life with eternal impact. He will go to work immediately!

A PLAN FOR OUR PRAYER

What do you pray for your husband? "Change him, Lord?" "Fix him, God?" "Get him, God?" You may smile, but often our prayers boil down to one of those three categories. All three cause us to focus on what's wrong with our husbands. Yes, true desire to see a changed heart in a husband can generate these prayers. But more often it's hurt, anger, bitterness, a critical spirit, or conditional love.

 Take a moment to write down what you pray for your husband. Be specific. Be honest too.

_____

_____

_____

Now take a look at the list you just compiled. Do any of your prayers fall under "Change him," "Fix him," or "Get him"? Let's alter the three prayer categories just a tad to see how they might redirect our prayer focus:

First, instead of praying, "Change him, Lord," pray, "Draw him, Lord." It's easy to slip into prayers that concentrate on all the ways we would like to see our husbands change. By the time we're done praying, we're overwhelmed at the enormity of the task we've just given God and angry with our husbands all over again. Charles Stanley gives wise counsel: "When we pray for someone, we must take our hands off the matter completely and let God work any way He desires."[5] This is important whether or not our husbands are in relationship with Christ. We must put our hope, our confidence, and our expectancy in God alone. This puts us in neutral gear, allows us to pray balanced prayers, and lets God work with our husbands. Nobody does it better!

How does John 6:44 encourage the prayer "Draw him, Lord?"

_____

_____

_____

It's easy to slip into prayers that concentrate on all the ways we would like to see our husbands change. By the time we're done praying, we're overwhelmed at the enormity of the task we've just given God and angry with our husbands all over again.

God draws us to Himself. Genuine change takes place as we respond to the Holy Spirit's drawing, convicting, sanctifying power. He puts a desire or a longing for God in our spirits, a longing that's beautifully captured in the following Scriptures. How do the psalmists describe their longing?

Psalm 42:1–2

_____

_____

Psalm 63:1–8

_____

_____

Psalm 84:1–2

_____

_____

God wants us to want Him and to want to be with Him. When our desire wanes, we can earnestly ask God to ignite a longing that brings us closer to Him again. He answers this prayer, knowing that our hearts are open and responsive to His loving influence. Then we can pray for our husbands what we willingly pray for ourselves: "Draw him, Lord, so that he'll be open to Your loving influence."

APPLY Do you hunger and thirst for God? What do you do when you feel spiritually dry or empty?

_____

_____

_____

Do you acknowledge with thanksgiving the Holy Spirit in you? Do you draw upon His resources in you? Would you say that you have a heart that's open and responsive to the Holy Spirit's influence? In what ways has He influenced your role as a wife, especially in these last twelve weeks of study?

_____

_____

_____

How would asking God to draw your husband to Himself alter the way you're praying for him now?

_____

_____

_____

Second, instead of praying, "Fix him, Lord!" pray, "Mature him, Lord." "Fixing" is automatic as we grow spiritually. It's called the sanctification process. Asking God to mature our husbands releases them to grow in accordance with God's plan and purpose, in keeping with His will and not our own. For you whose husbands are difficult to live with, pray this also for yourselves ("Mature me, Lord"). He'll prepare you to respond to the tougher

> **"How lovely is your dwelling place, O Lord Almighty! My soul yearns, even faints, for the courts of the Lord; my heart and my flesh cry out for the living God."**
>
> **Psalm 84:1–2 (NIV)**

aspects of your husband's character in a more balanced way, one that will testify to His presence in your life and circumstances. The love of Christ in our prayers and in our behavior has the supernatural potential to influence our husbands. If we refuse to lose heart and give up, we'll exhibit fruit rather than frustration, and that's something the Holy Spirit will work with!

📖 The following scriptures are Paul's prayers for the believers in the cities of Ephesus, Philippi, and Colosse. What did he pray for specifically in each passage that we could also pray for our husbands? (Please don't write off these passages if your husband doesn't believe in Christ. God will receive them as the desire of your heart.)

Ephesians 1:16–20

_____

_____

_____

Philippians 1:3–6, 9–11

_____

_____

_____

Colossians 1:3, 9–12

_____

_____

_____

APPLY Did you note the intensity of Paul's prayers, his thankfulness for the believers, the faithfulness with which he prayed, the specifics of his prayer? How do your prayers for your husband compare to Paul's? Would you pray differently for the areas in your husband's character that you would like to see mature? In what ways?

_____

_____

_____

Last, instead of praying, "Get him, God," pray, "Bless and protect him, Lord." It's hard to have a bad attitude toward our husbands when we're sincerely asking God to bless them and protect them. We know this is not a flesh–and–blood world (Ephesians 6:12). In the spiritual realm, our adversary, the devil, stands against us at every turn (1 Peter 4:8). Satan hates a believer humbled before the Lord pleading her husband's case. He really doesn't expect her to be savvy enough to do battle with him there. Could it be that she's no longer easily deceived?

📖 What do the following scriptures reveal about blessing and protection?

Job 1:9–10

_____

_____

_____

> *The love of Christ in our prayers and in our behavior has the supernatural potential to influence our men. If we refuse to lose heart and give up, we'll exhibit fruit rather than frustration, and that's something the Holy Spirit will work with!*

> *Satan hates a believer humbled before the Lord pleading her husband's case. He really doesn't expect her to be savvy enough to do battle with him there. Could it be that she is no longer easily deceived?*

Psalm 94:12–13 (this is not a "Get him, God" prayer!)

_____

_____

_____

John 17:15

_____

_____

_____

Ephesians 6:10–18

_____

_____

_____

APPLY Think about all the areas (physically, emotionally, psychologically, sexually, and spiritually) in which your husband needs to be covered by prayers of blessing and protection. List specific items under each area that you can be praying for him.

_____

_____

_____

 The prophet Samuel knew all that the Israelites had done against God, and yet he said in 1 Samuel 12:23, _"As for me, far be it from me that I should sin against the LORD by failing to pray for you"_ (NIV). Kay Arthur writes, "True prayer is submission to the will of the Father."[6] When we know where our husbands need prayer, I believe God holds us accountable to pray. Their needs, their temptations, their weaknesses, their failings, and their sin can be covered when praying, "Draw him" (where and why?), "Mature him" (how?), "Bless him" (in what ways?), and "Protect him" (from what or whom?). What is God telling you about your commitment to pray for your husband? How can you assist in drawing him to God, in contributing to his spiritual maturity, in being a part of God's blessing, in covering him with protection? Are you resistant to praying for your husband? If so, take your resistance to the Lord, and ask Him to reveal what has yet to be surrendered: "Not my will, but Yours be done." Amen.

OUR PART IN OUR PRAYER

When I send my husband off in the morning, I walk to the window and pray for him as his car passes our home. Doing this reminds me that he's vulnerable and that he needs the physical, sexual, psychological, spiritual, and relational protection that the Lord provides through prayer. And I want nothing to impede my prayers for him. How do we offer our prayers to the Lord? How do we ensure that they get past the ceiling and into the ears of God? Woven throughout Scripture are wonderful principles that help to shape our prayer lives. Here are some to consider:

📖 Read Hebrews 10:19–22; 1 John 1:9; 3:21–22. Pray with a clean slate. If we're in rebellion to God's Word, our fellowship with Him is broken, and His ears are closed to all our prayers, not just those for our husbands. When we humble ourselves and confess our sin, He throws wide the door, restores our fellowship, and attends to our prayers.

Is something hindering your prayers right now? If so, what is it? Will you expose it to His light right here and now and let Him cleanse you from all unrighteousness? Write it here.

_____

_____

_____

📖 Read John 15:1–11 and 1 John 5:14–15. Pray with the will and the purposes of God in mind. According to Kay Arthur, "We can misinterpret God . . . if we do not abide in Him and His words do not abide in us. That is why we must spend time alone with Him, why His Word is to dwell in us richly . . . so we fully know Him and His will."[7] We learn to desire what God desires for our husbands as we abide in Him, keep our eyes fixed on Him, and stay in His Word.

What do you want for your husband that you know agrees with God's desire for him?

_____

_____

_____

_____

📖 Read Mark 11:24. Pray specifically. Sometimes we don't know what to pray, so we pray in generalities such as "Lord, give my husband a good day." Yes, it takes a little more time to think of specifics and pray them, but that's what the Holy Spirit is for. Becky Tirabassi gives good instruction: "It has become my practice, without fear of being laughed at or scolded by God, to *ask* Him how I should pray when I am unsure of His will. . . . God says to 'call to Me, and I will answer you, and show you great and mighty things, which you do not know' (Jer. 33:3, NKJV). Almost to say, 'Just ask. It's no secret.' "[8] Great advice!

If you're not sure how to pray for your husband, take a few moments right now and ask God. Write your insights here:

_____

_____

_____

📖 Read Philippians 4:4–7 and 1 Thessalonians 5:16–18. Pray with the right attitude. Sometimes our husbands are hard to pray for. We may not even want to pray for them. Rather than pray and wait for God to work, we tend to criticize, nag, or freeze our men into change (which we know doesn't work, but we do it anyway). When we submit to God and pray

> "Dear friends, if our hearts do not condemn us, we have confidence before God and receive from him anything we ask, because we obey his commands and do what pleases him."
>
> **1 John 3:21–22 (NIV)**

obediently, our hearts soften. A fresh faith, hope, and expectancy in God rises in us that keeps a stream of peace coursing through our spiritual veins because God is God, and we can stop trying to do His job.

There is no other who will work in our circumstances like God will. How can this truth affect your attitude when you pray for your husband?

_____

_____

_____

📖 Read James 4:3. Pray with the right motives. Stop yourself every so often while in prayer and ask, "Why am I praying this prayer or making this request? What do I truly want from God?" Right motives reflect a right heart before God, which generates genuine prayer.

Do you ever check your motives when you pray for your husband? What have you discovered? How can understanding your motives make your prayers for him more effective?

_____

_____

_____

_____

📖 Read Ephesians 3:20, Hebrews 11:6, and James 1:5–8. Pray with a believing spirit and without doubt. Do you pray for your husband and then immediately doubt that God will answer your prayers? Do you doubt that He's able to do what you've asked? Do you believe that God's power was able to save your soul—but can't save your husband's? Do you believe He could change your life but can't change your husband's? Do you believe His power raised His own Son from the dead but can't resurrect your marriage? His is the only power that can do all these things!

What about your husband or your marriage do you find difficult to entrust to God? What can you do to resist doubt and embrace belief?

_____

_____

_____

📖 Read Hebrews 4:14–16. Pray with confidence. We can take anything to God—our weaknesses, our fears, our failings, our shame. Anything. We can go before Him boldly, confident that His mercy will meet us at His throne and that His grace will help us in our need.

Have you pictured God's throne as one of grace or punishment? Does the Hebrews passage change your picture and influence your approach to God? If so, in what ways?

_____

_____

_____

📖 Read Luke 10:19 and 2 Timothy 1:7. Pray with authority. As Stormie Omartian suggests, "We *don't* have authority over our husbands. However, we have been given authority 'over all the power of the enemy' (Luke 10:19) and can do great damage to the enemy's plans when we pray."[9] We stand against Satan and his strategies because God tells us to (Ephesians 6:10–12)—not with arrogance but with God-confidence, just as Jesus did.

How does approaching God with confidence compare to your typical approach?

_____

_____

_____

📖 Read Matthew 7:7–11 and Luke 18:1–8. Pray persistently. Don't give up until you know His answer! Charles Stanley writes, "God answers prayers in one of four ways: Yes. No. Wait. My grace is sufficient. Or in more personal terms, 'Yes, child, you may have it'; 'No, child, this is not good for you'; 'Wait, child, I have something better'; or 'My grace is sufficient for you' (2 Corinthians 12:9)"[10] Waiting on God's answers is the most difficult aspect of prayer, but Jesus wants us to be tenacious—to ask and keep on asking, to seek and keep on seeking, to knock and keep on knocking. He's doing something while we persist and persevere, and we persevere until we know His answer.

How easy is it for you to give up on a prayer? Are you tempted to stop praying a prayer that you know is in God's will? Why would you give up? Write the prayer here. Why should you persist in praying this prayer?

_____

_____

_____

📖 Read James 5:16. Pray for your husband with an earnest heart. The Amplified Version says, *"The earnest prayer of a righteous man makes tremendous power available."* Isn't that encouraging? Actually, it's exciting! Have you already experienced the working power and outcome of earnest prayer in your marriage? If so, you know that God's signature is written all over the experience. And so is His glory. May we ask the Holy Spirit to keep us walking in righteousness, so that when we offer up earnest, heartfelt, continued prayers for our husbands, they'll make tremendous power available and be dynamic in their working!

According to James 5:16, consider what an earnest prayer yields and why. How would you characterize your prayer for your husband? Does anything need to change? If so, what? How will you effect change?

_____

_____

_____

📖 Read Psalm 27:13 and Isaiah 64:4. Pray with expectancy, not with expectation. In his book *Your God Is Too Safe,* Mark Buchanan explains,

> Expectancy is the belief that God will do something. Expectation insists He do it in *just this way.* Sometimes expec-

"The earnest, prayer of a righteous man makes tremendous power available— dynamic in its working."

James 5:16 (AMP)

tation blinds us more to the God who is here right now than outright disbelief does. . . . But imagine a life buoyed by expectancy, by the conviction that the Lord will show Himself. How, when, where—we don't know that. We don't dictate the terms. . . . But by living with biblically girded expectancy, our lives stir to vibrant wakefulness."[11]

How would praying with expectancy instead of expectation be different from the way you're praying now?

_____

_____

_____

📖 Read 1 Thessalonians 5:17. Pray without ceasing. Cultivate an attitude of ceaseless prayer on your husband's behalf. Whenever the Lord brings him to mind, offer a meaningful prayer of praise, thanksgiving, and petition.

How often does your husband come to mind during the day? Key in on what you're thinking and then pray accordingly. You may discover that the prayer is as much for you as for your husband. Any insights?

_____

_____

_____

_____

Prayer isn't just speaking what's on our hearts—we listen for what's on God's heart. Neither can be conveyed without the powerful working of His Holy Spirit.

📖 Read Romans 8:26–27, Ephesians 6:18, and 1 Corinthians 2:9–14. Pray as led by the Spirit, who is always interceding for you. When we pray as the Holy Spirit leads us, we're submitted to Him and aligning our will with His. Sometimes our hearts are so disturbed or broken that we may not even know what to pray. We can only agonize or grieve. The Holy Spirit intercedes for us and sends to the Father's ear the prayer that's in accordance with His will. And then we listen—for insights, answers, wisdom, and guidance. Prayer isn't just speaking what's on our hearts—we listen for what's on God's heart. Neither can be conveyed without the powerful working of His Holy Spirit.

Do you take time to let the Holy Spirit lead your prayer? Do you wait to hear from God when you're done speaking? How can relying on the Spirit help you pray for your husband and about your relationship?

_____

_____

_____

_____

📖 Read John 14:13–14. Pray in the matchless name of Jesus. Praying "in the name of Jesus" is not just a collection of words to close a prayer. Invoking His name professes that we're in agreement with everything His character and His name represent. Recognizing the Lordship of Jesus Christ glorifies the Father. Using His name also invokes His power into our prayer. The bottom line in our prayer is not to accomplish what we want but to accomplish what God wants. And that can happen only through the Son.

Does understanding the use of Jesus' mighty name in your prayer change what and how you pray? If so, in what way?

_____

_____

_____

APPLY You can apply an excellent "formula" to your prayers. There's nothing wrong with a little structure, especially if we're not sure where or how to begin. It keeps us focused and also leaves plenty of room for the Holy Spirit to work. The one I use is the popular acronym ACTS: Adoration, Confession, Thanksgiving, and Supplication. Read through each of these steps prayerfully, applying what you've learned in today's lesson:

A—Acknowledge with **adoration** the Author of your marital covenant. Prayer begins with worshiping God. Jesus affirmed this when He taught His disciples how to pray (Matthew 6:9). God deserves and desires our acknowledgment, our adoration, and our praise for who He is. When we do this, we declare His Lordship in our lives, which prepares our hearts to be submissive to His Word and His will.

C—**Confess** any ill-will, coldness, or hostility toward your husband. Confess indifference. Confess critical, judgmental, and condemning tendencies. Confess self-righteousness. You may say, "But you don't know my circumstances!" None are bigger than God. The real question is—do you believe that God is bigger than your circumstances? Decide to trust Him with your husband and your circumstances. Then watch Him work as you continue to pray faithfully, and don't give up.

T—**Thank** God for your husband—for who he is and for what he's doing for you and your family. This opens up the door for God's love in you to unconditionally accept your husband, to release him to the Lover of his soul, and to let God be God in his life, even if he doesn't yet know Christ as Savior. This frees you to love your husband as he really is.

S—Make your **Supplications** known to God. Ask God to show you your husband through His eyes. Then ask Him what to pray for him. You may be surprised by what you're given. Ask your husband as well how you can pray for him. Then be faithful, devoted, and constant in your prayer (Romans 12:12).

GOD'S POWER IN OUR PRAYER

Most of us desire a prayer life that exalts Christ, one that allows Him to loom large in our minds as the All-Sufficient One who gets things done His way and in His timing (see 1 John 5:14–15). Often our temptation is to tell God what to do with our husbands and on what timeline. One way to keep us in line with the will of God is praying back to Him verses that apply to our husbands, to us, or to our circumstances. We personalize them by including them into our prayers, adding the names of those for whom we're praying. When we add the Word of God to our prayer life, it helps to align our thoughts with God's thoughts. We pray with the mind of Christ (see 1 Corinthians 2:16) and

> *"And I will do whatever you ask in my name, so that the Son may bring glory to the Father. You may ask me for anything in my name, and I will do it."*
>
> *John 14:13–14 (NIV)*

Praying for Your Husband

DAY FOUR

Praying Scripture recalibrates our human perspective into spiritual perspective. It strengthens our trust in God and encourages us to wait patiently for Him to work His way.

not with our own or one influenced by the lies from the Enemy. Beth Moore tells us,

> In praying Scripture, I not only find myself in intimate communication with God, but my mind is being retrained, or renewed (Romans 12:2), to think *His* thoughts about my situation rather than mine. Ultimately, He resumes His proper place in my thought life as huge and indomitable, and my obstacle shrinks. This approach has worked powerfully every time I've applied it. It takes belief, diligence, and *time*, but the effects are dramatically liberating and eternal.[12]

Praying Scripture recalibrates our human perspective into spiritual perspective. It strengthens our trust in God and encourages us to wait patiently for Him to work His way.

📖 God told the Israelites, *"Man does not live on bread alone but on every word that comes from the mouth of the LORD"* (Deuteronomy 8:3, NIV). Jesus spoke this truth to Satan when assaulted with temptation for forty days in the desert (see Matthew 4:4). He relied on the Word of God at every turn. It sustained Him and thwarted the Enemy's plan. And it will do the same for us. But the Word of God wasn't all He relied on. Jesus was full of the Holy Spirit, led and controlled by Him. When the Enemy's onslaught of temptation confronted Jesus, He had His two resources ready for use: the Word of God and the power of God's Holy Spirit.

Ephesians 6:17 describes God's Word as the sword of the Spirit. It's the only offensive weapon among the pieces of God's armor that we put on. When we rely on His sword to define our prayers, His Spirit wields them with power against whatever would come against us. The sword of the Spirit slices through lies, fear, doubt, depression, confusion, weariness—you name it. We can depend on the sword and the power of the Spirit to guide us, sustain us, prepare us, protect us, comfort us, get us on God's track, and keep us there.

 Writing your prayers for your husband is an effective way of learning and applying Scripture. I recommend that you start a journal, and separate it into five categories of prayer emphasis: spiritual, physical, sexual, psychological, and relational. As you continue to read and study, God will draw your attention to verses He wants you to apply to your husband. He will also guide your attention to those scriptures that you can pray for yourself. Write them in your journal as personalized prayers. Then, in a particular time of need, you'll know right where to go to pray truth for you both.

To get you started, I've selected several wonderful truths in each category that you can personalize for your husband. By way of example, I'll begin with a passage on salvation. Then you can continue by personalizing the rest of the passages into prayer. Some of the passages will be familiar. Meditate on each (ponder the spiritual truth) before writing out your prayers here. Whether your husband is a believer or an unbeliever, pray believing!

SPIRITUAL
John 6:44 and 2 Peter 3:9 (for an unbelieving husband)
Father, I may not understand Your timing, but You said that You're not slow in keeping Your promise. Thank You that You're patient toward my husband, not wanting him to perish but to come to repentance. Help me to

be patient, too, Lord. Draw him to Jesus by your Spirit. While I wait on Your perfect timing, use me as Your instrument to reflect Christ's love and blessing. I pray this in the name that is above all names, Jesus Christ. Amen.

John 17:15 and Ephesians 6:10–18 (for your husband's protection from the evil one). This is one of the most important prayers you can pray every morning for him, for yourself, and for your children.

_____

_____

_____

Psalm 119:9–11 (for his protection from sin)

_____

_____

Ephesians 2:10, Philippians 1:6, and Colossians 1:9–12 (for his spiritual growth)

_____

_____

_____

PHYSICAL
Psalm 91:16 and Isaiah 58:11 (for his health)

_____

_____

_____

Psalm 30:2 and Malachi 4:2 (for his healing)

_____

_____

_____

SEXUAL
Proverbs 5:15–19 and 1 Corinthians 6:18–20 (for his protection from sexual sin)

_____

_____

_____

PSYCHOLOGICAL
2 Corinthians 3:17–18 and Colossians 3:1–4 (for his self-concept)

_____

_____

_____

Isaiah 26:3–4, Matthew 11:28–30, 2 Corinthians 10:3–5, and Philippians 4:4–8 (for his mental and emotional health)

> *"Jesus answered, 'It is written: MAN DOES NOT LIVE ON BREAD ALONE, BUT ON EVERY WORD THAT COMES FROM THE MOUTH OF GOD.'"*
>
> *Matthew 4:4 (NIV)*

_____

_____

_____

RELATIONAL

Ephesians 5:25, Colossians 3:19, and 1 Peter 3:7 (for his role as husband)

_____

_____

_____

Proverbs 17:6 and Colossians 3:21 (for his role as father)

_____

_____

_____

Proverbs 23:4–5, Colossians 3:22–24; 4:1 (for his work)

_____

_____

_____

Psalm 1:1–3, Proverbs 27:17, and 1 Corinthians 15:33 (for his companions)

_____

_____

_____

Proverbs 3:3–4; 31:23 (for his public image)

_____

_____

_____

 Pray for your husband—for his provision and for his protection. Ask the Holy Spirit to give you insight into how to pray for him specifically. Ask Him to provide scriptures that speak directly to your husband's needs. Write them in your journal. Then pray boldly, persistently, and with authority, believing and not doubting that God is working on behalf of you and your husband.

Praying for Your Husband

DAY FIVE

PRAYING, WAITING, STANDING

Not many of us enjoy waiting our turn in long lines (or even short ones!). We tap our toes, shift restlessly, murmur under our breath, comment impatiently to a complete stranger, keep our eyes on our watches, and grouse about how much longer we'll have to wait.

Life is about waiting. Life is also about change. Many of us are waiting for change, especially in our marriages. We wait restlessly and tap our toes, murmur under our breath, remind God to look at His watch, and grouse about how much longer we'll have to wait for change to come to our men and our marriages.

Whether we realize it or not, waiting is a discipline that God builds into our relationship with Him. He intends it to refine our character, build our strength and endurance, and perfect our faith. But when we pray and wait, and wait and pray some more, and nothing happens—when there is no visible, viable, tangible change—what then?

We continue to pray and wait—and stand.

📖 What does it mean to wait and stand? Read what the following scriptures say about waiting and standing. Be aware of the nuances of waiting and standing in these passages as well. What do you learn?

Psalm 62:5–8

_____

_____

Isaiah 50:7 and Philippians 3:12–14

_____

_____

Ephesians 6:10–18

_____

_____

In our prayerful waiting, we stand tall, fixed, and immovable in the knowledge that God is for us. And we refuse to forget it. Even if our husbands stand against us, we must believe that God is working inexhaustibly for our good, because that's what His Word says (see Romans 8:28–29). His guarantee is His Son's life in us and everything He has to offer. And although we don't know if, when, or how our circumstances will change, we know that the One who towers over them is sovereign in them. That's our hope, and that's why we pray and wait and stand—all the while pressing on to _"lay hold of that for which Christ Jesus has also laid hold of me"_ (Philippians 3:13, NKJV).

In every marriage there are seasons of challenge, hardship, and tragedy. And we're called to pray and wait. But do we stand? If our eyes are fixed on the circumstance or on ourselves, we'll crumble under every negative human thought and emotion. But if our eyes are on the sovereign Lord, He will balance our human emotions with Himself and place in our souls a desire for His greater purpose. This is the bottom line of life in Jesus Christ: If we've made Him our primary relationship, then no matter what we encounter in our marriages, we can still know His securing peace, because we believe that His purposes will prevail. And that gives us the strength to pray and wait and stand.

As I close out this last lesson, I'm thinking of your marriage and how God yearns to complete you and your husband in Himself. As you continue to draw nearer to Him and to your husband, wait faithfully on your faithful

> ### When we pray and wait, and wait and pray some more, and nothing happens—when there is no visible, viable, tangible change—what then? We continue to pray and wait—and stand.

Extra Mile

NO FEAR

Read Exodus 14:1–14 and 2 Chronicles 20. Exodus 14 records that as the Israelites left Egyptian captivity, Pharaoh and his army were in hot pursuit. How did the Lord encourage the frightened entourage? What similarity do you see in 2 Chronicles 20 when Jehoshaphat faced a vast army? How can these two passages help you face what seems like insurmountable circumstances?

God. Stand firm in His presence. Stand immovable on His principles-and stand triumphant in His power. He'll see that you remain strong and steadfast, victorious on your knees.

 Lord of Glory, bless each woman who has just complteted this study. May its application last a lifetime. Thank you that Your Spirit will bring to her remembrance all that You've taught her and will continue to teach her about loving her husband. Heal where there yet needs to be healing. Lovingly discipline when course-correction is necessary. And may You touch the heart of her husband, steadily drawing him nearer to You as You continually add depth to their marriage—for as long as they both shall live. Amen.

Works Cited

1. Stormie Omartian, *The Power of a Praying Wife* (Eugene, OR: Harvest House Publishers, 1997), 13.

2. Hank Hanegraaff, *The Prayer of Jesus* (Nashville: W Publishing Group, 2001), 84.

3. James Reimann, ed., *My Utmost for His Highest: The Golden Book of Oswald Chambers* (Grand Rapids, MI: Discovery House Publishers, 1992), August 28 devotional.

4. Stormie Omartian, *The Power of a Praying Woman* (Eugene, OR: Harvest House Publishers, 2002), 250.

5. Charles Stanley, *The Glorious Journey* (Nashville: Thomas Nelson Publishers, 1996), 481.

6. Kay Arthur, *Lord, Teach Me to Pray in 28 Days* (Eugene, OR: Harvest House Publishers, 1982), 64.

7. Ibid., 93.

8. Becky Tirabassi, *Let Prayer Change Your Life* (Nashville: Thomas Nelson, 1992), 109.

9. Omartian, *The Power of a Praying Wife,* 14.

10. Stanley, *The Glorious Journey,* 495.

11. Mark Buchanan, *Your God Is Too Safe* (Sisters, OR: Multnomah Publishers, 2001), 149-150.

12. Beth Moore, *Praying God's Word* (Nashville: Broadman and Holman Publishers, 2000), 8.